The Ages of Iron Man

The Ages of Iron Man

Essays on the Armored Avenger in Changing Times

Edited by JOSEPH J. DAROWSKI

McFarland & Company, Inc., Publishers
Jefferson, North Carolina

LIBRARY OF CONGRESS CATALOGUING-IN-PUBLICATION DATA

The ages of Iron Man : essays on the armored Avenger in changing
    times / edited by Joseph J. Darowski.
        p.   cm.
    Includes bibliographical references and index.

    ISBN 978-0-7864-7842-2 (softcover : acid free paper) ∞
    ISBN 978-1-4766-2074-9 (ebook)

    1. Iron Man (Fictitious character).   2. Comic books, strips,
etc.—United States.   3. Iron Man (Motion picture).   4. Literature and society—United States.   I. Darowski, Joseph J., editor.

PN6728.I76A38 2015
741.5'973—dc23

                                                            2015021203

BRITISH LIBRARY CATALOGUING DATA ARE AVAILABLE

Front cover illustration © 2015 David Grigg/Thinkstock

Printed in the United States of America

*McFarland & Company, Inc., Publishers
    Box 611, Jefferson, North Carolina 28640
    www.mcfarlandpub.com*

To Alex and April

Table of Contents

Introduction

Joseph J. Darowski

Iron Man's presence in popular culture rose significantly following the character's portrayal by Robert Downey, Jr., in Marvel Studios' 2008 film *Iron Man*. Though the film, and Downey Jr.'s performance, considerably increased the general cultural awareness of Iron Man, the character goes back to the early days of Marvel Comics' superhero renaissance. After Jack Kirby and Stan Lee found success with *The Fantastic Four* in 1961, a quick succession of superhero adventures were produced to ride out the new popularity of the industry's rejuvenated genre. The Incredible Hulk, Spider-Man, Thor, Iron Man, the X-Men, the Avengers, and Daredevil all had their initial appearances in the next few years. Iron Man, and his alter-ego the billionaire industrialist Tony Stark, had been a prominent figure in Marvel's comic book universe, but was not considered an A-list character, such as Spider-Man, until recently. Nevertheless, his adventures have been published consistently since his first appearance in *Tales of Suspense #39* (March 1963).

As with many aspects of the early Marvel era when the Marvel method of comic book creation allowed for greater collaboration between writers and artists in terms of storytelling, it is not perfectly clear who was responsible for all the aspects of the character's creation. While Larry Lieber scripted the first issue and Don Heck was the artist, Stan Lee had developed the concept of the character and Jack Kirby, who drew the cover image for the issue, worked on the visual design.

But, as with all long-running comic book series, hundreds of creators have since had a hand in telling Iron Man stories and defining the character. The decades-long run of Iron Man adventures has allowed unique takes, evolving depictions, and distinct artistic styles to characterize different eras of Iron Man stories. Also influencing the Iron Man stories through the years

1

is the inevitable association between social issues and the entertainment that is consumed by a society. As would be expected, Iron Man stories created during the Cold War are very different from the Iron Man stories in a post–9/11 world in part because the creators and readers have different expectations for what issues a hero should be facing in those distinct eras. This collection examines the efforts creators and publishers have made to maintain Iron Man's relevancy to the contemporary audience while publishing his stories for five decades. Audiences are not static, and if the entertainment they consumed did not evolve to reflect their tastes it would become a relic of a previous era. Like any popular culture product, Iron Man comic books are reflective of the time period when they were produced.

With a character such as Iron Man, there are more than fifty years of stories, and analyzing the stories created and consumed in different periods is enlightening for a cultural critic. The contributors to this collection have each selected a contained period of Iron Man comic books and examine a distinct facet of those storylines and how the narratives are reflective of the moment in American history when they were produced. Tony Stark/Iron Man is an intriguing character for this type of analysis due to his relationship with the American military. This aspect of the character has been a delicate negotiation for comic book creators across the years, at times supporting military actions, at times condemning them. Iron Man's origin is explicitly tied to the Vietnam War and his role as a weapons manufacturer, but creators have not always chosen to highlight or glorify the American military industrial complex.

One of the most fascinating eras for Iron Man stories are the first decade of his adventures. As one of the most political of Marvel's early superheroes, Iron Man was often entrenched in Cold War issues, whether it was battling Russian enemies, fighting in war-torn Asian territories, or addressing America's evolving attitudes towards the military in the 1960s. As such, the first several essays in this collection address unique aspects of this significant period in the development of the Tony Stark/Iron Man character.

In "'The Iron-Clad American': Iron Man in the 1960s," Brian Patton presents the early history of Iron Man and analyzes the links between the narratives and the culture at that time. Craig This follows with an examination of a narrower social issue of the time in "Tony Stark: Disabled Vietnam Veteran?" He examines how the early Iron Man stories parallel emerging social issues surrounding returning war veterans.

Three essays look at America's Cold War enemies as reflected in the comic books of the era. The primary concerns of any era inevitably appear in the popular entertainment that is produced, and American comic books are certainly no exception. Natalie R. Sheppard addresses the intersection of evolving gender roles and international Cold War tensions in "'Gorgeous new menace': Black Widow, Gender Roles and the Subversion of Cold War Expectations of Domesticity." The Black Widow was a Russian spy who defied American gender norms. In "Fu Manchu Meets Maklu-4: The Mandarin and Racial Stereotypes," Richard A. Iadonisi examines the problematic Asian stereotypes that are pervasive in one of Iron Man's arch-enemies, the Mandarin. José Alaniz looks at how the significant anxiety between the United States and the Soviet Union influenced the portrayal of Russian characters in Iron Man comic books. "'Does Khrushchev Tell Kennedy?' Superpowered Rivalry and Silver Age Iron Man" provides a thorough investigation of Iron Man comic books in the 1960s in light of international concerns of the era.

Will Cooley and Mark C. Rogers write of Tony Stark's role as a member of the military-industrial complex. "Ike's Nightmare: Iron Man and the Military-Industrial Complex" explores the rhetoric and policies in America surrounding the rise of a defense industry and how the comic books negotiated shifting attitudes towards such an industry throughout the 1960s. While several previous essays established how foreign powers were portrayed, Cooley and Rogers address more domestic issues and their presentation in Iron Man's early comic books adventures.

Charles Henebry also notes Tony Stark's undeniable links to the military-industrial complex, but identifies how Marvel rehabilitated the character and moved Stark/Iron Man away from that unpopular profession in the 1970s. "Socking It to Shell-Head: How Fan Mail Saved a Hero from the Military-Industrial Complex" analyzes how fan response guided the creators producing *Iron Man* to shift the character's profession and also his role in the United States.

In "Countdown to #100: Escapist Heroism and the Challenges of Modernity in the Late 1970s," John M. Vohlidka looks at five issues of *The Invincible Iron Man* that encapsulate many of the issues both America and Iron Man were facing in the late 1970s. In the buildup to the 100th issue of Iron Man's eponymous comic book series the stories addressed hot-button issues such as technology, communism, globalization and traditionalism.

Undoubtedly one of the most famous attributes of Tony Stark is the character's struggle with alcoholism. Jason Sacks analyzes the story that made this trait an indelible part of Stark's character in his essay "Demon in a Bottle and Feet of Clay: David Michelinie and Bob Layton on Iron Man." Michelinie and Layton had been tasked with updating Iron Man, and in the process they cast him more in the mold of Marvel's other flawed heroes by giving the character a debilitating addiction.

In "War Machine: Blackness, Power and Identity in *Iron Man*," Julian C. Chambliss provides a thorough examination of one of Marvel's most notable African American characters. James Rhodes was introduced in Iron Man comic books, and even wore the Iron Man armor at times, before he was given his own suit of armor. Rhodes has a long and interesting history, and Chambliss provides insightful analysis of this important figure in Iron Man's cast of characters.

Jean-Philipe Zanco considers several Iron Man stories through the lens of economic models. "From Armor Wars to Iron Man 2.0: The Superhero Entrepreneur" aligns the changing issues Stark faces both as Iron Man and as the head of a multinational corporation with the stages of economic development facing the country at the times the stories were produced.

"Cold Warrior at the End of the Cold War: John Byrne's 'War Games' in an Era of Transition" looks at storylines written by John Byrne. Joseph J. Darowski considers a period in which a new American identity was being established following the decades-long Cold War and how a character that had been so clearly defined as an anti-communist force is reestablished with a new motivation in the early 1990s.

John Darowski uses the Marvel mini-series *Civil War* to examine audience expectations of heroes and villains in mainstream superhero comic books in "'I would be the bad guy': Tony Stark as the Villain of Marvel's *Civil War*." Marvel's *Civil War* featured superheroes battling superheroes, with the divided sides being led by Captain America and Iron Man. In ad campaigns while the mini-series was being published Marvel Comics invited fans to consider "Whose Side Are You On?" and readers overwhelmingly supported Captain America's side of the issues, casting Iron Man in the role of villain. Darowski explores what this means for the narrative, fan reaction, and for the character of Iron Man.

The final two essays in the collection focus on two more recent Iron Man storylines, "Extremis," written by Warren Ellis, and "The Five Nightmares," written by Matt Fraction. "Feminizing the Iron: Tony Stark's Rescue," by Jason Michálek, uses the lens of masculinity and femininity in contemporary culture to analyze the relationships of Tony Stark and characters such as Pepper Potts (Rescue) and Maria Hill. Rikk Mulligan's "Iron Icarus: Comics Futurism and the Man-Machine System" explores contemporary issues of technology and culture as represented in Iron Man's superhero narrative.

Tony Stark/Iron Man is a fascinating character for analysis, as evidenced by the essays in this collection. Ideally this collection can serve as a resource and launching point for further investigation into one of the most popular superheroes appearing in America popular culture today.

"The Iron-Clad American"
Iron Man in the 1960s

BRIAN PATTON

Tales of Suspense and the Rise of Marvel Comics

Iron Man made his first appearance in *Tales of Suspense* #39, which bore a cover date of March 1963, although it actually appeared on newsstands in the final month of 1962 (Wells 77). The character's debut came in the midst of a remarkable period of creativity on the part of writer-editor Stan Lee and his several artist collaborators. This period saw publisher Martin Goodman's comic book line emerge from near extinction at the start of the decade and begin a rapid ascent toward the industry dominance it enjoyed by 1969 as the "Marvel Comics Group," a brand emblazoned on all of the company's covers and house ads within two months of Iron Man's introduction. *Tales of Suspense*, the monthly title in which Iron Man's adventures shared cramped space with those of Captain America through March 1968, was one of a handful of repurposed SF/fantasy titles of the sort that had enabled Goodman's comics line to limp through the company's lean years. Goodman had made the unfortunate decision to shut down his distribution firm, Atlas News, in favor of a deal with the American News Company shortly before American News went out of business in 1957. Left without a means of getting his comics to their readers, Goodman accepted a highly restrictive deal with Independent News, a distributor owned by a major competitor in the comics field, National (DC), under the terms of which Goodman's company could distribute only eight titles per month, down from the 30–40 that had previously been the case.

Goodman and his editor, Stan Lee, managed to nurse the struggling enterprise through these difficult times, securing space on spinner-racks by keeping 16 bi-monthly titles in print and following a variety of popular trends. The period's fascination with science fantasies and creature-features prompted Goodman and Lee to produce, from 1958 onwards, a series of fantasy anthologies such as *Journey Into Mystery*, *Tales to Astonish*, and *Tales of Suspense*—all of which would linger well into the self-proclaimed "Marvel Age of Comics," long after the bug-eyed monsters and presumptuous scientists had given way to Marvel's new generation of superheroes. Iron Man's debut adventure, "Iron Man is Born!" was followed by two stories of the sort more typical of *Tales of Suspense* to that point: a science fiction story entitled "The Last Rocket!" and a Viking ghost story, "Gundar!" The rapidly developing "Marvel universe"—a single, coherent imaginary world in which all of the company's new (and revived) superhero characters lived and battled—began encroaching on these back-up features beginning with the January 1964 issue, when one was reframed each month as a "Tale of the Watcher," narrated by a toga-clad alien first introduced in the pages of *The Fantastic Four*. These "tales" were finally pushed out altogether when the new Captain America feature was introduced several months later.

Along with most other comic book publishers, Marvel had abandoned the superhero genre by the early 1950s, by which time readers' interest was more readily caught by romance, western, crime, and horror comics. When National began to achieve success from 1956 by reimagining and updating some of its wartime heroes and assembling some of its older and newer creations into the popular Justice League of America in 1960, Goodman directed Stan Lee to follow suit. Lee and his artist collaborators responded, over the next few years, with a succession of genuinely innovative creations, beginning with the Fantastic Four in 1961. By the time Iron Man made his debut late in 1962, the Marvel roster already included the Hulk, Thor, Ant Man, and Spider-Man. Within a few months, it would expand further to include Dr. Strange as well as the X-Men and the Avengers, two hopeful rivals to National's own team, the Justice League. Marvel's new superheroes offered a degree of realism that distinguished them from their competitors' creations; while ultimately on the side of good, they were not always the unassailably upstanding citizens that National's heroes tended to be. For example, Peter Parker/Spider-Man's first instinct on discovering his superpowers is to use them for his own ends, not to make the world a safer and better place for others. Only the tragic killing of his beloved Uncle Ben, a cruel karmic payback for Parker's own self-centeredness, prompts his guilty entry into a life of costumed crime-fighting. The Hulk, Marvel's most unusual superhero, was a monstrous misanthrope, at times violent and unpredictable, more an antiheroic hybrid of Frankenstein's creature and Mr. Hyde than a virtuous crusader for justice. On the whole, Marvel's new heroes were a tormented lot, variously plagued by guilt or self-doubt, and assuming the superhero mantle at a considerable personal cost reckoned at length in the angst-filled thought balloons that flourished on the pages of their melodramatic adventures.

Like his predecessors in the Marvel stable, Iron Man is an anguished figure for whom the burden of heroism is a heavy one: the armor that is the source of his power is also a prison of sorts, a life-saving device whose secret nature forces his isolation from others. As Stan Lee puts the matter, employing his typically overblown style, Tony Stark must struggle through life "not daring to confess his love to the girl he cares for … not knowing when the mechanical chest device he wears will fail, ending his life in an instant.… Nor does he know when or where his next deadly threat will come from! This is Tony Stark, rich, handsome, successful Tony Stark … one of the most tragic heroes the world has ever known!" (Lee, "Hawkeye, the Marksman"). In characteristic Marvel fashion, Iron Man's action-filled adventures were framed by an ongoing soap opera in which Tony Stark strove to achieve some semblance of a normal private life, only to find himself caught in a love triangle involving himself, his secretary, Pepper Potts, and his chauffeur, Happy Hogan.

"Iron Man Is Born!"

While the Marvel brand had not yet been established when Iron Man debuted in early 1963, the cover of *Tales of Suspense* #39 (Mar. 1963) declares that this "most sensational super-hero of all" derives from the same "talented bull-pen where The Fantastic Four, Spider-Man, Thor and your other favorite super-heroes were born!" (Lee, "Iron Man is Born"). Despite the hyperbole, though, Iron Man was a second-tier character during this decade, not given his own title until 1968, when Marvel's acquisition by Cadence Publications freed the company from its restrictive distribution arrangement with Independent News and enabled a significant expansion of the company's range of titles. The character was initially designed by Marvel's premier artist, Jack Kirby, who also provided the cover art for this first issue (Manning 11), but most of the interior art from 1963 through 1965 was handled by Don Heck, a lesser light whose work is typically overshadowed by the more distinctive visual styles of Kirby (The Fantastic Four, Thor) and Steve Ditko (Spider-Man, Dr. Strange). A three-issue stint by Ditko late in 1963 saw the character abandon a bulky early look in favor of his definitive, sleek red-and-gold costume, and the arrival of new artist Gene Colan in the January 1966 issue brought a moodier and more expressionistic visual style to the series. Stan Lee is the credited writer of the Iron Man stories until the March 1968 issue of *Tales of Suspense*, a credit occasionally shared with others, presumably owing to Lee's staggering workload at the time. The script of this first story is attributed to Lee's brother, Larry Lieber, based on Lee's plot, and some later stories would involve similar collaborations with Robert Bernstein (credited as R. Berns) and Don Rico (as N. Korok). From March 1968, when the Marvel line expanded and several new creators joined the company, Archie Goodwin assumed the writing duties on the Iron Man series.

As the title, "Iron Man Is Born," indicates, this debut adventure is the inevitable origin story. Tony Stark is introduced in his closely-guarded laboratory, conferring with an American general regarding his latest invention, a "tiny transistor" that boosts the power of a small magnet "so tremendously that it will open that locked vault!" The heavy guard is necessitated by Stark's importance to the U.S. military: as one guard informs another, "the commies would give their eyeteeth to know what he's working on now!" Having established Stark's genius as an arms manufacturer and his importance to America's Cold War efforts, the narrative moves on to his credentials as a millionaire playboy. In a beach-set panel reminiscent of the Charles Atlas ads familiar to generations of comic book readers, we see "Anthony Stark … rich, handsome, known as a glamorous playboy, constantly in the company of beautiful, adoring women…." He is "both a sophisticate and a scientist! A millionaire bachelor, as much at home in a laboratory as in high society!" Stark travels to Vietnam, where his "midget transistors" are needed to aid the outnumbered South Vietnamese. Following a successful live demonstration, though, Stark trips a booby trap and is left a captive with shrapnel fatally close to his heart. His captor, Wong-Chu—a bestial, bullying "Red guerrilla tyrant" introduced earlier in the story—plans to trick Stark into spending his last days working for him in exchange for life-saving medical attention; however, Stark is too clever to buy the ruse: "my last act," he thinks, "will be to defeat this grinning, smirking, Red terrorist!" Aided by another of Wong-Chu's prisoners, the great physicist Professor Yinsen, Stark employs his expertise in transistor technology to design and build the armor that will save his life and enable him to escape his imprisonment. Yinsen describes the clunky grey suit of armor as a "mighty electronic body"; Stark controls it with his own brain waves, so that the armor is, in effect, an extension of his body, a complex and powerful tool he wields—although he wields it rather awkwardly to begin with, "like a baby learning to walk!" However, he does master its "transistor-powered air-pressure jets," which enable him to fly, and its "magnetic turbo-insulator," which redirects bazooka shells aimed at him, along with a host of other gadgets, including a miniature buzz-saw and, more humbly, a pair of suction cups for hanging discreetly from a ceiling. The climactic battle between Iron Man and Wong-Chu allows Tony Stark to escape and revenge the death of Yinsen, who sacrificed his life giving Iron Man the crucial extra moments required to sufficiently charge his armor; however, that clash also takes on an unambiguously ideological dimension when the armored man declares, "This is Iron Man who opposes you, and all you stand for!" (Lee, "Iron Man is Born"). The declaration confirms Iron Man's role as a Cold Warrior, an unpaid and unofficial citizen-soldier in the contest between East and West.

Iron Man, Marvel Comics and the Cold War

Marvel's return to the superhero genre in the early 1960s coincided with a particularly intense period of Cold War hostility between the U.S., the Soviet Union and Communist China in a conflict pursued through proxy wars and propaganda. U.S. observers watched with concern as Soviet and Chinese influence spread in the Middle East and Southeast Asia while, much closer to home, Fidel Castro's Cuban revolution led to the establishment in 1959 of a socialist state closely aligned with the Soviet Union a mere 90 miles south of Florida in the gateway to the strategically significant Gulf of Mexico. The Soviets' 1957 launch of Sputnik 1—the world's first artificial satellite—was a propaganda coup that prompted an international contest to send ever more effective satellites and rockets into space and eventually to land men on the moon. Just as the first generation of superheroes had joined the ideological war against the Axis powers by battling caricatures of the enemy, so too did these new heroes engage in a ceaseless game of one-upmanship with cartoonish Soviet foes. The "Marvel Age" itself was, in effect, born of the Space Race: the four unlikely astronauts who become the Fantastic Four make their premature foray into space, despite the unknown effects of cosmic rays, because, as Susan Storm explains to the reluctant Ben Grimm, "we've got to take that chance … unless we want the commies to beat us to it!" (Lee, "The Fantastic Four"). In reality, the Soviets had already achieved that success a few months earlier, in April 1961, when cosmonaut Yuri Gagarin made the first manned flight in space—an awkward fact on which "The Fantastic Four!" remains silent, thereby revealing a stronger commitment to boosting national morale than maintaining historical accuracy.

Susan Storm's passing reference to "the commies" is indicative of the casual prejudice that characterizes a wide variety of popular cultural forms of the time. The Berlin Wall, whose construction began in 1961, became an apparent physical manifestation of a great ideological East/West divide most familiarly known as the "Iron Curtain." "Each strand of their barbed wire," writes Tom Engelhardt, "each new watch tower, offered proof that the globe was split into two clearly defined parts, 'half slave and half free' as the phrase went. The United States was now the leader of what was called [...] the Free World, while its enemy ruled a vast slave-labor empire from Poland to the Korean peninsula" (95). All of Marvel's new heroes of the early 1960s some-how reflected and contributed to American perceptions of its Cold War ene-mies, but none more explicitly than Iron Man, whom historian Bradford Wright identifies as "the most political of Marvel's superheroes" (222). Reflect-ing back on some of his co-creations in 1975, Stan Lee dubiously claimed that "Marvel Comics has never been into politics" or beholden to an "official party line" before offering a near-apology for the moral simplicity of the portrait of the Vietnam conflict in 1963's "Iron Man Is Born!" (*Son of Origins* 47). A disinterested observer would find much evidence to counter those claims in the pages of *Tales of Suspense* between 1963 and 1968. Far from being apolit-ical, Iron Man was, in the words of Matthew Costello, "the most ardent of Marvel's Cold Warriors" (63), entering routinely into battles that were largely, and simplistically, ideological in nature: contests between a virtuous West and a treacherous East. *Tales of Suspense* #42 (Jun. 1963), for instance, pitted Iron Man against the Red Barbarian, depicted on both the cover and the splash-page as a brutish, snarling, low-browed ogre decorated with military medals, carrying a luger and enjoying an opulent feast reminiscent of Henry VIII, including a goblet, grapes, and a recently chomped giant drumstick. The Red Barbarian recalls the monstrous caricatures of Germans and espe-cially Japanese that were typical of the comics of the Second World War. His servile underlings address him as "Excellency"; in a fit of impatience, His Excellency hurls a large joint of meat at one minion, knocking him out cold, and douses another with the contents of his goblet before reaching for his gun. When another character enters, noting, "You are well named, Red Bar-barian!" he is stating the very obvious (Bernstein, "Trapped..."). Bullski the Merciless, the Soviet commissar who aims to defeat Iron Man by donning the guise and weaponry of Titanium Man, is another instance of this type: a Soviet ogre, an imperious bully built like a tank, who crushes an iron pipe in his bare hands and treats the imprisoned scientists who work under him like slaves. "I'll crush the spirit of resistance or rebellion," he warns, "just as easily as I crush this iron pipe!" (Lee, "If I Must Die...").

Many of Iron Man's foes in these 1960s stories are spies, terrorists, or uniquely enhanced soldiers in the direct service of the Soviet government, whose explicit aim is to damage American military capability and/or morale by destroying or bettering Stark's celebrated weaponry. The list of Iron Man's ideologically driven communist foes includes the Crimson Dynamo, the Black Widow, the Unicorn, Half-Face, and Titanium Man—Iron Man's would-be Soviet counterpart whose extended bouts with Iron Man are staged as international spectacles pitting the chosen champions of East and West against each other. An additional dash of realism and topicality was provided early on by then Soviet Premier Nikita Khrushchev, who made several appearances between 1963 and 1965 as "the 'Mr. Big of the Iron Curtain'" (Bernstein, "Iron Man Faces..."), the ever-thwarted mastermind behind the Soviet plots against Iron Man, Stark Industries, and the USA. Like the purely fictional Red Barbarian and Bullski the Merciless, Marvel's Khrushchev is a monster, albeit on a more modest scale. Perpetually scowling and prone to fits of "uncontrollable rage" (Korok, ""The Crimson Dynamo..."), the Soviet Premier demonstrates the capacity for cruelty and treachery needed to succeed within the Soviet political system, plotting against the very agents he employs and even threatening the parents of the Black Widow in order to coerce her into continued service when she declares, "I'm through serving your evil purposes!" (Lee, "Hawkeye..."). Communist China is a similarly inhumane place, a haven for bullies with no tolerance for the failure that inevitably greets their devious schemes.

Standing in sharp contrast to these grim portraits of life under communism is "the iron-clad American" (Lee, "The Tragedy...") who does battle on his nation's behalf. He surprises Professor Vanko, the Crimson Dynamo, by being merciful in victory, thereby demonstrating that "Americans are not murderers" (Korok, "The Crimson Dynamo...") and paving the way for Vanko's defection. The Black Widow—another Soviet agent on her way to defection and redemption—is similarly struck by Iron Man's willingness to risk his life to save those of two Soviet agents. "That's the trouble with you commies!" he insists, "You just don't dig us!" (Korok, "The Black Widow"). Whereas his communist foes are paranoid and humorless, dehumanized by the collectivist ethos of their social and political system, Iron Man embodies a humane, individualist solution to what ails them.

Perhaps surprisingly, the Iron Man of the 1960s was a more engaged Cold Warrior even than Captain America, the iconic hero of the Second

World War with whom he shared the pages of *Tales of Suspense* until 1968. Captain America, of course, was a product of a very different cultural moment and a very different war: he began his career delivering a spectacular blow to the jaw of Adolf Hitler on the cover of the debut issue of *Captain America Comics* in 1941 and enjoyed a fleeting revival in 1953–1954 as a red-baiting "Commie Smasher!" (Unknown)—although the brevity of that comeback is perhaps telling. When the U.S. entered the war in Europe and the Pacific several months after that eye-catching encounter between Captain America and Hitler, the colorful and virtuous first generation of superheroes adapted readily to the propagandistic narratives of 1940s comic books. However, World War II lent itself more easily to a four-color palette than America's post–1945 conflicts in Korea and Vietnam did. The lengthy Korean stalemate, which unfolded in a country whose complex colonial history was unfamiliar to many, provided few instances of the sort of triumphalism typical of the popular heroic narratives of World War II. Compared to the "exuberant and sublime comic books of World War II," notes historian Bradford Wright, "those of the Korean War tended to be grim and ironic" (*Comic Book Nation* 115), with some presenting the later war "in almost nihilistic terms" (117). While a handful of American comics focused on the subsequent conflict in Vietnam, the general tendency for the larger superhero publishers, National and Marvel, was to look elsewhere; even Marvel's sole war title of the time, *Sgt. Fury and His Howling Commandos*, was set during World War II (Wright, "The Vietnam War" 438), as were many of the early adventures of Captain America in *Tales of Suspense*. Captain America had fought World War II in a bold and brightly colored campaign, but his forays into Vietnam two decades later were scarce indeed.

Nonetheless, Marvel comics engaged enthusiastically in the propagandistic dimension of the Cold War during the 1960s, and nowhere so evidently as in the Iron Man series, where Susan Storm's "commie" slur is echoed variously in Iron Man's ironic gibes directed toward his opponents from "Commieland" (Lee, "If I Must Die...".). The epithets "commie" and "Red" are routinely employed, along with other variations, such as "Ivan" and "Volga boatman" (Lee, "By Force of Arms"), and mocking references to *The Communist Manifesto* (Lee, "Crescendo") and the supposedly just and egalitarian nature of a communist system, in which "the leaders of the People's Republic" claim to be "the friends of the masses" (Lee, "What Price Victory?"). The unquestioning confidence proclaimed by Iron Man in his contests with America's enemies (like that of Captain America a generation earlier) typifies a triumphalist tone that would diminish significantly over the course of the 1960s. That confidence declares an idea of the nation on whose behalf these heroes fought: virtuous, just, and uniquely destined to lead the world into better times. According to Matthew Costello, post–1945 American mainstream cultural discourse was shaped by a national consensus whose key themes, endlessly reiterated, were i) the primacy of individualism, ii) the possibility of unending progress, and iii) a providential role for America in the world. "Promulgated by government, professional, and academic elites, and enforced by loyalty oaths, Congressional hearings, and public censure, this consensus was constructed throughout the 1940s and 1950s and became nearly hegemonic by the start of the 1960s" (45). At the very heart of this postwar consensus, he adds, was anticommunism, a claim well supported by the first few years' worth of Iron Man Stories (58).

In his earliest manifestation, Iron Man's allegiance to "the land I love" (Lee, "The Uncanny Unicorn") is absolute and beyond question, as Tony Stark affirms while preparing to risk his personal safety by revealing his secret identity to a Congressional committee: "No one has the right to defy the wishes of his government … not even Iron Man!" (Lee, "The Return…"). Of course, as the 1960s wore on, American virtue, progress and exceptionalism were subject to increasingly compelling challenges from within the nation itself: voices of dissent became ever more insistent, from the Civil Rights movement, the feminist movement, and opponents to U.S. involvement in Vietnam. Following the Tet Offensive of 1968—which provided a dramatic demonstration of the National Liberation Front's continued strength and will to fight, and undermined confidence in U.S. government claims regarding the progress of the war—the efficacy of Tony Stark's transistor-aided weaponry would have appeared doubtful at best. Nor would the morality of his role in the Vietnam conflict or his close relationship with the U.S. military be taken for granted, as it was early on. As Bradford Wright has noted, significantly divergent political positions became evident in readers' published letters responding to the Iron Man and Captain America stories in *Tales of Suspense*, and Marvel's response to the more fractious political environment was to move quietly away from Cold War themes toward the end of the decade and embrace instead the liberalism espoused by Stan Lee in his September 1968 "Stan's Soapbox" column. There, in response to requests "for the Bullpen's opinion about such diverse subjects as Viet Nam, civil rights, the war on poverty, and the upcoming election," Lee insisted that "we share the same diversity of opinion as Americans everywhere," and affirmed only a commitment to "tolerance and respect" (Lee, "Stan's Soapbox"), a vague position more or less repeated in his preface to his first Iron Man story when it was reprinted in 1975's *Son of Origins of Marvel Comics*. Clearly, though, Bill Mantlo and George Tuska, the writer and artist of the *Iron Man* series in 1975, felt that the character's Cold War origins required a more direct response, which they provided in a story whose publication roughly coincided with the final U.S. withdrawal from Vietnam and the fall of Saigon. "Long Time Gone" features Tony Stark revisiting his earlier actions in a self-accusing mode: "And what about you, Tony Stark? Once you were do or die for America and Mom's apple pie! You didn't do much soul-searching back then, did you? As Iron Man you beat the commies for democracy without ever questioning just whose democracy you were serving...." The story—which recounts a series of incidents earlier in the Vietnam war—veers into the sort of war-is-hell nihilism Harvey Kurtzman had brought to his groundbreaking war comics for EC in the 1950s and concludes with Iron Man embracing a new mission, "to avenge those whose lives have been lost through the ignorance of men like the man I once was" (Mantlo, "Long Time Gone").

Transistorized Arms and the Man

While Iron Man bears much resemblance to the other Marvel heroes of his time, he differs in one key respect: where his peers are all variously super-powered—having been transformed through radiation or magic or some other extraordinary occurrence—Tony Stark is an ordinary mortal blessed with extraordinary technical ingenuity: a gifted inventor whose superhuman powers are put and removed on with his colorful suit of armor. Minus that armor, Iron Man is simply a man, albeit an unusually handsome, rich and clever one. The peculiar nature of Iron Man's power results in an especially heavy emphasis in the series on state-of-the-art technology. From the start, Stark's inventions are notable for both their tremendous power and their diminutive size. His particular expertise in these early years is in transistor technology, which was relatively new at the time, but increasingly a presence in ordinary people's lives. The first transistor radios appeared in the mid–1950s, and by 1962 they were available at comparatively modest prices, significantly altering the way people listened to music, owing to their small size and portability. Stark's technology, then, is at the cutting edge of a familiar trend: a newer, more powerful version of a modern-day marvel. It is worth noting that the issue of *Tales of Suspense* featuring Iron Man's debut also includes a full-page ad inviting readers to enroll in the National Radio Institute and send for a catalogue entitled "Amazing Field of Electronics," and that similar ads—for an "All-Transistor Wrist Watch Type Radio" (*Tales of Suspense* #50 [Feb. 1964]) and a shortwave radio that "Brings the world wherever you are!" (*Tales of Suspense* #61 [Dec. 1964])—appear over the next couple of years.

As a scientist-hero, Tony Stark is particularly well-matched to his moment. Soviet cosmonaut Yuri Gagarin's successful orbit of the earth in April 1961 prompted U.S. President John F. Kennedy to propose a month later that America aim to achieve a manned moon landing by the decade's end. This appeal inaugurated the Space Race and greatly intensified the push toward applied science that had brought the National Aeronautic and Space Administration (NASA) and the National Defense Education Act (NDEA) into being in 1958, shortly after the launch of the Soviet satellite Sputnik 1.

Iron Man's first suit of armor—the clunky, battle-grey version forged from scrap iron during his captivity in Vietnam—was powerful and effective, but as inelegant as a tank. Modifications followed quickly, though, and within two years Iron Man was sporting a version of the now familiar red and gold costume—"smooth, supple, form-fitting, and with the strength of ductile iron!" (Lee, "The New Iron Man..."). In the context of the Cold War, the sportier, lightweight design was evidence of superior American technological savvy, just as the gadgetry that featured in the James Bond films from 1964's *Goldfinger* onward staked a comparable claim for British ingenuity. The point is made explicit in the Iron Man series when Commissar Bullski's team of scientists is devising the Titanium Man suit in imitation of Iron Man's original: "We cannot make it as small as Iron Man's!" Bullski acknowledges, "We have not his unequalled knowledge of miniature transistors!" (Lee, "If I Must Die..."). The best the Soviet experts can achieve is a much heavier and more awkward outfit, and only the brute strength of Bullski enables him to manipulate it. Suggestively, the early modifications to Iron Man's armor also place considerably more emphasis on the human body beneath the suit, moving him away from his earlier, robotic appearance. Stark's humanity is undiminished by the technology that makes him Iron Man. In or out of costume, the technologized hero manifests his heroism as an individual. In all of his roles—playboy, entrepreneur, inventor, warrior—the Tony Stark of the 1960s embodies the liberal, capitalist values of the nation on whose behalf he fights.

WORKS CITED

"All-Transistor Wrist Watch Type Radio" [advertisement]. *Tales of Suspense* #50 (Feb. 1964). New York: Vista.

Costello, Matthew. *Secret Identity Crisis: Comic Books and the Unmasking of Cold War America.* New York: Continuum, 2009.

Engelhardt, Tom. *The End of Victory Culture: Cold War American and the Disillusioning of a Generation.* 1995. Amherst: University of Massachusetts Press, 1998.

"Learn Radio Television Electronics" [advertisement]. *Tales of Suspense* #39 (Mar. 1963). New York: Vista.

Lee, Stan. *Son of Origins of Marvel Comics.* New York: Simon and Schuster, 1975.

_____. "Stan's Soapbox." *Iron Man* #6 (Oct. 1968). New York: Atlas Magazines.

Lee, Stan, R. Berns [Robert Bernstein] (w) and Don Heck (a). "Iron Man Faces the Crimson Dynamo!" *Tales of Suspense* #46 (Oct. 1963). New York: Vista.

_____. "Trapped by the Red Barbarian!" *Tales of Suspense* #42 (Jun. 1963). New York: Vista.

Lee, Stan (w) and Gene Colan (a). "By Force of Arms!" *Tales of Suspense* #82 (Oct. 1966). New York: Vista.

_____. "The Return of Titanium Man!" *Tales of Suspense* #81 (Sept. 1966). New York: Vista.

_____. "The Tragedy and the Triumph!" *Tales of Suspense* #94 (Oct. 1967). New York: Vista.

Lee, Stan (w) and Steve Ditko (a). "The New Iron Man Battles ... 'the Mysterious Mr. Doll!'" *Tales of Suspense* #48 (Dec. 1963). New York: Vista.

Lee, Stan (w) and Don Heck (a). "Hawkeye and the New Black Widow Strike Again!" *Tales of Suspense* #64 (Apr. 1965). New York: Vista

_____. "Hawkeye, the Marksman!" *Tales of Suspense* #57 (Sept. 1964). New York: Vista.

_____. "If I Must Die, Let It Be With Honor!" *Tales of Suspense* #69 (Sept. 1965). New York: Vista.

_____. "The Uncanny Unicorn!" *Tales of Suspense* #56 (Aug. 1965). New York: Vista.

_____. "What Price Victory?" *Tales of Suspense* #71 (Nov. 1965). New York: Vista.

Lee, Stan (w) and Jack Kirby (a). "The Fantastic Four!" *The Fantastic Four* #1 (Nov. 1961). New York: Canam.

Lee, Stan, N. Korok [Don Rico] (w) and Don Heck (a). "The Black Widow Strikes Again!" *Tales of Suspense* #53 (May 1964). New York: Vista.

_____. "The Crimson Dynamo Strikes Again!" *Tales of Suspense* #52 (Apr. 1964). New York: Vista.

Lee, Stan, Larry Lieber (w) and Don Heck (a). "Iron Man is Born!" *Tales of Suspense* #39 (Mar. 1963). New York: Vista.

Manning, Matthew K. *Iron Man: The Ultimate Guide to the Armored Super Hero.* New York: DK, 2010.

Mantlo, Bill (w) and George Tuska (a). "Long Time Gone." *Iron Man* #78 (Sept. 1975). New York: Marvel Comics.

"Powerful 2-Band AM Shortwave Radio licensed by ... RCA" [advertisement]. *Tales of Suspense* #61 (Jan. 1965). New York: Vista.

Simon, Joe and Jack Kirby (w & a). *Captain America Comics* #1 (Mar. 1941). Meriden, Conn.: Timely.

[Unknown] (w) and John Romita (a). *Captain America Comics* #76 (May 1954). New York: Prime.

Wells, John. *American Comic Book Chronicles: The 1960s, 1960–1964.* Raleigh, North Carolina: TwoMorrows, 2012.

Wright, Bradford. *Comic Book Nation: The Transformation of Youth Culture in America.* Baltimore and London: Johns Hopkins University Press, 2001.

_____. "The Vietnam War and Comic Books." In *The Vietnam War: Handbook of the Literature and Research*, edited by James S. Olson. Westport, Conn. & London: Greenwood Press, 1993. 427–54.

Tony Stark

Disabled Vietnam Veteran?

CRAIG THIS

Stan Lee created Tony Stark as the "quintessential capitalist": a weapons manufacturer, industrialist and capitalist (Lee). Tony Stark has undeniably fulfilled that role, but also many others. He has been an anti–Communist and a weapons industrialist in the early *Tales of Suspense* storylines (Hogan). In Marvel Comics' *Civil War*, he symbolically represented the viewpoint that the United States government should register and regulate the movement of immigrants (superheroes) in the wake of the 9/11 attacks in the United States (Langley; White). In Warren Ellis's *Iron Man: Extremis,* he was a focal point for examining the problem of the merging of technology and humans (Hogan). In fact, an entire book, *Iron Man and Philosophy*, is dedicated to various interpretations of Tony Stark/Iron Man (White). However, an interpretation that has been insufficiently examined is disabled veteran. With Marvel's launching of the Iron Man/Tony Stark character in 1963, which coincided with the United States escalation of the Vietnam War, and the origin story including Stark being wounded and disabled by a landmine in the jungles of Southeast Asia, he could be viewed as a disabled veteran. Yes, Tony Stark/Iron Man is a superhero story, but it is also the story of the disabled veteran trying to reintegrate back into society. It is a story that is told too infrequently.

The disabled veteran has rarely been the protagonist in popular literature, though there are certainly exceptions such as Hemingway's *Farewell to Arms,* Remarque's *The Road Back,* or Barker's trilogy of World War I stories: *Regeneration, The Eye in the Door,* and *The Ghost Road.* Even in written history, the disabled veteran has pretty much been ignored (Gerber, *Disabled*

Veterans in History). A few memoirs do exist, such as *Fortunate Son: The Healing of a Vietnam Vet* by Lewis B. Puller, Jr. Disabled veterans, however, have been featured more prominently in films, such as *The Best Years of Our Lives* and *Born on the Fourth of July*. Kathleen McClancy argues that part of the appeal of the disabled Veteran, particularly the Vietnam Veteran in film, is because it was the first "televised war" as people received nightly video images of the war on the evening news. Additionally, the visual image of the Veteran missing a limb, wearing an eye patch or seated in wheelchair has a much more profound impact on the viewing public than the written word.

The comic book, though, improves on the images of film and the written word of books by combining "text and static images to communicate to its audience [and conveying] messages through two different means" (McCloud 9). The use of visuals and texts, argues comic scholar Scott McCloud in *Understanding Comics,* evokes the reader's empathy. Thus, the comic book portrayal of Tony Stark as disabled veteran can become more powerful than a portrayal of a disabled veteran in film or book. The reader sees, reads, and empathizes with his attempt to be "heroized, remasculinized and reassimilated back into society at all costs" (Norden 105).

Tony Stark: Soldier?

The question, though, is: is Tony Stark a soldier? To answer that, the reader must look at the first few pages of *Tales of Suspense* #39 (Mar. 1963); Tony Stark accompanies some soldiers in an inspection of Stark Industries weapons when they come under fire:

> SOLDIER: Take cover. There's the enemy! You'll see your gun in action now.
> NARRATION: Battle-filled minutes later.... But, the jungle holds a thousand perils! Some natural, others man made. And tripping over a small, concealed string leads to disaster.
> TONY STARK: A booby trap! Ohhhhh... (Lieber)

Injured and apparently left for dead, Tony Stark is taken prisoner by the red guerrillas where the reader learns that Tony Stark has shrapnel near his heart that will kill him. The guerrilla leaders offer surgery that will save his life if he will build them "the most fantastic weapon of all time" (Lieber). Tony Stark does, but the weapon is Iron Man and its life-giving heart of iron. In this brief moment, Tony Stark symbolizes two important themes or lingering images of the Vietnam War: the prisoner of war and the disabled veteran.

It could be argued that Tony Stark is not really a disabled veteran because he is not serving in the military. He is a civilian—a military contractor, who just happened to be in the wrong place at the wrong time. But, it can be argued that Tony Stark/Iron Man is a soldier—actually, a modern twist of an old soldier—a knight.

In describing the inspiration for Iron Man, Stan Lee is credited with saying,

> What if a guy had a suit of armor, but it was a modern suit of armor—not like years ago in the days of King Arthur—and what if the suit of armor made him as strong as any superhero? [Mangels 4].

The gray suit of iron would give way to gold and then gold and red, but Iron Man/Tony Stark was a modern day knight—a soldier. And, for the purposes here, a wounded soldier, a wounded warrior of the Vietnam War. And, as with those disabled veterans, his prosthetics—his artificial heart and his suit—become part of him.

Disabled Vietnam Veterans

Of the three major wars of the 20th century in which the United States was fully involved almost from start to finish—World War II, Korea and Vietnam—the Vietnam War had the largest percentage of wounded soldiers as well as the largest ratio of wounded to killed. Sociologist Paul Starr in *The Discarded Army: Veterans After Vietnam* writes:

> In World War II, the ratio of wounded to killed was 3.1 to 1, in Korea 4 to 1, but in Vietnam it was 5.6 to 1. The Army, which bore the brunt of the casualties, reports that 81 percent of its wounded survived in Southeast Asia, compared with 74 percent in Korea and 71 percent in World II. [...] Among the wounded Army men discharged for disability, the proportion of amputees has risen from 18 percent in World War II to 28.3 percent in Vietnam. [...] Paralysis of the extremities accounted for only 3.1 percent of wounded Army disability separations in World War II; for Vietnam this figure has been 25.2 percent. [...] The rate for leg amputations in Vietnam has been 70 percent higher than in Korea and 300 percent of above World War II; for functional loss of lower extremities (paraplegia), the incidence has been 50 percent higher than in Korea and 1,000 percent over World War II. [...] In World War II, only 5.7 of the amputees had multiple amputations or other major injuries. In Vietnam, the proportion has been 18.4 percent. [...] Among patients with burns over half their bodies, nearly 60 percent formerly died, whereas now fewer than 30 percent are lost [54–55].

The emergence, then, of Tony Stark as a wounded veteran at this point in time serves as a powerful metaphor for the war in Vietnam. True, Tony Stark/Iron Man fit the Marvel aesthetic that comics scholar Charles Hatfield writes about, "...soap opera-like [...with] unresolved problems. Marvel's heroes [...] had baggage. They shared memories and carted them around, seldom forgetting" (139). Tony Stark fit this "Marvel aesthetic," like other Marvel characters—Peter Parker/Spider-Man, Bruce Banner/The Hulk, and so on. But, the unresolved problems and carting around memories sounds a lot like a war veteran, who cannot escape the damages of war, who is haunted by post-traumatic stress disorder (PTSD). First and foremost, though, Tony Stark is dealing with the physical realities of war—a war wound.

In *Tales of Suspense* #41 (May 1963), Tony Stark narrates his situation:

> There's the metal plate I must wear constantly around my chest. If the plate isn't regularly charged with booster shots of electricity, my shrapnel-pierced heart would soon stop beating [Bernstein, "The Stronghold..."].

Tony Stark, like so many disabled veterans, is dependent upon technology for his continued survival and daily existence. Think of the soldier with the prosthetic arm or leg or using a wheelchair for mobility. However, what makes Tony Stark an interesting study is that not only is he dependent on an artificial heart, but he also creates a prosthetic body—the Iron Man suit—that not only makes him a whole man once again, but actually makes him better than his original self.

"The comic book," wrote John Hogan, "is one context in which humanity's relationship with technology is often explored" (199). And, again, this relationship with technology is part of the "Marvel aesthetic." Whether it is the Bruce Banner and his relationship with radiation that turned him into the Incredible Hulk or the Fantastic Four dealing with the effects of cosmic rays after going into outer space, Marvel Comics seemingly explore the relationship of society and technology. That is also the story of the disabled veteran in American history—the individual learning to deal with a prosthetic arm or leg or dealing with a wheelchair or some other piece of technology to make their body whole again.

In that regard, Tony Stark, then, is the disabled veteran since his story is the exploration of his relationship with technology. In fact, over the course of the Iron Man comics, Hogan sees three different storylines of this relationship. The first storyline is that of technology to keep Tony Stark alive. The second storyline is that of technology as a status symbol. The third storyline is technology and human become cyborg (Hogan).

The first storyline—keeping Tony Stark alive—the one that chronologically runs parallel to the Vietnam War (*Tales of Suspense*) provides the reference for this analysis and enables us to see the superhero as disabled veteran.

"Superhero comic books," writes Hogan, "… give us the greatest insight into society. Analyzing the superhero is the perfect means of analyzing the culture" (200). And, as Arthur Asa Berger wrote, "there is a fairly close relationships, generally, between a society and its heroes; if a hero does not espouse values that are meaningful to his readers, there seems little likelihood that he will be popular" (151). Now, the Vietnam War was not popular by any stretch of the imagination. Soldiers returned home to be spat on and disillusioned soldiers burned their uniforms and joined the anti-war movement (MacPherson).

However, the anti-war movement grew alongside the push for Civil Rights in this country and the acceptance and inclusion of the outsider, the one who is different. The disabled veteran was seen as an outsider, as one who had been discarded by his country. He was seen as the image of both a failed imperialistic and nationalistic system. He was also reviled for being a symbol of American imperialism and jingoism around the world. Yet, this broken and discarded body appeared in the cultural period of the 1960s and 1970s and may have prompted a greater acceptance of the outsider and the push towards greater diversity and inclusion in the United States.

The launch of Marvel Comics in the 1960s seemed to ride this wave towards greater acceptance and inclusion of diversity as it shifted the emphasis on the superhero away from the nationalistic and jingoistic exploits of Superman and Captain America to the soul-searching, consciousness-raising new superhero. The Fantastic Four, the X-Men, Spider-Man, Incredible Hulk and Iron Man, among others, all represented this new superhero. While Superman and World War II-era Captain America embodied "truth, justice and the American way" (whatever that may be), Marvel Comics ushered in a new era of comic book heroes—an era that preached tolerance, acceptance, and inclusion of outsiders and those who were different. Comic book content shifted during this period "from oblique narrative metaphors for social problems toward direct representations of racism and sexism, urban blight and political corruption" (Fawaz 356). The Marvel Comics superheroes and their storyline were offering cultural criticism lobbied at contemporary sociopolitical conditions. Tony Stark/Iron Man, as the returning disabled Vietnam War veteran, was at once both the byproduct and image of a failed war and failed policies.

Other cultural criticisms and challenges to the government and failed policies occurred during this period, such as the Civil Rights movement and "liberal and radical feminism, environmentalism, black nationalism and gay liberation" (Fawaz 357). Many of these emerged in 1963 with the escalation of the Vietnam War and began to subside in 1975 with the end of the Vietnam

War. This period, 1963–1975, coincided with the launch of both Iron Man and another set of superheroes, who were different and outsiders: the X-Men. Iron Man continued his successful run during this period while the X-Men were abruptly canceled and then revived in 1975, ironically, as the Vietnam War ended. Nevertheless, the X-Men, like Iron Man, focused on mutant or mutated characters and the social and cultural difference that had been highlighted during this period.

Avenger Adapt!

War creates mutants and freaks. War seeks to create physical and psychological victims (Scarry). However, what has changed in the past century is not so much the physical and psychological damage, but the fact that these wounds no longer result in a quick death (Boyle). As a result there are more and more disabled veterans who live than in the past. Complicating those matters is the relationship of the disabled veteran to the state.

Disabled veterans are an unavoidable result of war. For the most part, up until the Vietnam War, compensation had been the method by which governments dealt with disabled war veterans. That is because historically the relationship between the veteran and the state has been transactional. The veteran is hired or conscripted to take up arms on behalf of his or her country. If he or she is killed, the state pays for the funeral. If he or she is wounded, the state compensates that veteran for his or her disability.

In the United States, the war veteran, and, in particular, the disabled war veteran has had a long and contentious relationship with the government. While many disabled veterans have sought aid from the government, others have also been reluctant to do so. Nevertheless, the need for aid and the sometimes slow response of the government to provide that aid has led to the creation of multiple special interest groups that lobby the government on behalf of disabled veterans: Grand Army of the Republic (1866); Veterans of Foreign Wars (1914); the American Legion (1919); Disabled American Veterans (1920); Blinded Veterans Association (1945) and Paralyzed Veterans of America (1946). Despite advocating for compensation, disabled veterans in the United States have advocated more for accommodation. Consequently, in the Vietnam era, the United States government shifted away from compensating disabled veterans and instead focused on changing society to accommodate disabled veterans. Although the Americans with Disabilities Act would not be enacted until the 1990s, Tony Stark as disabled veteran aligns with this shift in focus from compensation to adaptation (Gerber).

From Compensation to Adaptation

Disability Rights Movement historians Paul Longmore and Lauri Umansky noted that between 1968 and 1990, the United States altered its definitions of disabilities and moved from a compensation model to one of adaptation or accommodation (Longmore and Umansky). The compensation model viewed disabilities as a medical problem and focuses on money and support for research to cure "the problem." The accommodation model views disabilities as a social problem and "highlights the need for social change: legal protection, increase access, more social support, less prejudice" (Ilea 171). By society changing and thus accommodating the disable Vietnam veteran, it meant that the veteran would be "heroized, remasculinized and reassimilated back into society" (Norden 10). Tony Stark/Iron Man accomplished all three.

Of the three, cultural norms assert masculinity as the key and the one on which the other two are built. The post–World War II discourse labeled male veterans as feminine because they were "not normal."

> [Gender] domination [of physically disabled men] depends upon a double-bind: men with physical disabilities are judged according to the standards of hegemonic masculinity, which are difficult to achieve due to the limitations of their bodies. Simultaneously, these men are blocked in everyday interactions from opportunities to achieve this form of masculinity. The most significant barriers they face occur in the key domains of hegemonic masculinity: work, the body, athletics, sexuality, and independence and control. Because men with physical disabilities cannot enact hegemonic standards in this realism, they are denied recognition as men. As failed men, they are marginalized and occupy a position in the gender order similar to gay men, men of color, and women [Gerschick 189].

Yes, Tony Stark's injury does marginalize him, but his injury is hidden: people do not see the heart. It does prevent him from doing things a "normal" man would do. In *Tales of Suspense* #40 (Apr. 1963), Tony Stark is dancing with a woman named Jeanne when the following exchange occurs:

> JEANNE: A moonlight swim! That should be great fun! Let's go, Tony!"
> TONY STARK: Oh, er, count me out, Jeanne. I've had a hard day, and a sudden tiredness just came over me. So you run along without me! I am going back to the hotel!
> NARRATION: But little does Jeanne, or any other persons know that Tony Stark has left the gay party for a most unusual date with … an electric cord. (Bernstein, "Iron Man versus Gargantus")

The marginalization is not a missing limb, or being blind, or being confined to a wheelchair. The Iron Man suit does serve as a prosthetic. It does help him compensate for his deficiency. It helps him accommodate and adapt to life. But, the suit does much more. It restores his masculinity. It enables him to be a hero.

Superhero comics, as Noah Berlatsky writes, have a "hyper-masculine, muscle-bound body, swathed in day-glo tights; an uber-manly man ... out of the costume, on the other hand, the hero is a feminized sissy-boy, whose painful secret prevents him from having any meaningful relationship with the leading lady" (100). This sums up precisely the relationship between Tony Stark and his alter ego Iron Man as disabled veteran. Tony is marginalized, unable to have a relationship with women because of his secret—bad heart— but his costume, is hypermasculine, muscle bound, and is day-glo colors of red and yellow.

Tim Nelson concurs, "The superhero genre has always provided reassurance for insecure young men, and its connection to the cult of body building should come as no surprise" (251). Who might be more insecure than a disabled veteran whose war wound makes him feel less than normal? While Nelson's analysis focuses on Marvel Comics' character The Vision, his analysis can be useful in examining Tony Stark/Iron Man. Nelson notes that The Vision, although an android, conforms to the appropriate "muscular look" of other male superheroes. The same can be said of the Iron Man suit. Iron Man began as a gray, bulky robot version, but by 1968 that look had given way to the muscular, lean suit we know today and that, like The Vision (an android), resembled the appropriate muscular look for a superhero.

The Vision also spoke to the incongruity of the superhero. The Vision appears to be a muscleman, and is, but he is also an intellectual. So, too, is Tony Stark—genius inventor, scientist, businessman, capitalist—but in the outfit, he is a muscleman. Like the disabled veteran, the body may be broken, but the mind is not. The disabled veteran, through the character of Tony Stark, began to challenge the myths of appearance in American society. This, in turn, led to a greater emphasis on accommodating, not compensating, the wounded warrior.

Accommodation meant assimilation back into society and for the veteran that meant also heroizing the veteran. The disabled veteran is:

"a freak of nationalism. A patriot who neither died in the service of his country no continued fighting for it ... [and because of his disability, the veteran becomes] ... the exemplar of passivity and dependence imagined as the very anti-thesis of the self-reliant 'American'" [Etter 70].

This view, prevalent before Vietnam, kept the focus on compensation, not accommodation. However, part of the shift in attitude during Vietnam was from victim to hero. Disabled veterans, wounded in service to the country, were viewed as heroes. This masculinity enables him to become and reinforces his heroism. The shift away from compensation to adaptation of the Vietnam Veteran began with seeing the war wound as heroic not victimization. Tony Stark had been injured in service to his country. He was a hero, not a victim. However, the prosthetic of the suit enables his heroic adventures. Page after page of first *Tales of Suspense* and then *Iron Man* heralded his role as hero, as victor, as triumphant. As Tony Stark says to Kala, Queen of the Netherworld:

> Iron Man can sink a battleship by ripping out its bottom ... knock supersonic speed bombs out of the air with a single punch ... or break a huge space missile in two with his bare hands..." [Bernstein, "Iron Man versus Kala"].

Iron Man's heroism is further witnessed in *Tales of Suspense* #46 (Oct. 1963):

> IRON MAN: The rocket isn't falling naturally. Someone—something is causing this and I've got to find out who!
> MAN IN CROWD WATCHING: Look! Iron Man's here! He's trying to reach the Y-9 before it crashes.
> ANOTHER MAN IN CROWD WATCHING: He won't make it! Those guys are as good as dead!
> IRON MAN: Got to save those men—that missile—no matter what! Only one thing to do ... meet the craft in mid-air and lessen the speed of its descent! This way I can buffer the fall so the men aren't injured.
> PILOT: Iron Man managed to slow the ship down!! But he took the full brunt of the impact himself.
> IRON MAN: I ... I did it! They're safe! [Bernstein, "Iron Man Faces..."].

Although his body was disabled, once inside the Iron Man suit—his prosthetic—he is a hero. He is nearly assimilated back into society. The final assimilation takes place when he is not only accepted by society but called upon to act in society. In *Tales of Suspense* #40 (Apr. 1963), Iron Man goes to save a crowd from leopards and lions that have escaped from a circus. However, he does not anticipate the public's reaction:

> MAN: Wait! Iron Man is here! He'll take care of the rampaging animals.
> WOMAN #1: Oh! How dreadful looking he is!
> WOMAN #2: Ugh! He looks like a creature in one of those science fiction films!
> CHILD: Momma! Momma! (Sob) Save me from the ugly man!
> CHILD #2: Dad, please don't let him come near me.
> IRON MAN: Great Scott! I never noticed before but my appearance terrifies women and children as if I were a monster [Bernstein, "Iron Man versus Gargantus"].

Yes, Tony Stark is a hero and masculinized, but still not fully reassimilated. He changes the color scheme of his costume, first all gold and then crimson and yellow, and in *Tales of Suspense* #41 (May 1963), Tony Stark is fully assimilated:

> NARRATION: The following day, near the national hospital for orphans.... Presently, as Iron Man arrives at hospital.
> IRON MAN: To begin my demonstration kids . . I'll do a juggling act, but not with oranges or basketballs! No with automobiles [Bernstein, "The Stronghold..."].

Iron Man does a series of tricks for the kids—juggling automobiles, having a cannon ball shot with him. The monster that was shunned is now accepted and assimilated into society. He is no longer called upon by just the military to help solve crises. Iron Man is called upon by the police to help solve crimes and he works alongside the X-Men and the Avengers to help save earth from super villains.

Conclusion

Tony Stark/Iron Man, whether or not it is agreed he was a soldier, did represent the disabled veteran in American history. He was wounded in the jungles of Southeast Asia and returned to this country, where he used his prosthetic—his Iron Man suit—to overcome his war wound. This suit enabled him to reassimilate back into society. And, his story, which is like that of so many other disabled veterans, is the story that we see represented in *Tales of Suspense* during the period of the Vietnam War, 1963–1975. Tony Stark/Iron Man then serves as a work of popular literature demonstrating, through monthly installments, the reintegration of the Vietnam veteran back into society.

WORKS CITED

Barker, Pat. *The Eye in the Door.* New York: Dutton, 1994.
_____. *The Ghost Road.* London: Viking, 1995.
_____. *Regeneration.* New York: Dutton, 1992.
Berger, Arthur Asa. *The Comic Stripped American.* New York: Walker and Company, 1973.
Berlatsky, Noah. "Comics in the Closet." *The Comics Journal,* #295 (2008): 100–104.
The Best Years of Our Lives. Dir. William Wyler. Samuel Goldwyn Company, 1946.
Born on the Fourth of July. Dir. Oliver Stone. Ixtlan, 1989.
Boyle, Brenda. "Phantom Pains: Disability, masculinity, and the normal in Vietnam war representations." In *Disability and/in Prose,* edited by Brenda Jo Brueggemann and Marian E. Lupo. London: Routledge, 2008, 83–97.

Etter, William. "Cripple, Soldier, Crippled Soldier: Alfred Bellard's Civil War Memoir." In *Disability and/in Prose,* edited by Brenda Jo Brueggemann and Marian E. Lupo. London: Routledge, 2008, 70–82.

Fawaz, Ramzi. "'Where No X-Man Has Gone Before!' Mutant Superheroes and the Cultural Politics of Popular Fantasy in Postwar America." *American Literature:* 83.2, Number 2, (June 2011): 355–388.

Forrest Gump. Dir. Robert Zemeckis. Paramount Pictures, 1994.

Gerber, David A. "Creating Group Identity: Disabled Veterans and American Government." *OAH Magazine of History.* (July 2009): 23–29.

_____, ed. *Disabled Veterans in History.* Ann Arbor: University of Michigan Press, 2000.

Gerschick, Thomas J. "Sisyphus in a Wheelchair: Men with Physical Disabilities Confront Gender Domination." In *Everyday Inequalities: Critical Inquiries,* edited by Jodi O'Brien and Judith A. Howard. Malden, MA: Blackwell Publishers, 1998, 189–212.

Hatfield, Charles. "Jack Kirby and the Marvel Aesthetic." In *The Superhero Reader.* Jackson: University of Mississippi Press, 2013, 136–154.

Hemingway, Ernest. *A Farewell to Arms.* 1929. New York: Scribner, 2012.

Hogan, Jon. "The Comic Book as Symbolic Environment: The Case of Iron Man." *ETC.* (April 2009): 199–212.

Ilea, Ramona. "The Mutant Cure or Social Change: Debating Disability." In *X-Men and Philosophy,* edited by Rebecca Housel and J. Jeremy Wisnewski. Hoboken: John Wiley and Sons, 2009, 170–202.

Langley, Travis. "Freedom versus Security: The Basic Human Dilemma from 9/11 to Marvel's Civil War." Henderson State University, 2007. Web.

Lee, Stan. *Son of Origins of Marvel Comics.* New York: Simon & Schuster, 1975.

Lee, Stan and Robert Bernstein (w) and Don Heck (a). "Iron Man Faces the Crimson Dynamo." *Tales of Suspense, #46* (Oct. 1963). New York: Marvel Comics.

_____. "Iron Man versus Gargantus." *Tales of Suspense, #40* (Apr. 1963) New York: Marvel Comics.

_____. "Iron Man versus Kala, Queen of the Underworld." *Tales of Suspense, #43.* (Jul. 1963). New York: Marvel Comics.

_____. "The Stronghold of Doctor Strange." *Tales of Suspense, #41* (May 1963). New York: Marvel Comics.

Lieber, Larry (w) and Don Heck (a). *Tales of Suspense #39.* New York: Marvel Comics, March 10, 1963.

Longmore, Paul K. and Lauri Umansky (eds). *The New Disability History: American Perspectives.* The History of Disability Series. New York: New York University Press, 2001.

MacPherson, Myra. *Long Time Passing: Vietnam & The Haunted Generation.* New York: Signet, 1984.

Mangels, Andy. *Iron Man: Beneath the Armor.* New York: Del Rey Books, 2008.

McClancy, Kathleen. "Back in the World: Vietnam Veterans through Popular Culture." Doctoral Dissertation, Duke University, 2009.

McCloud, Scott. *Understanding Comics: The Invisible Art.* New York: Harper Paperbacks, 1994.

Norden, Martin F. "Bitterness, Rage and Redemption: Hollywood Constructs the Disabled Vietnam Veteran." In *Disabled Veterans in History,* edited by David A. Gerber. Ann Arbor: University of Michigan Press, 2000, 96–116.

Nelson, Tim. "'Even an Android Can Cry.'" *Journal of Gender Studies,* 13.3 (November 2004): 251–257.

Puller, Lewis B., Jr. *Fortunate Son: The Healing of a Vietnam Vet.* New York: Grove Press, 1991.

Remarque, Erich. *The Road Back.* 1931. New York: Random House, 2013.

Scarry, Elaine. *The Body in Pain: The Making and Unmaking of the World.* New York: Oxford University Press, 1997.

Starr, Paul. *The Discarded Army: Veterans After Vietnam.* New York: Charterhouse, 1973.

White, Mark D. "Did Iron Man Kill Captain America" In *Iron Man and Philosophy,* edited by Mark D. White. Hoboken: John Wiley & Sons, 2010, 64–79.

_____.ed. *Iron Man and Philosophy.* Hoboken: John Wiley & Sons, 2010.

"Gorgeous new menace"

Black Widow, Gender Roles and the Subversion of Cold War Expectations of Domesticity

NATALIE R. SHEPPARD

In 1963 a wealthy playboy scientist superhero debuted on the pages of *Tales of Suspense*. Antagonized by several communist villains out to steal the his private property and technology in order to advance the communist agenda of enslaving the free world, Iron Man was one of an early wave of superheroes published by Marvel Comics. Iron Man is often pitted against the communist scourge in these early issues rather than against American criminals or intergalactic threats. Though most superheroes of the Cold War were fighting communists as well, they are especially suited to Iron Man, who represents the self-made man that capitalism exalts. Often just revealing a character to be a communist, or a citizen of a communist nation was a narrative shorthand establishing each issue's nemesis. The communist enemy would either be temporarily defeated or reformed by Iron Man at the end of each 13-page issue, signifying America's victory over the reds. Each month Iron Man appeared, extolling the virtues of American patriotism while denouncing the tyrannical communist governments. While this pattern was appealing, it did not represent the reality of the Cold War, which was fought largely through propaganda, espionage, and by proxy nations rather than in an epic battle between the USSR and the USA. Matthew J. Costello writes,

> By the end of the 1950s, most Americans accepted that they existed in a virtuous society of free individuals, with the best form of government and the greatest possible economic system in the free market.... If this was to con-

tinue, Americans needed to be vigilant against the tide of totalitarian control that flowed outside their borders and lapped at their shores [49–50].

In an era where Cold War paranoia and espionage fear was at its height, it is no surprise that one of Iron Man's most revealing villains is the KGB super-spy Black Widow, Natasha Romanov.

Black Widow is more than the standard communist brute with whom Iron Man typically battled. As both a villain and a heroine, Black Widow is explicitly subversive to American domesticity and womanhood. With the notable exception of Wonder Woman, female superheroes are often created as female derivatives or love interest of the male heroes. Supergirl, She-Hulk, Batwoman, and Ms. Marvel are all feminized versions of their male counterparts; Superman, Hulk, Batman, and Captain Marvel, respectively. In other cases, the female superheroine is created to balance a group and provide a mother/sister/wife dynamic. Invisible Girl, Marvel Girl, and Wasp all fall into this category. This type of heroine not only serves to add a romantic element to otherwise masculine stories, but also reinforces domestic ideals in women. In the cases of both classes of heroines, the women generally value love and marriage over truth and justice, and are always the weakest members of the group. This focus on the woman as domestic caretaker existed outside of comic books, as well. Television shows such as *Leave It to Beaver* and *The Donna Reed Show* emphasized the importance a woman should place on her family and on being a good wife.

This new obsession with the nuclear family stemmed from the years following World War II, when the country was desperate for stability and security. Jeffrey K. Johnson points out that,

> Prominent Americans warned the U.S. Public to carefully observe their neighbors because anyone could be a communist agent attempting to destroy the American way of life. Because Americans constructed postwar society to be rigid and conformist, the notion of the outsider was terrifying" [78].

Created in 1964 by Stan Lee, Don Rico, and Don Heck, Black Widow is subjected to these same anxieties of traditional domestic femininity, but also on the cusp of second-wave feminism, which was just gaining speed in 1963 with the release of *The Feminine Mystique*. Caught between these two ideals of what a woman "should" be Black Widow subverts each of them as both heroine and villainess.

In fact, the very name Black Widow distinguishes her from the male derived heroes, and her villainy depends on her lack of domesticity. She is evil because, unlike American women, she isn't ruled by love and emotion. Just as her namesake arachnid devours the heads of her male counterparts, so too does Black Widow subvert the patriarchal power structure which was vital to the culture of the Cold War. Black Widow is more than sexy, she is powerful. Not only because she is an expertly trained super-spy, but because she operates outside of the norms of society. As a villain, this type of woman may be attractive and alluring, but she spells doom for any man she comes across. As a heroine, Black Widow is entirely unique because she fails to surrender her femme-fatale characteristics in favor of domesticity, the more commonly seen route chosen by Marvel's female superheroes in this era.

Black Widow's lack of traditionally feminine characteristics establishes Soviet women as a tier "less than" American women because they lack American domestic values. Black Widow is portrayed as independent, powerful, and promiscuous; three things that endanger the patriarchal status quo in America. The pages of Iron Man contain very few women, but most of them are the love interests of Tony Stark. They fit squarely within the expectations of American women, particularly Pepper Potts, the only woman who is shown opposite of Black Widow. As secretary, Pepper Potts fills the role of platonic caretaker to the bachelor Tony Stark, but longs to become romantically involved.

Potts is often contrasted with Black Widow. Where Pepper Potts wears bright colors like yellow and robin's egg blue, Black Widow is shown wearing dark greens and blues. In addition, Black Widow is nearly always shown wearing a fur, which emphasizes her coldness, and a pillbox hat with a partial veil that obscures her face, suggesting she is hiding something. Where Black Widow is brilliant and cunning, Pepper Potts relies on feminine intuition. Black Widow is forced to work for her communist masters, while Pepper Potts gladly shows up to work as Tony Stark's secretary. Where Pepper Potts hides her attraction to Stark while still nurturing him, Black Widow fakes an attraction in order to destroy him. Pepper Potts is largely powerless, and in *Tales of Suspense* #64 (Apr. 1965) the threat that communist women pose against American women is acted out when Black Widow kidnaps Pepper Potts in order to get to Iron Man. Pepper Potts plays the traditional role of damsel in distress while the woman with power is portrayed as intelligent and sexy, but ultimately evil.

Black Widow's beauty is remarked upon numerous times, but always in conjunction with her coldness as a fundamental flaw. This fact is established as early as Black Widow's first appearance. On the cover and title pages of *Tales of Suspense* #52 (Apr. 1964), she is described as "the gorgeous new menace" and introduced as "the breathtaking beauty." Among Iron Man's villains, Black Widow is unique because she is physically beautiful. In comic books physical beauty often reflects moral virtue, but in the case of Black Widow her beauty is her weapon. Black Widow's partner in this first adventure, Boris Turenov, is far more typical of the physical representation of Iron Man's Russian villains; he is both tall and wide, with a large forehead, square jaw, bad teeth, and beady eyes. Unlike the villains of Asian countries, whose racial differences were caricaturized in order to easily designate them as other, Russian villains were often drawn as sub-human with Neanderthal features, reflecting the depravity of the Soviet communist system. Physical beauty, in the case of men, at least, is directly correlated to how virtuous a character is. Black Widow, however, is both physically alluring and morally bankrupt. After Iron Man defeats Boris, Stark's pal Happy Hogan asks why they don't go after the escaped Black Widow. Stark responds "In a way, I pity her! All that beauty outside.... But inside ... nothing!" (Lee and Korok, "The Crimson Dynamo..."). This coldness of women is one associated specifically with femme-fatale characters, who are in many ways so seductive because they are unfeeling and manipulative. Unlike American female characters of the Cold War who were shown as both patriots and willing participants in the patriarchy, female soviet spies are often portrayed as breathtakingly beautiful, but for whom all domesticity has been denied by the Soviet system. Though her beauty is momentarily distracting to Iron Man, she is ultimately not a danger to the hyper-patriotic superhero. The unwillingness of Iron Man to go after Black Widow demonstrates the little threat he believes she poses to him. Not only is she a mere woman, someone his patriarchal society demands he protect, but he knows that her own government will punish her much more severely than he ever could.

Black Widow escapes unscathed from her battle with Iron Man, but it is not his vengeance she fears. The final panel of *Tales of Suspense #52* shows Black Widow "On some fog-filled street in some crowded city ... lonely ... abandoned ... always hiding!" But it is her communist masters she fears, not Tony Stark. The thought bubble reveals Black Widow's motives, stating "I must keep moving ... I know too well the penalty for failure!!" (Lee and Korok, "The Crimson Dynamo..."). Even loyal citizens of the Soviet Union fear their own government more than the American superheroes.

In the very next issue, Black Widow attempts to redeem herself by stealing a new Stark invention, the anti-gravity beam, and defeating Iron Man with the help of two Soviet stooges. In the climactic final battle, the anti-gravity beam loses power and puts the two Soviet men in danger. Iron Man saves them, causing Black Widow to ask "What manner of men are these Americans, who risk their lives for their enemies?" Iron Man responds "That's the trouble with you commies! You just don't dig us!" (Lee and Korok, "The Black Widow..."). The juxtaposition of Black Widow, a spy, with Iron Man, a superhero, is a powerful contrast between the underhanded, sneaky Soviets and the upstanding, honorable Americans. Iron Man acts in a virtuous way even towards his enemies, saving their lives despite the fact that they attempted to steal his technology and, presumably, kill him. Black Widow, as a spy, uses lies and manipulation to steal and commit acts of violence. In these first few appearances, Iron Man and Black Widow are polar opposites and natural enemies, just as the USA and the USSR are foes on the global stage. Iron Man's heroism reinforced the idea of America as the protector of the free world, while Black Widow represented the insidious and subversive communist scourge.

Like Black Widow, the present-day superhero Hawkeye began as a villain. Hawkeye first appears in *Tales of Suspense* #57 (Sep. 1964), which opens with Clint Barton, before his Hawkeye days, performing trick bow and arrow shots on Coney Island. Eventually, Hawkeye enters the world of superheroes out of envy, not a sense of justice or morality. He is a far cry from Iron Man, who has a seemingly unwavering moral compass, but his decision to become a superhero is not in itself a bad choice. He wants to be admired for doing good works, rather than as a circus sideshow. However, his plan goes awry when, after catching a thief, he is caught with the jewels and thought to be a purple-clad criminal. Black Widow sees Hawkeye running from the police and offers him a ride. Hawkeye is immediately infatuated, assuring Black Widow that "Whatever you're lookin' for, gorgeous, you can bet your bottom dollar ... I'm it!" The reader is then told that "thus, smitten by the Black Widow's fatal beauty, the man called Hawkeye enters into a dramatic alliance which is to change the course of both their lives, and Iron Man's as well!" (Lee, "Hawkeye, the Marksman"). With the help of Black Widow's technology, Hawkeye nearly defeats Iron Man. But at the last second, Black Widow is injured and Hawkeye chooses to save her rather than complete the mission, crying out "She has to live!! She has to be mine!! She's the only one I've ever loved!!" (Lee, "Hawkeye, the Marksman"), as he runs into the mist. Unlike Iron Man, who is already a successful capitalist, Hawkeye is much more vulnerable to Black Widow's seduction because he is a working man. Though he begins on a path sanctioned by American values, the communist Black Widow appears a more appealing option. She doesn't even have to say anything before Hawkeye promises that he's her man. Once again, her beauty and attractiveness is all she needs.

Hawkeye is a man doomed by bad luck and bad decisions, but he is not a villain at heart. When Hawkeye tells Black Widow in *Tales of Suspense* #60 that "My heart rebels at the thought of treason!" she responds "It will not be treason, my bold hero! I only serve the cause of peace!" (Lee, "Suspected...").

Hawkeye sees the best in people, and he saw the best in Black Widow at her worst. He believes her when she says that hers is a mission of peace because that is what he wants to believe. He wants to believe that this woman he loves is not evil. He wants to believe that he is doing the right thing. And maybe she does, too.

Black Widow's power in the relationship further subverts the domesticity women in America were subjected to. Most female heroines of the time were young, pining after older heroes, and performing domestic tasks for the Avengers or whatever superhero team they were on. Mike Madrid writes of superheroines that "their need for love is often of greater or equal importance than their quest for justice. If Mr. Right popped the question, a heroine could easily retire that mask and cape and settle down to a life as a wife and mother" (57). Other Marvel heroines such as The Wasp, Invisible Girl, and Marvel Girl certainly follow this pattern,[1] but not Black Widow. Instead, Black Widow is the older, cleverer woman who seduces the young but naïve Hawkeye. The situation is completely reversed; *he* is introduced as *her* love interest. Rather than a young, naïve girl becoming a heroine out of admiration for an older man in a position of power, we see a strong young man lured into villainy by an older, intelligent woman. Before the appearance of Hawkeye in *Tales of Suspense* #57 (Sep. 1964), Black Widow had already fought Iron Man several times and, while she may not have defeated him, she escaped capture from both Iron Man and her disappointed communist leaders. She did this all with no superpowers or gadgets, and each time was outdone by her lack of physical strength. Hawkeye is a devoted dupe who goes along with her master plan. Black Widow orchestrates and plans the attack, then looks on from afar as stronger men battle beneath her. Black Widow may use her feminine sexuality and wiles to manipulate the men around her, but in these early appearances she is just as ambitious and powerful as the male heroes.

Black Widow is introduced as a spy, not a supervillain. She first appears in civilian clothing and has no superpowers and no special technology to give her an advantage over her adversaries. What she does have is her sexuality, and she weaponizes that aspect of her femininity. Black Widow uses not only her beauty (Pepper Potts, after all, is beautiful too), but her knowledge of her beauty, her self-confidence. Where Pepper laments of Tony Stark ever noticing her, Black Widow fully expects Stark not only to notice her, but to be completely in awe of her. Everything from her dress to her actions are carefully constructed to attract men to her, and to their doom. However it is not only her sexuality that Black Widow uses to defeat Iron Man, but American expectations of domestic women. Black Widow is able to distract Tony Stark because he doesn't believe a woman, much less a woman as gorgeous as Black Widow, can be a villain. During the battle, Black Widow pretends to be helplessly trapped beneath some machinery, playing the expected role of damsel in distress to Iron Man's noble knight. Even her escape is only permitted her because Iron Man doesn't believe she could possibly be a real threat. Black Widow then not only weaponizes her own femininity, but also uses society's expectations of women against those who subscribe to America's patriarchal system.

In *Tales of Suspense* #64 (Apr. 1965) Black Widow evolves from spy to supervillain. Her communist leaders design a costume and, despite Black Widow's protestations of "I'm through serving your evil purposes!" (Lee, "Hawkeye and..."), force her to wear it. The new blue and fishnet costume enables Black Widow to climb walls and shoot a nylon rope from her wrist, allowing her to swing from building to building like a spider. When she was asked to design a mask for her new costume, Black Widow tells her lover, "I made one to resemble yours, Hawkeye ... for you shall again be my partner!" (Lee, "Hawkeye and..."). In the span of only seven issues, Natasha has gone from thinking "It is fortunate that he is taken with my beauty! I will be able to twist him around my little finger!" (Lee, "Hawkeye, the Marksman") to telling Hawkeye that "I had to come back ... to see you once more!! To feel your strong arms around me!" (Lee, "Hakweye and..."). Her new costume and technology allow Black Widow to enter the battle as an equal to the men; however, her motives aren't pure. Just as Hawkeye entered into superheroism out of envy, Black Widow is coerced into becoming a supervillain by her superiors. Just as Hawkeye's intentions as a hero were easily subverted, so too are Black Widow's.

Hawkeye serves as yet a more drastic warning against the allure of communist temptation. Unlike Iron Man, who is only momentarily distracted by Black Widow, Hawkeye falls in love with her and ultimately it is this love that leads to his becoming a villain. It is only after becoming forcibly separated from Black Widow that Hawkeye comes to his senses and joins the Avengers. In *The Avengers* #16 (May 1965), the Avengers are understandably hesitant to let Hawkeye join them, but he tells them that he always wanted to be a hero until Black Widow seduced him. He goes on to assure his new friends that "I'll make up for what I've done! I'll devote my life to making amends!" (Lee, "The Old Order..."). Still in love with Black Widow, Hawkeye hopes to make amends for them both. It is Iron Man who officially announces the addition of Hawkeye to the Avengers, symbolizing his ultimate forgiveness of and newfound trust in Hawkeye, though others remain suspicious of Hawkeye's true intentions.

Hawkeye reformed and became a part of a superhero team, but what of Black Widow? "Fortunately, opportunities for redemption abounded" Peter Lee writes of femme-fatales in this era of comic books, "Women who rediscovered their capacity for love and romance inevitably found their way to the Western powers" (39). In spy fiction and film noire, the femme-fatale often fell in love with the hero, and would be passed over in favor of the more wholesome woman such as Pepper Potts or else completely reformed by her newfound warmth. However, it is fellow criminal Hawkeye, not Iron Man, whom Black Widow falls for. It is Hawkeye's love for Black Widow which warms her icy heart and causes her to defect to America. It is this love that causes her to tell her communist commanders that she's through serving their "evil purposes" (Lee, "Hawkeye, and...").

Unlike the Avengers, however, the Soviets are much less understanding, and force her to continue fighting for them by threatening her parents and making her a weapon. When even this doesn't work, the Soviets are finally forced to use brainwashing. Brainwashing is the expression of true evil in communist nations, as it gives the Soviets a method of policing free thought. It further supports the dichotomy of American liberty and Soviet slavery. Though Black Widow is bodily and physically free, her mind is still under the control of the Soviets. It is under these circumstances that Black Widow is sent on her final mission to defeat the Avengers with a new crew of Soviet goons to do her bidding in *The Avengers* #30 (Jul. 1966). As a villain, Black Widow is still the woman in charge. But after seeing Hawkeye, the brainwashing wears off and she helps him defeat her communist former comrades (Lee, "Frenzy..."). From that moment on both Black Widow and Hawkeye remained firmly on the side of the good guys.

Despite their, to this point, character-defining romance which was a plot line unto itself, Hawkeye and Black Widow were not meant to be. The love for Hawkeye that made Black Widow defect to the United States was doomed, in part because Black Widow put her heroic expectations above her romantic life. Sent on a top secret mission by SHIELD, Black Widow was forced to play the double agent and made to appear a traitor to the Avengers. This breaks Hawkeye's heart, and he takes to brooding as Black Widow singlehandedly destroys a communist mass mind control device behind the bamboo curtain. Although Hawkeye's love is what causes Black Widow to defect to the United States and begin a new life as superhero rather than a villain, it is her own strength that causes her to continue on that path. Black Widow sacrifices her love when her new country needs her, and it is ultimately this decision that establishes her as a true hero despite running counter to expectations of domestic femininity. Once again, Hawkeye is placed in the traditionally feminine role when he pines over her seeming reversion to villainy, while Back Widow values justice and her career over her love life.

Despite turning into a heroine, Black Widow rarely appears on the pages of Iron Man stories after this conversion. She appeared as a villain five times in a span of only twelve issues, but even her defection takes place on the pages of *The Avengers*. Part of this is because even after becoming a heroine, Black Widow remains an independent and powerful woman who subverts feminine domesticity. Black Widow goes off on her own secret mission and single-handedly saves the free world from communist control while Hawkeye laments his lost lady love. Black Widow would also not be an appropriate heroine for Iron Man to fight alongside because she was a spy. Her knowledge of espionage was a crucial component to her character. Pairing Black Widow with Iron Man would have bolstered her own reputation, but diminished him. As a superhero representing American ideals, the unscrupulousness of a former spy would have made his own actions less heroic. Black Widow operates on a different, unseen level of heroism, which is why she works for SHIELD, the superhero equivalent to the CIA, rather than the Avengers following her defection. The Avengers are all paragons of virtue and American idealism. SHIELD is a department dedicated to doing whatever is necessary for the preservation of freedom. Tony Stark, weapons manufacturer, is more valuable to SHIELD than Iron Man. SHIELD is not led by a handsome, flag-clad American icon like Captain America, but by a gritty, more-realistic former CIA agent. This type of agency is better suited to the super-spy character that Black Widow embodies. At SHIELD Black Widow can continue to exhibit femme-fatale characteristics while remaining a heroine.

During the years following World War II emphasis was placed on women returning to their rightful place in the home as protectors of their families. Black Widow was created as an enemy of this ideal, a subversion of the warm, nurturing American woman. Her femme-fatale characteristics are portrayed as a direct threat to American domesticity, just as communism was perceived as a direct threat to capitalism and the American way of life. Black Widow's independence and feminine power foreshadow the influence second-wave feminism would have on American culture and comic books, but renders her an inappropriate partner for Iron Man, who is too visible as an American icon to be seen approving the characteristics of the femme-fatale spy. Black Widow's romance with Hawkeye is one of the central insights to her character, revealing her true power and intelligence. As a feminist character, Black Widow subverts the conservative expectations of the past and embraces the future of feminism as an independent, powerful, and complex heroine.

Notes

1. Please see "Invisible, Tiny, and Distant: The Powers and Roles of Marvel's Early Female Superheroes" by Joseph J. Darowski in the essay collection *Heroines of Comic Books and Literature: Portrayals in Popular Culture* for further discussion of this topic.

Works Cited

Costello, Matthew J. *Secret Identity Crisis: Comic Books and the Unmasking of Cold War America*. New York: Continuum, 2009.

Johnson, Jeffrey K. *Super-history: Comic Book Superheroes and American Society, 1938 to the Present*. Jefferson, NC: McFarland, 2012.

Lee, Peter. "Decrypting Espionage Comic Books in 1950s America." In *Comic Books and the Cold War 1946–1962: Essays on Graphic Treatment of Communism, the Code and Social Concerns*. Edited by Chris York and Rafiel York. Jefferson, N.C.: McFarland, 2012. 30–44.

Lee, Stan, Jack Kirby, and Don Heck. *Avengers 16, 29–30*. Vol. 1. New York: Marvel Comics, 1963–1966.

Lee, Stan (w) and Don Heck (a). "Frenzy in a Far-Off Land!" *The Avengers* #30 (Jul. 1966). New York: Marvel Comics. *Marvel Unlimited*. Web.

_____. "Hawkeye and the New Black Widow Strike Again." *Tales of Suspense* #64 (Apr. 1965). New York: Marvel Comics. *Marvel Unlimited*. Web.

_____. "Hawkeye, the Marksman!" *Tales of Suspense* #57 (Sep. 1964). New York: Marvel Comics. *Marvel Unlimited*. Web.

_____. "Suspected of Murder!" *Tales of Suspense* #60 (Dec. 1964). New York: Marvel Comics. *Marvel Unlimited*. Web.

Lee, Stan (w) and Jack Kirby (a). "The Old Order Changeth!" *The Avengers* #16 (May 1965). New York: Marvel Comics. *Marvel Unlimited*. Web.

Lee, Stan (w), N. Korok (w), and Don Heck (a). "The Crimson Dynamo Strikes Again!" *Tales of Suspense* #52 (Apr. 1964). New York: Marvel Comics. *Marvel Unlimited*. Web.

Madrid, Mike. *The Supergirls: Fashion, Feminism, Fantasy, and the History of Comic Book Heroines*. Ashland, Or.: Exterminating Angel, 2009.

Wright, Bradford W. *Comic Book Nation: The Transformation of Youth Culture in America*. Baltimore: Johns Hopkins University Press, 2001.

Fu Manchu Meets Maklu-4

The Mandarin and Racial Stereotypes

Richard A. Iadonisi

From his inception, Iron Man is a product of Cold War ideology. The villain who opposes Iron Man in his inaugural issue is Wong-Chu, "the Red guerrilla tyrant" who goes from one South Vietnamese village to the next vanquishing each village's champion in hand-to-hand combat (Lee, "Iron Man is Born"). Early issues of *Tales of Suspense* continue to evoke the Communist menace as Soviet villains Crimson Dynamo, the Titanium Man, and Black Widow make appearances. When Stan Lee and Don Heck sought another villain to oppose their fledgling hero, they looked beyond the Soviet Union and opted to create the Mandarin, a foe from Communist China. Given the fact that, in the minds of many, China had come to rival Russia as a threat to the United States,[1] we would expect the Mandarin to be as much a symbol of Cold War tension as other characters. However, his relationship to Communism is vexed by the numerous racial stereotypes that writers and artists invoke.

Perhaps the dominant stereotype represented by the Mandarin is the blatantly racist image of the Yellow Peril. According to Daniel A. Métraux, Professor of Asian Studies at Mary Baldwin College, although "[t]he expression initially referred to Japan's sudden rise as a military and industrial power in the late nineteenth century," it came to be used for all Asia and "took on a broader more sinister meaning." The leap from "military and industrial power" to threat to global security is apparently not a great one, and soon led to a "fear held by Western society—in particular British and American societies—that Orientals would one day unite and conquer the world," as Gary Hoppenstand explains (280).

It did not take long for popular culture to grab hold of the Yellow Peril stereotype and personify it. The first of these manifestations to gain wide readership was Sax Rohmer's Dr. Fu Manchu, initially appearing in 1913. Following Rohmer's lead, both pulp fiction and comic strip writers such as Philip Nowlan and Alex Raymond created their own versions of the Yellow Peril, Nowlan in his Buck Rogers strip, which debuted in 1929 and Raymond in Flash Gordon with Ming the Merciless, first appearing in 1934. Perhaps the first major comic book character to carry on this tradition, and the immediate precursor to the Mandarin, was Yellow Claw, who had a brief initial run in an eponymous 1956 and 1957 comic.

In many ways, the Mandarin is an amalgamation of the worst traits of his forbears. One of the most common stereotypes associated with China in the popular imagination, as historian Harold Isaacs notes in his book *Images of Asia*, stems from Genghis Khan's ironically Mongol (rather than Chinese) hordes, an "undifferentiated crush of humanity" (45). Although it began in twelfth century Mongolia, this stereotype was applied to the Japanese during World War II and to the Chinese during and after the Korean War. Implied in the numerous agents in Fu Manchu's employ, this imagery is less subtle in Nowlan's strips as Buck Rogers is pitted against the Red Mongols, an obvious allusion to Genghis Khan's Mongol hordes. Still more obvious is Yellow Claw, who, according to the Marvel Universe Wiki, "was actually Plan Tzu, the 19th Century descendant of and rightful successor to the legendary warlord Temujin, a.k.a. Genghis Khan" ("Yellow Claw").

As for the Mandarin, the connection with the Mongol hordes is even more explicit and extensive. In his first appearance, in *Tales of Suspense #50* (Feb. 1964), the cover depicts a line of soldiers advancing down a flight of stairs in the background. In the foreground are a hand wielding a spear and another holding a pistol while the blade of a sword is also displayed. As if the implication that the Mandarin is a modern day Khan is too subtle, Iron Man refers in the course of the story to his foe as a "weak apology for Genghis Khan" (Lee, "The Hands..."). The Mandarin's origin in *Tales of Suspense #62* (Feb. 1965) repeats this symbolic genealogy by claiming his "father was a direct descendent of Genghis Khan" (Lee, "The Origin"). Decades later, readers learn that the Mandarin has a son, and that son is bequeathed with the Mongol leader's birth name Temujin (Grell, "Book of...").

Just like Genghis Khan, the popular culture manifestations of the yellow peril are associated with conquering. Fu Manchu, "the yellow peril incarnate in one man" (*The Insidious Fu Manchu* 26), is bent on world domination, Ming has conquered a world, albeit the distant planet Mongo, and Yellow Claw initially heads the Atlas Foundation intent on conquest. Thus, as a narrative successor to these others, the Mandarin will also plot to rule the world. And plot he does. Skeptics may argue that world domination is not an unusual aspiration for a supervillain, yet a useful distinction can be made by comparing the Chinese supervillain to his Soviet counterparts. Crimson Dynamo and the Titanium Man are agents of world domination, important cogs, but cogs nonetheless, in the Communist machine. The Mandarin, conversely, is agency rather than agent, thus at odds with Communism. The Mandarin, who wields ten power rings, finds his rings while wandering after his palace is confiscated by Communists in *Tales of Suspense #62* (Feb. 1965). In *Tales of Suspense #86* (Feb. 1967) Chinese troops, sent to demand the Mandarin's help, are routed by the villain. Much later, he teleports Communist soldiers to the moon to die (*Invincible Iron Man #266* [Mar. 1991]), conquers one-third of China and even invades the U.S.S.R. (*Invincible Iron Man #10* [Nov. 1998]). As would-be conqueror, the Mandarin is reviled by both democratic America and Communist China. Though Chinese, he performs what to many Americans would be considered admirable: rebuffing, repelling, subduing, and even destroying the Communists who oppose him. While "hawks" in the United States were frustrated by restrictions on U.S. military tactics (such as Korean War troops being ordered to halt all pursuits of enemy combatants at the Yalu), the Mandarin is able to meet and defeat the Communists in their own territories, accomplishing what the United States could not.

As Ming the Merciless's name suggests, another common stereotype of Asians in general and Chinese in particular is that they are cruel. Isaacs notes that cruelty is one of the dominant images his research turned up, and it goes back, once more, to Genghis Khan and his men who butchered, beheaded, and tortured their way across Asia and into Europe (105). The Boxer Rebellion, during which missionaries and Chinese Christians were attacked and killed, fostered this idea of cruelty, of the Chinese as "the killers of girl infants" and "the torturers of a thousand cuts" (64) who employed "devilishly ingenious methods of inflicting pain and death" (106). Even given that villains are typically sadistic, it becomes evident that the Mandarin elevates cruelty to a higher level than most of his comic-book peers. This malevolence begins shortly after his birth as, following the death of his parents, he inherits a great fortune only to have his aunt attempt to kill him so the fortune will be hers (Lee, "The Origin..."). This twist on the "killers of girl infants" idea is the first of many instances in which "Asian" and "cruel" are synonymous.

When Denny O'Neil is authoring the Iron Man stories, in one issue, the Mandarin's minion Radioactive Man seeks to get revenge for the pain inflicted on him. However, the Mandarin uses one of his power rings to command the hapless minion to strike himself in the face and to break his own thumb. This issue ends with the Mandarin forcing Iron Man to remove his own helmet, pick up a handy sword, and cut his own throat "slowly" (O'Neil, "This Ancient Enemy"). Dispensing death with no remorse and even a certain glee is a trademark of this villain who, in one issue, uses his matter rearranging ring on a disloyal underling after offering him false hope (Byrne, "...Like All Secrets..."). Even a Communist leader is appalled by the Mandarin, of whom he says, "He would as gladly rule a land of corpses as be opposed in any way" (Byrne, "Retribution").

Where the Mandarin far outdoes the previous incarnations of the Yellow Peril is in the fear held by many whites that Asians' hunger for military and/or economic conquest is "only matched by their hunger for the Anglo-American woman" (Hoppenstand 280). Although the Mandarin has Genghis Khan's blood from his father's side of the family, his mother is "a high born English-woman" (Lee, "The Origin..." Consequently, the supervillain's implicitly sex-ually predatory father has succeeded in "polluting" white blood. This Western fear of Asian sexual hunger is further emphasized in *Invincible Iron Man #27* (Apr. 2000). Writer Joe Quesada, along with artist Sean Chen, depicts the Mandarin appearing before a drunken Tony Stark and taunting him with the following speech: "I've destroyed your life! I've killed your friends! I killed your woman! Oh, and what I did to her before she welcomed death—such pleasure you will never know!" ("The Dream Machine"). The strong sugges-tion that the Mandarin rapes Stark's girlfriend Rumiko Fujikawa at once underscores and defuses fears of Asians preying on white women when we learn that the sequence was a dream and by our awareness that the woman is Japanese. Still, the stereotype's "footprint" remains to demonize the other while the villain's comment that Stark will never know the pleasure the Man-darin experienced demonstrates how readily white masculinist desires can be projected onto that other.[2]

Various writers even go so far as to resurrect the "torturers of a thousand cuts" stereotype. In one of his earlier appearances, the Mandarin reacts to a blow from Iron Man by promising the hero will "die a thousand deaths" (Lee, "Death Duel...") while in *The Invincible Iron Man Annual #1* (August 2010), Matt Fraction has the Mandarin, directing and starring in his own filmic autobiography, tell the actor playing Iron Man, "I'll kill you for your crimes—kill you. Kill you a thousand times" ("Mandarin:..."). The repetition of the word "kill" followed by the word "thousand" may seem like mere hyperbole, but the fact that the Mandarin actually does end the life of the actor suggests otherwise.

The fact that neither the Korean War nor the Vietnam War went well for the United States may explain another way in which the Mandarin is stereotyped. Isaacs observes that images of the ineffectual Chinese troops of World War II were replaced as a result of defeats of U.S. soldiers in 1950 by images of "a formidable foe" (216) comprised of "dangerous fighting men" (227). Faced with such troublesome images, Americans may well have responded favorably to the resurrected stereotype of the emasculated and asexual Asian male. This stereotype doubtless owes its origins to the typically smaller stature of Asian men and more specifically to their braided queues, long silk gowns, and long fingernails, the latter two commonly associated with mandarins. Initially at odds with the comic book villain's great powers, the Mandarin is nonetheless feminized occasionally. Occasionally, he is depicted with long hair. Moreover, while wearing the armor of the Golden Avenger, both Tony Stark and James Rhodes address him as "Mandy," a diminutive that is at best androgynous. More tellingly, at one point, the narrative voice uses the same appellation, reinforcing and granting authority to the Mandarin's feminization. The Mandarin's often (but not always) long fingernails add to this coding, never more so than when they are featured on the cover of an issue, as they are in *Invincible Iron Man #241* (Apr. 1989). This cover depicts a huge hand with the obligatory fingernails poised to attack a comparatively tiny Iron Man.[3] It is also worth noting that the writers implicitly feminize the Mandarin by contrasting the many women who come into and out of the life (and, presumably, bed) of playboy Tony Stark, and the lack of any but the most fleeting relationships on the part of the villain. Instead of othering serving to express our unspoken desires, here it serves to allay the Communist threat.

Yet another common stereotype is that of the "heathen Chinese," and it comes as no surprise that the Mandarin is frequently depicted as a heathen. Rather than referring to God or even a god, it is "the gods" who play a role in the action or who are called upon. Indeed, the Mandarin owes his very life to heathen beliefs, as the aunt who determined that she would kill him was stopped in her plan by "the gods" who chose to intervene (Lee, "The Origin..."). In *The Invincible Iron Man #100* (July 1977), the Mandarin will "claim [his] birthright as heir to the great Ghenghis (sic) Khan" and "fulfill [his] destiny, his fate decreed by the gods!" (Mantlo, "Ten Rings...") while in different issues he makes such remarks as "Truly, the gods guide my hand" (Kaminski, "Friends...") and "By the will of the gods, I have been granted new hands" (Kaminski, "Hands...") In an issue written by Denny O'Neil, the heathen villain cannot comprehend why his scheme failed since "the signs were all propitious. The very stars told me the time for the return of Mandarin greatness is at hand—the very stone of the Earth cried out a prophesy of triumph," and he ridicules Radioactive Man, expecting "nothing [but cringing, groveling, and whimpering] from one born in the Year of the Rabbit" (O'Neil, "This Ancient..."). In another issue, having defeated four warriors, the Mandarin boasts, "I have focused my *chi* beyond the power granted me by these rings. I have walled about my soul with hoops of steel" (Byrne, "The Hollow Man"). Because chi (perhaps best translated here as "energy flow") underlies many traditional Chinese martial arts, its use in this context may appear nonpejorative. Yet when the word is posed antithetically with the word "soul," which the Mandarin's chi allows him to seal off, the heathen/Christian dichotomy emerges leaving little doubt as to which side the villain seeks. Emphasizing the Mandarin's heathen observances enables the writers to distance him from the Chinese Communists, who, of course, are recognized atheists.

The Mandarin's first appearance, in *Tales of Suspense #50* (Feb. 1963), refers to his castle deep "in seething, smoldering, secretive Red China," with "secretive" the most loaded of the words in this description, for it calls to mind the stereotypes of the inscrutable Oriental (Lee, "The Hands..."). As the issue unfolds, readers learn that the Mandarin's rings are actually made from the power source of a crashed space ship from the alien planet Maklu–4. Along with tapping into late 1950s and early 1960s interest in science fiction (and science is important here, for it connects the Mandarin with his Yellow Peril predecessors Fu Manchu, Ming, and Yellow Claw, all of whom are masters of science), technology in the service of evil (the rings) seems suitable to oppose technology in the service of good (Iron Man's armor). Yet, unlike Crimson Dynamo and the Titanium Man, whose armor is merely technological, the Mandarin must be othered. As the character's role in the series expands, so does the emphasis on his magical, mystical abilities. Yet again, the Mandarin is but one more in a line of evil mysterious Asians. Fu Manchu "is an adept in certain obscure arts and sciences which *no* university of today can teach" (*The Insidious Fu Manchu* 24). Meanwhile, when artist Joe Maneely designs covers for issues of The Yellow Claw each cover is headlined by the question, "Who ... or *What* ... Is He??!" and the italicized "what" reinforces the character's mysterious otherness. While Maneely's covers of the first two issues trumpet the villain as "the most dangerous man of all time," when Bill Everett and John Severin create the cover of issues three and four, respectively, the stereotype shifts from Yellow Claw's danger to his inscrutability as he is described as the "master of mystery."

The sense of mystery surrounding "the inscrutable Mandarin" (Stan Lee uses this very phrase in *Tales of Suspense #76* (Apr. 1966)) is highlighted by his various powers. Although the focus is often on the Mandarin's karate skills and power rings, he, like Ming and Yellow Claw before him, is a master of magic. One of his rings endows its bearer with the ability to compel others to do his bidding, and he uses this hypnotic power often.[4] This clichéd mystical ability is later supplemented when the Mandarin obtains "the might of the fabled Eye of Yin" (Gerber, "Strike"). In a story line beginning in *The Invincible Iron Man #260* (September 1990), the Mandarin meets up with the ancient wizard Chen, and as the story arc continues, so does the magic and mystery. The very next issue finds the wizard and the Mandarin in China's Valley of the Sleeping Dragon where they come upon a gate guarded by "hereditary guardians of a secret so incomprehensible all but a handful dismiss it as the stuff of dreams and fairy tales" (Byrne, "Untitled"). A later story, this one by Len Kaminski and Tom Morgan, presents the narrative voice informing readers that the Mandarin used sorcery to re-grow the hands he lost in the story arc described above ("Appetite for Destruction"). Foregrounding mystery marks the Asian as other while foregrounding magic signals another critical move that the comics make by fixing that other as pre-technological (i.e., backwards) and therefore pre–Communist.

However, in each of these instances, magic alone is somehow not enough. Just as the same ring that possesses powers associated with magic was forged from alien technology, the Eye of Yin is not only "the sole monument to a race of sorcerers who strode this planet in dark days long past," but also "[t]he Yin had learned their sorcerous skills—from a race of beings … who, undoubtedly—were ancient visitors from another world" (Gerber, "Strike"). Similarly, writer John Byrne and artist John Romita, Jr. (and later Paul Ryan and Mark D. Bright) walk the fine line of magic and technology in the Chen-Mandarin stories, eventually revealing that the wizard is a dragon/alien from the ship from which the Mandarin fashioned his rings (*The Invincible Iron Man #261* (Oct. 1990)), and Kaminski and Morgan's narrative informs readers that the Mandarin "styled himself a technocrat, and sought conquest through science" even though sorcery is "power beyond that of *mere* technology" ("Appetite for Destruction"). Despite the writers' efforts to foreground technology as a way of making the Mandarin at once more formidable and more like Iron Man (a doppelganger), magic, the characteristic that others the villain, seems to win out.

Thus far, we have focused on pejorative stereotypes and images, and how they function to establish the Mandarin as a descendent of the Yellow Peril tradition as other as well as distancing him from Communism. Yet, numerous writers and artists accomplish the same goals by coopting positive images and stereotypes Americans possess regarding Asians in general and the Chinese in particular. As Isaacs observes, positive attributes are rooted in economics, tracing their roots back to Marco Polo's self-serving travelogues describing Chinese culture, art, and wisdom (63). Hoppenstand notes that this trend continued when Europeans, beginning to trade with China, "realized that Chinese craftsmanship was superior to theirs" (281), while Isaacs attributes Western beliefs in the Chinese as superior people to "China's ancient civilization, its great age and its aged greatness" (89).

The Mandarin's parentage offers insight into this stereotype. On the one hand, he inherits a propensity for despotism from Genghis Khan, and this attribute is contrasted with Iron Man's affiliation with American democracy. On the other hand, the fact that the Mandarin's mother is "high born" raises issues of socioeconomic class disparities. In *Tales of Suspense* #62 (Feb. 1965) the Mandarin refers to Iron Man as "a low-born clod" (Lee, "The Origin…"). Nearly twenty years later, in *The Invincible Iron Man #180* (Mar. 1984) the Mandarin comments on Iron Man's "ignobility" (O'Neil, "The Ancient Enemy"), and in *The Invincible Iron Man #10* (Nov. 1998), the Mandarin dismisses the Russian people as "a peasant race," explaining that he is invading Russia so he can restore "the empire of the Tsars." He even expresses his appreciation for feudalism and "the manual labor of the peasants generate[s] power, which flow[s] ever upward—growing greater at each level, until it rest[s] in the hands of the truly deserving—the noble classes" (Busiek and Chen, "Revenge"). The view of the Chinese as a superior people is undercut, of course, because the Mandarin is the one claiming that superiority. And it is further muddled because he, by aligning himself with autocrats (the Tsars) and embracing the classic Marxist dialectic of base and superstructure (the proletariat spending themselves for the nobility), the Mandarin is at odds with Communism in its theoretical form; from a practical perspective, and certainly in the minds of the reading public, the villain's views are virtually identical to those of Communist leaders. More revealing, unlike the villain, who is born titled and entitled, Tony Stark's nobility comes from his actions. Stark seems to embody the American Dream as he amasses great wealth and power through hard work.

This notion of the Mandarin as symbolic of Chinese superiority is also evident in his very name. The common definition of a mandarin is a bureaucrat of Imperial China. Consequently, at a time when Communist China, by virtue of its nuclear capabilities and surprising skill and resolve in the Korean War, is asserting itself as a legitimate threat to the U.S., the decision is made to create not a tool of the formidable Communists in the mold of the Crimson

Dynamo or Titanium Man; rather, the villain's name takes readers back to the days when China and its resources were being apportioned to Western powers. In 1974, this strategy is employed yet again when Sunfire, the Japanese superhero, says to the Mandarin, "I see in you a fallen warlord" (Friedrich, "Confrontation"), a move echoed in 1989 when the narrative voice applies the word "warlord" (Michelinie and Layton, "China See!"). Even as late as 1998, this idea crops up as the Mandarin criticizes Iron Man because he himself has "the mind of a warlord," an attribute the hero lacks (Busiek and Chen, "Revenge..."). Ideologically, Americans in the 1950s and the early 1960s were shaken by the Soviet Union's advances in the space race and by China's forays into atomic weapons as well as the Chinese Army's emergence as a fighting force with which to be reckoned. Unwilling to acknowledge the superiority of any nation, particularly a Communist, non-white one, Americans surely were tempted to gaze with fondness at the China of old, and both warlords and mandarins, as figures of the pre–Communist takeover echo an earlier, colonial China. The broad stereotype at play is that of the country as both a land of untapped riches and an ancient civilization, one incapable of change, static in contrast with the West's dynamism.

Isaacs comments on another admirable stereotype of the Chinese, who are often praised for their "filial piety" (63). Yet this image is also reimagined by the writers of *Iron Man*. For what type of ancestor worship do we see? The Mandarin honors Genghis Khan's dreams of conquest and world domination, of course. In 2002, the Mandarin's son, Temujin, is told by his mentor Master Po, "It is the duty of a son to honor the memory of his father" by "destroy[ing] Iron Man and establishing "a great dynasty" (Grell, "Book ... Part One") that will fulfill the Mandarin's "dream of China's return to the glory of Empire" (Grell, "Book ... Part Two"). As the story line continues, and Robin Laws replaces Mike Grell as writer, the stereotype persists when Temujin speaks of "[his] filial duty" and "the vengeance that duty demands" (Laws, "Manhunt"). Once more the seeming desire to distance the Mandarin from Communist ideology rears up as "filial piety" is code not only for "world conquest" or "revenge" but also for "dynasty"—a return to the days before Red China existed.

According to Isaacs' research the highest positive attribute Americans have of the Chinese is their "high intellectual quality" (73) which stems from their role as the inventors of "such things as paper, moveable type, the compass, porcelain, [and] gunpowder" (90). Today, this stereotype is another form of the Yellow Peril: the Asian scholar who achieves perfect test schools and gains admission to the top colleges supplanting real [white] Americans. Americans' belief in and fascination with this stereotype has long been evident in popular culture. Fu Manchu, for instance, "has the brains of any three men of genius. [H]e is a mental giant" (*The Insidious Fu Manchu* 24) who boasts of his four doctorate degrees (*The Bride of Fu Manchu* 181). Ming possesses tremendous intellectual capabilities, and the Yellow Claw is a scientific genius. As for the Mandarin, his genius is often employed in the service not of establishing a new world order, a worker's paradise, but of returning "this ancient land ... to the full height of its greatest glories" (Byrne, "Untitled"), "bringing to the world the wisdom and harmony of [his] Mandarin ancestors" (O'Neil, "This Ancient..."), and "restor[ing] China to the days of old" (Kaminski, "Hands..."). Consequently, he must be an inventive genius not only because Tony Stark is brilliant, and a suitable supervillain needs powers commensurate with those of the hero, but also because Western readers expect the Mandarin to conform to the trope which simultaneously connects him with ancient China and distances him from the common view of Chinese Communists as highly efficient but repressed "worker ants."

Matthew S. Hirshberg argues that Americans viewed the cold war in terms of binary opposites: Americans were democratic, free, and good unlike the Soviet Union which was Communist, oppressive, and evil. China's place in this schema was as a Soviet puppet, equally oppressive and evil (261). However, the stereotypes employed in *Iron Man* do more than reinforce binaries. As Homi Bhabha argues, stereotyping is a mechanism for members of a dominant culture to fix their views and experiences of colonial subjects and present them as representative of an entire population. These fixed views are part of the colonizers' desire to understand their colonial subjects, so that that understanding can be used to construct a new social reality. In this reality, skin color becomes a fetishized object that the colonizers use to represent whatever they need it to. In the case of the Mandarin, "yellow" signifies that which is despotic, cruel, inscrutable, treacherous, mystical, heathen, ancient, and even feminine. More than that, as these various images collide and collapse, he signifies that which we despise and admire in ourselves.

WORKS CITED

Bhabha, Homi. "The Other Question: Homi K Bhabha Reconsiders the Stereotype and Colonial Discourse." *Screen* 26.6 (Nov. 1983): 18–36.
Busiek, Kurt and Sean Chen (w) and Eric Cannon and Sean Parsons (a). "Revenge of the Mandarin, Part Two." *Invincible Iron Man #10* (Nov. 1998). New York: Marvel Comics.
Busiek, Kurt (w) and Sean Chen and Sean Parsons (a). "Trouble in Paradise." *Invincible Iron Man #4* (May 1998). New York: Marvel Comics.
Byrne, John (w) and John Romita, Jr. (a). "Armor Wars II." *The Invincible Iron Man #261* (Oct. 1990). New York: Marvel Comics.

_____. "Back from the Grave!" *The Invincible Iron Man #259* (Aug. 1990). New York: Marvel Comics.

_____. "Laser Tag!" *The Invincible Iron Man #260* (Sept. 1990). New York: Marvel Comics.

_____. "Retribution." *The Invincible Iron Man #266* (Mar. 1991). New York: Marvel Comics.

Byrne, John (w) and Paul Ryan (a). "The Hollow Man." *The Invincible Iron Man #269* (June. 1991). New York: Marvel Comics.

Everett, Bill (a). "Sleeping City." *Yellow Claw #3*(Feb. 1957). New York: Atlas (Marvel) Comics.

Fraction, Matt (w) and Matt Wilson (a). "Mandarin: The Story of My Life." *The Invincible Iron Man Annual #1* (Aug. 2010). New York: Marvel Comics.

Friedrich, Mike (w) and George Tuska (a). "Confrontation." *The Invincible Iron Man #69* (Aug. 1974). New York: Marvel Comics.

_____. "A Madness in Motown!" *The Invincible Iron Man #59* (Jun. 1973). New York: Marvel Comics.

_____. "Who Will Stop ... Ultimo?" *The Invincible Iron Man #69* (Aug. 1974). New York: Marvel Comics.

Garber, Steve (w) and George Tuska (a). "The Mandarin Strikes Back!" *The Invincible Iron Man #57* (April 1973). New York: Marvel Comics.

Grell, Mike (w) and Michael Ryan and Sean Parsons (a). "Book of the Ten Rings, Chapter Two." *The Invincible Iron Man #54* (June 2002). New York: Marvel Comics.

Grell, Mike (w) and Ryan Odagawa and Derek Fridolfs (a). "Book of the Ten Rings, Chapter One." *The Invincible Iron Man #53* (June 2002). New York: Marvel Comics.

Harriman, W. Averell. Letter to John F. Kennedy. 22 Jan. 1963. *John F. Kennedy Presidential Library and Museum.* John F. Kennedy Presidential Library and Museum, N.d. Web. 9 Sept.2013.

Hirshberg, Matthew. S. "Consistency and Change in American Perceptions of China." *Political Behavior* 15.3(1993): 247–263.

Hoppenstand, Gary. "Yellow Devil Doctors and Opium Dens: The Yellow Peril Stereotype in Mass Media Entertainment." In *Popular Culture,* edited by Jack Nachbar and Kevin Lause. Madison: University of Wisconsin Press, 1992. 277–91.

Isaacs, Harold. *Images of Asia.* New York: Capricorn, 1962.

Kaminski, Len (w) and Tom Morgan (a). "Appetite for Destruction!" *The Invincible Iron Man #300* (Jan. 1994). New York: Marvel Comics.

_____. "Friends and Other Enemies." *The Invincible Iron Man #310* (Nov. 1994). New York: Marvel Comics.

_____. "Hands of the Mandarin, Part III: The Conqueror." *The Invincible Iron Man #311* (Dec. 1994). New York: Marvel Comics.

Laws, Robin (w) and Michael Ryan and Sean Parsons with Rich Perrotta (a). "Manhunt, Part 4." *The Invincible Iron Man.* #68 (July 2003). New York: Marvel Comics.

Lee, Stan (w) and Adam Austin (a). "Here Lies Hidden .. the Unspeakable Ultimo!" *Tales of Suspense#76* (Apr. 1966). New York: Marvel Comics.

Lee, Stan (w) and Don Heck (a). "The Death of Tony Stark." *Tales of Suspense #61*(Jan. 1964). New York: Marvel Comics.

_____. "The Hands of the Mandarin!" *Tales of Suspense #50* (Feb. 1964). New York: Marvel Comics.

_____. "The Origin of the Mandarin!" *Tales of Suspense #62* (Feb. 1965). New York: Marvel Comics.

Lee, Stan (w) and Gene Colan (a). "Death Duel for the Life of Happy Hogan!" *Tales of Suspense #86* (Feb. 1967). New York: Marvel Comics.

Lee, Stan and Larry Lieber (w) and Jack Kirby and Don Heck (a). "Iron Man Is Born!" *Tales of Suspense#39* (Mar. 1963). New York: Marvel Comics.

Maneely, Joe (a) and Al Feldstein (w). "The Coming of the Yellow Claw! *Yellow Claw#1* (Oct. 1956). New York: Atlas (Marvel) Comics.

Mantlo, Bill (w) and George Tuska (a). "Ten Rings to Rule the World!" *The Invincible Iron Man #100* (July 1977). New York: Marvel Comics.

Métraux, Daniel A. "Jack London, Asian Wars and the 'Yellow Peril.'" *History News Network*. George Mason University Department of History. 2013. Web. 16 Oct. 2013.

Michelinie, David (w) and Alan Kupperberg and Bob Layton (a). "Master Blaster!" *The Invincible Iron Man #242* (May 1989). New York: Marvel Comics.

Michelinie, David and Bob Layton (w) and Denys Cowan and Bob Layton (a). "China See!" *The Invincible Iron Man #241*(Apr. 1989). New York: Marvel Comics.

O'Neil, Denny (w) and Luke McDonnell and Steve Mitchell (a). "The Ancient Enemy." *The Invincible Iron Man #180* (Mar. 1984). New York: Marvel Comics.

_____. "Though My Life Be Forfeit...." *The Invincible Iron Man #181* (Apr. 1984). New York: Marvel Comics.

Quesada, Joe (w) and Sean Chen. "The Dream Machine part 2." *Invincible Iron Man #27* (Apr. 2000). New York: Marvel Comics.

Rohmer, Sax. *The Bride of Fu Manchu*. New York: Mattituck Reprint Co., 1933.

_____. *The Insidious Fu Manchu*. New York: McBride, Nast, & Co., 1913.

Severin, John (a). "Living Shadows." *Yellow Claw*#4 (Apr. 1957). New York: Atlas (Marvel) Comics.

"Yellow Claw." *Marvel Universe Wiki*. Marvel Comics, 2014. Web. 30 Nov. 2014.

NOTES

1. A scant three months after the "Missiles of October" brought the world to the brink of nuclear war, Under Secretary of State for Political Affairs W. Averell Harriman advised President John Kennedy that the threat of a nuclear-capable China was so worrisome that "joint U.S./Soviet measures" should be considered.

2. Rumiko's one-time affair with Tiberius Stone (*Invincible Iron Man #4* (May 1998)) adds another stereotype—that of the Asian vixen—to this tableau and it also feeds into white masculinist desire—this time for exotic sexuality.

3. In fairness, the Mandarin gracing the cover of issue *#180* (Mar. 1984) has short, rounded fingernails.

4. It seems that whenever hypnosis is depicted in popular culture as an attribute of Asians, it is a force of evil. See, for instance, Dr. Yen-Lo in Richard Condon's 1959 novel *The Manchurian Candidate* and the 1962 film of the same name. In the hands of a hero like the Shadow, of course, it is not hypnosis but a force for good—"the power to cloud men's minds."

"Does Khrushchev Tell Kennedy?"

"Superpower" Rivalry and Silver Age Iron Man

José Alaniz

The Americans have created their own image of the Soviet man and think that he is as you want him to be. But he is not as you think.
—Nikita Khrushchev[1]

The infamous "kitchen debate," an iconic engagement of the early Cold War, took place in Moscow on July 24, 1959. It pitted then–US Vice President Richard Nixon (in the USSR to open a first-ever American National Exhibition in Sokolniki Park) and Soviet Premiere Nikita Khrushchev. The sold-out exhibit—a landmark of the post–Stalin Thaw era—featured U.S. products, technology and even a fully-stocked "typical American kitchen." Touring the site with the world's press in tow, the two superpower rivals fell into a heated exchange regarding the relative merits of capitalism and communism.

Apart from anything else, it was great television. At the height of the flare-up, captured live on the new technology of color videotape, Khrushchev harangued his visibly ruffled guest about the bright Soviet future:

[A]merica has been in existence for 150 years and this is the level she has reached. We have existed not quite 42 years and in another seven years we will be on the same level as America. When we catch you up, in passing you by, we will wave to you (waves mockingly, to off-screen cheers). Then if you wish we can stop and say: Please follow up. Plainly speaking, if you want capitalism you can live that way. That is your own affair and doesn't concern us. We can still feel sorry for you but since you don't understand us—live as you do understand.

Polite and smiling, Nixon punched back. With translators struggling to keep up, sparks flew in the ensuing repartee and crosstalk:

> N: There are some instances where you may be ahead of us, for example in the development of the thrust of your rockets for the investigation of outer space; there may be some instances in which we are ahead of you—in color television, for instance.
> Kн: No, we are up with you on this, too. We have bested you in one technique and also in the other.
> N: You see, you never concede anything.
> Kн: I do not give up [Khrushchev-Nixon Debate].

The "kitchen debate" typified—and for viewing audiences, incarnated—the high-stakes drama between "us" and "them"; the *New York Times* account described it as "more like an event dreamed up by a Hollywood script writer than a confrontation of two of the world's leading statesmen" (Salisbury).[2] The skirmish crystallized a predominant frame for the representation of the Cold War in both countries: the superpower face-off. Indeed, as argued by Everette E. Dennis, in this period U.S. attention was often "riveted on matters of competition…. Closely linked to the general idea of national security and resultant 'red scares' has been a general capitalism-vs-communism emphasis in our view of the rest of the world" (50).[3] Russian historian Viktor Malkov adds:

> The collision of these opposing national-imperialist interests found a particular keenness [ostrota] also due to the global expansion of the two absolutely antithetical ideologies represented by the Soviet model and Americanism. Both these ideologies took on a Biblical significance and served as the primary (though not sole) motivating factor for both peoples [394].

An epochal rivalry with global reach found expression in all venues and outlets, including popular culture; no less so in the ideologically-freighted medium of U.S. superhero comics. Marvel's Iron Man stories (launched in 1963), a series "designed as a Cold War allegory" (Ackerman), featuring what Bradford W. Wright called "the most political of Marvel's superheroes" (222), emblematized the early Silver Age's approach to that rivalry—from, of course, a deeply pro–US perspective.

Premiere Khrushchev himself appeared more than once in Iron Man stories, looking and acting suitably odious: the toad-like dictator schemes to double-cross the Crimson Dynamo once he's accomplished his mission (lest he threaten his own rule); he coerces the reluctant superspy Black Widow into doing his dirty work by threatening her parents with harm. The Premiere cuts a decidedly unappetizing figure in these tales, an emblem of the untrust-worthy, power-mad communist fiend.

All the same, the patriotic jingoism with which the series began (in the jungles of Vietnam, no less) would by the mid–1960s start to yield to a more nuanced treatment with the shift in national attitude to the war in Southeast Asia. In fact, Iron Man/Tony Stark, like no other Marvel figure, embodied fluid Cold War era anxieties, disavowals and paradoxes regarding many of the era's concerns—U.S. capitalism, the military-industrial complex, com-munism, democracy, and manhood—as only a superhero could. In this essay I trace how the series reflected such changes through its evolving depiction of Russians, Eastern Europeans and the Soviet Union—and how, through all the variations, the trope of life-or-death rivalry remained.

The Cold War

What needs to be forever remembered is that in these decades, through countless events—from the deterioration of the U.S./Soviet alliance of World War II to Winston Churchill's "Sinews of Peace" aka "Iron Curtain" speech in Fulton, Missouri in 1946, from the announcement of the Truman Doctrine in 1947, the policy of Containment and Domino Theory, to the nuclear arms race, from the McCarthy Red Scare and blacklists of the late 1940s to the exe-cution of the Rosenbergs in 1953 to the 1954 Senate hearings on juvenile delinquency that led to self-censorship in the Comics industry, from the space race set off with the 1957 launch of Sputnik to the 1960 downing of Gary Powers' U2 spy plane to warnings voiced by Dwight D. Eisenhower on the growing outsize influence of the military industrial complex in his farewell speech of 1960 to the Cuban Missile Crisis of 1962 and beyond (to say nothing of the proxy conflicts in Southeast Asia and Central America, among many others)—Cold War thinking fostered a Manichean view of world affairs that largely shaped foreign and domestic policy, often to the detriment of all.[4] As David Painter reminds:

> Any assessment of the wisdom of the Cold War must take its costs into account. The United States, the Soviet Union, and many other countries suf-fered great harm from waging it. With its insatiable demand on resources, its exacerbation of ideological and political intolerance, its emphasis on external threats, and its consequent neglect of internal problems, the Cold War deformed the U.S., Soviet and other societies, distorted their priorities, and dissipated their wealth [118].

Among the more insidious effects of Cold War binarism was the chilling effect it produced on political dissent, including outright legal persecution such as the House Un-American Activities Committee, the Hollywood Ten controversy and blacklisting of Leftists. In a less-known example, David Caute traces how the 1948 passage of the Smith-Mundt Act, allocating $30 million in cultural and educational initiatives against "Soviet propaganda" and promotion of the U.S.'s image and values abroad, led the State Department to demand that publishers certify all books purchased by the United States Information Service[5] for overseas libraries were not written by communists or fellow travelers (24–27). Such priorities made it easy to mask mere political patronage as "national security." Businessmen too got in on this action: Lary May charts the ways in which anti-communist Cold War culture as promoted by the Hollywood film industry in its Red Scare phase was "sparked by corporate leaders who hoped to convert national values and popular imagery away from doctrines hostile to modern capitalism" (127). Fear—the overarching mood of this era—was parlayed to advantage, and profit.

The obverse of fear for many Americans, as noted by Matthew Costello, amounted to an inflated vision of themselves as "virtuous, free individuals on a progressive global mission to defend the world from the evils of totalitarian communism" (57), taking their post-war affluence as confirmation of right-mindedness (58). (To the extent that such problems as the enduring second-class status of many African-Americans and other minorities contrasted with that "virtuous" vision, they were ignored.)

If we were good, our geopolitical rivals must be evil incarnate—or so went the logic, fomenting what historian Stephen Cohen called a "wicked witch image" of the USSR (28). What he called Sovietophobia, an "exaggerated fear of [the] Sovie threat ... endanger[ed] democratic values, distort[ed] budgetary priorities and menac[ed] our national security by enhancing the prospect of nuclear war" (17).[6] To a degree perhaps not so unimaginable in a post–9/11 world (in which other bogeymen have taken the stage), the Cold War rivalry colored every aspect of national discussion, from defense to sports to the nuclear family[7] to language itself:

> [M]uch American commentary on Soviet affairs employs special political terms that are inherently biased and laden with double standards. Consider a few of them. The United States has a government, security organizations and allies. The Soviet Union, however, has a regime, secret police and satellites. Our leaders are consummate politicians; theirs are wily, cunning or worse. We give the world information and seek influence; they disseminate propaganda and disinformation while seeking expansion and domination [Cohen: 27].

Besides fear and advantage, the readiness of millions of U.S. citizens to resort to such loaded terms—despite in most cases never having met a Russian and even in the face of contradicting evidence—suggests not only the efficacy of government propaganda and media representations of the Soviet Union, but an underlying psychosocial mechanism as well.

Stereotyping to Ideology to Representation

The popular dehumanization of Russians/Soviets as Capitalism's great Other, in extreme cases as "inhumane, vicious torturers who enjoy inflicting pain and murdering children,"[8] brings us to the insights of Social Identity theory as articulated by British social psychologists Michael Hogg and Dominic Abrams.[9] In a book chapter titled "From Stereotyping to Ideology," they define the former as "generalizations about people based on category membership" often used to differentiate one's own "ingroup" from another "outgroup" perceived as homogenous and devalued (65).

The Social Identity approach to stereotyping emphasizes the role played by self-categorization and identity formation in a structuralist sense, linking it to the need for self-esteem. According to Hogg and Abrams: "It now becomes clear why ingroup stereotypes tend to be favorable and outgroup ones derogatory and unfavorable: self-categorization imbues the self with all the attributes of the group, and so it is important that such attributes are ones which reflect well on the self" (74). To go against such dichotomous "us. vs. them" thinking requires the overcoming of some powerful cultural crosscurrents, particularly when media seems to speak with one voice on the denigrated outgroup; perception becomes a comfortable, comforting salve to the ego, not easily dislodged. In fact, the human psyche itself appears strongly disinclined to rouse the "Red King" from his slumber:

> Social representations have an enormous inertia in so far as experiences and perceptions are distorted to conform to the representation. If people are indeed naïve scientists, it is a science very unlike Popper's characterization in terms of "conjecture and refutation" … Rather, people try to *verify*, not refute, their hypotheses and conjectures, and by all accounts are highly successful at this. There is abundant evidence that preconceptions (Moscovici's "social representations") distort reality in such a way as to preserve intact the preconception, and furthermore that they can even *create* a reality that fits … [Hogg and Abrams: 80, emphasis in original].[10]

These processes of identity formation, in turn, play a critical role in building the support structures of ideology, defined as "a systematically interrelated set of beliefs and propositions whose primary function is explanation" (82). We see here the psychosocial mechanism behind much of Cohen's "wicked witch image" of the Soviets: a "virtuous" USA (made up of "virtuous" individuals) can only be defined against a "villainous" USSR (comprised of a homogenous mass and a "villainous" leadership). In his more psychoanalytically-inflected reading of ideology, Slavoj Žižek initially emphasizes the unconscious aspects of such beliefs, all the more efficacious for seeming "natural":

> The very concept of ideology implies a kind of basic, constitutive naïveté: the misrecognition of its own presuppositions, of its own effective conditions, a distance, a divergence between so-called social reality and our distorted representation, our false consciousness of it.... We find, then, the paradox of a being which can reproduce itself only in so far as it is misrecognized and overlooked: the moment we see it "as it really is," this being dissolves itself into nothingness or, more precisely, it changes into another kind of reality [28].[11]

These concepts in hand, let us examine how they manifest (and undergo complication) in superhero comics at the dawn of the Silver Age.

Marvel Comics and the Cold War

As we would expect, and as documented by Wright, Costello, Paul Fellman and others, the vast majority of post-war U.S. comics wholly embraced a Cold War vision. Echoing the rhetoric of containment and the Truman Doctrine, 1950s stories on the Korean conflict tended to portray a "Communist enemy [who] commonly took advantage of peace talks to launch treacherous surprise attacks on the United Nations forces" (Wright: 120). Fellman's diagnosis of the national maladies evinced by these comics gravitates to the psychosexual:

> The stories, images and dialogue of the series revealed an America that was proud of her military and confident of her moral superiority. Nonetheless, America's lonely position at the top made her citizens just as nervous, paranoid and violent as they often imagined the Soviets to be. This America, captured in the pages of youth entertainment, was a deeply disturbed society that tried its best to hide any problems with a puff of the chest or a self-congratulatory pat on the back.

The superhero genre, especially after the congressional hearings which shocked the industry towards reform, engaged in robust "commie-bashing." Marvel's revival of its superhero line (1953–55) had a starkly anti-communist bent, with Captain America now a "Commie Smasher" and the Sub-Mariner swearing "never again [to] be conned into anything by a Red," according to Wright (121).[12] As he concluded: "The series offered no further discussion of

Cold War issues beyond the message that Communists were evil, overweight, and poor dressers" (123).

We should note that Marvel's initial revival of the superhero along this "jingoistic" Cold War model proved a commercial failure, unlike the relatively more weighty approach of earlier 1950s series such as *Kent Blake of the Secret Service*.[13] Nonetheless, the publisher under the editorship of Stan Lee retained a strong anti-communist posture with its new superheroes line that signaled the "Marvel Age of Comics" in 1961.

Many of these new heroes—the Fantastic Four, the Hulk, Spider-Man, Daredevil—emerged out of Atomic Age anxieties over radiation. But regardless of their origin, and despite the irreverent tone of the stories which became Marvel's hallmark, they stood in lock-step with the nation's values, ever-vigilant of the Red menace. As Costello wrote:

> Constantly under threat from the USSR, these superpowered Cold Warriors both articulated and represented the anti-ideological, [sic] free-market individualism that was its core. The strength of the [liberal] consensus is apparent in the moral certainty with which Marvel's heroes battle communists and their stand-ins, physically, verbally, and visually. Celebrating free markets, independent scientists, and individual rights, Marvel's Cold Warriors continually faced and triumphed over secret societies, communist agents, and their superpowered Soviet counterparts, frequently leading Soviet agents to defect once freed from totalitarian controls [61].[14]

Though as noted, this picture evolved over the course the 1960s, especially as popular support for the war in Vietnam eroded after such debacles as the 1968 Tet Offensive. Fearful of alienating his adolescent and college-age readership, Lee sought a vague, non-committal "centrist" approach to politics.[15] By 1975 (in a very different USA), Lee even took to issuing apologies for the excesses of the earlier anti-communist material. Commenting on Iron Man's origin and first nemesis, the North Vietnamese general Wong Chu, he wrote:

> Now it's important that you bear in mind that this yarn was written in 1963, at a time when most of us genuinely felt that the conflict in that tortured land really was a simple matter of good versus evil and that the American military action against the Viet Cong was tantamount to St. George's battle against the dragon. Since that time, of course, we've all grown up a bit, we've realized that life isn't quite so simple, and we've been trying to extricate ourselves from the tragic entanglement of Indochina [45].

Let us turn to some of what Lee meant by "we've all grown up a bit," as seen through the changing image of Russo-Soviet characters in Iron Man stories from 1963–1965. While the tone toward such figures may have softened, I

aim to show, the predominant frame of superpower rivalry—reified as superhero slugfests—stayed firmly in place.

Iron Curtain, Iron Man

More than any other 1960s Marvel Age figure, Tony Stark/Iron Man represented the triumphalism of U.S. technological and ideological might, evinc-
ing "the extent to which Marvel endorsed Cold War assumptions" (Wright:
222). He even sprang directly out of that conflict, in "Iron Man Is Born!"
(*Tales of Suspense* Vol. 1 #39, Mar. 1963, Lee/Larry Lieber/Don Heck). While
touring Vietnam to demonstrate his micro-transistors to the military, inven-
tor/industrialist Tony Stark falls victim to a Vietcong attack, which impales
shrapnel deathly near his heart. Captured by the sadistic Wong Chu, Stark
works to fashion a hi-tech suit to save his own life and strike back. Working
with brilliant professor and fellow prisoner Yin Sen, Stark succeeds in creating
the Iron Man armor. At the cost of Yin Sen's life, he vanquishes the VC and
escapes.

Iron Man/Stark, as Costello notes "the most ardent of Marvel's Cold
Warriors" (63), came to embody U.S. techno-entrepreneurial acumen and
militarist swagger. For Fellman, in fact, the "businessman and iron-clad communist killer combined was the perfect superhero for the new America" and
"an Iron warrior who stood up against the Iron curtain."

Even while not donning his armor, the dashing Stark projected a vision
of potent sexuality, equal parts Hugh Hefner and Howard Hughes.[16] Stark
the ladies' man and corporate titan, no less than Iron Man the superhero,
redeemed a post-war U.S. masculinity under severe duress, at home and on
the world stage. This was the era, after all, when the vigorous Russian body
of Yurii Gagarin (launched into orbit by the Soviets on April 12, 1961) out-
shone the gravity-bound American body of pilot Gary Powers (whom the
Soviets captured after downing his U2 spy plane in their own airspace on
May 1, 1960). The fantasy of Stark the playboy industrialist/superhero com-
pensated for such geopolitical humiliations. As Genter argues, "Despite the
life-threatening injury he has received in the war against communism and
despite the personal compromises he must make in his relationship with the
military, Stark is able to reconstitute his wounded masculinity through his
sexuality" (969).[17] Even a disabled U.S. male was better, more virile, than a
Communist one, the series insisted.[18]

But one facet of Iron Man resonates more than any other with Cold War
culture: its depiction of technology. In the series it took on aspects of what

Ben Saunders calls "techno-faith," a mode of thought which privileges technology's role in transforming the world to human—I would add national—will (106).[19] For Saunders, then, it's no surprise that "Marvel's most technologically enhanced Silver Age superhero was also the most politically hawkish" (107), given the intense competition of the space race. Despite such challenges, Fellman notes that

> Marvel Publishers had by this point made one theme very clear in the Iron Man series: that the communists could not surpass American weapons technology on their own merit. The "Reds" could only wish to catch up to America, and to do so required espionage and sabotage. Communists, in the comic book Cold War, were obviously inferior to their democratic counterparts.

One may read Silver Age Iron Man stories, in fact, in just this way: as formulaic rehearsals of the USA's moral (but also and especially technical) superiority over foreign (especially Russian) nemeses.

Of those the series, especially in its Lee/Heck/Colan period, had no shortage. From 1963 to 1966, fully one-third of Iron Man tales featured communist antagonists (Costello 63). Such material so pleased the editors of the *New Guard,* a journal sponsored by the conservative Young Americans for Freedom, that in 1966 they lauded Marvel for "the fact that the heroes run to being such capitalistic types as arms manufacturers (Tony Stark, whose alter ego is Iron Man), while the villains are often Communists (and plainly labeled as such, in less than complimentary terms)" (Howe: 94).

This did not mean, however, that readers saw no variation in those depicted. Russian communist antagonists of the 1960s, from the incorrigible (Red Barbarian, Titanium Man) to the reformed (Crimson Dynamo, Black Widow), represented the broad spectrum of U.S. opinion, from animosity to open-mindedness, that characterized different phases of the Cold War leading up to détente.[20] But their representations did share some commonalities: topicality in the form of "silly" canned dialogue referencing current events in the conflict; the unchanging mendacity of the Soviet leadership, contrasted with the decency of the common people; an at times racialized typage as uninspired—though much more dehumanizing—than the ubiquitous clichéd onion dome architecture used to depict "Eastern Europe"[21]; all crystallized through the trope of superpower rivalry. Let us examine some of these features in broad strokes before turning to more detailed case studies from early Iron Man stories (1963–1965).

In this period we observe much of what I'm calling "silly canned dialogue" threading Cold War memes into plot throughout the series, perhaps in a bid for respectability and relevance, but often amounting to mere politicized "trash talk." We could in fact characterize it as an anti-communist version of Spider-Man's smart-alecky banter as he engages foes.

The use of such language ranged, on the U.S. side, from puerile jibes (as when Tony Stark receives "a letter from commieland" or a caption describes a Russian supervillain as a "commie colossus") to mocking one-liners ("Does Kennedy tell Khrushchev? You'll find out *soon enough!*" and "This is the *pay-off,* comrade!").[22] Others offer sarcastic rejoinders on the USA's "inferiority" ("not bad for a mere *American,* huh?") or engage in crude ethnic baiting ("Don't turn your back on *me,* Ivan!"). Throughout, the tone is of one-upmanship. After Iron Man, somewhere in a vaguely-rendered "Red satellite country," lifts a car over his head and smashes it (in an homage to the cover of *Action Comics* #1), he jeers, "They don't build 'em so strong behind the iron curtain, *do* they?"[23]

The Russians' discourse runs the gamut from hackneyed ("By Lenin's beard!") to oxymoronic: "*Hah! Once again your decadent capitalistic inno-cence has betrayed you!*" With striking uniformity, the main Russian characters speak and act as devious, power-hungry louts—even those who eventually change their ways and join the free world. When Anton Vanko dons the Crimson Dynamo armor, he connives for his victory over Iron Man to make him a "national hero, powerful enough to replace even the leader himself!" Every Russian, then, is portrayed as a potential dictator, waiting for his chance at mastery over others.[24]

The entire communist system, in fact, appears designed solely to allow brutish leaders to vie with each other for power—and dominate cowed citizens. This despite the fact that such a state of affairs even works against the rulers' interests, prompting their most talented to defect to the West. The communist overlords must therefore suppress all the more brutally the "natural" yearning of all "normal" people for individual freedom, lest, as Costello argues, it "be vulnerable to opposition from inside whenever its ability to control its subjects weakens" (67). The journey of Natasha Romanova (aka Black Widow, who would eventually become the most developed of Marvel's Russian characters) precisely reflects this thinking. In "Hawkeye and The New Black Widow Strike Again!" (*Tales of Suspense* Vol. 1 #64, Apr. 1965, Lee/Heck), the Widow defies her Soviet masters, swearing she's "*through* serving your evil purposes!" (3)—until the state threatens her parents with harm unless she does its bidding (4). The blackmailed Widow resumes her mission. Through such depictions, and epithets like "Red Fascism," communists in the early Silver Age were often likened to Nazis.[25]

To show that Soviet corruption reached to the very top, the Widow's criminal coercion is carried out by none other than Nikita Khrushchev him-self,[26] who as mentioned made several cameo appearances in the series (far more than U.S. leaders). Shot through with Cold War presumptions, these appearances were nothing if not simplistic, even grotesque, distortions of the man—as a brief detour into political biography will demonstrate.

Nikita Sergeyevich Khrushchev (1894–1971), the successor to Joseph Stalin as leader of the USSR, served as Premiere from 1955 to 1964. In his brief time in office, Khrushchev initiated a "de-Stalinization" campaign cou-pled with economic and cultural reforms which came to be known as "the Thaw." Under such policies, millions of political prisoners were freed from prison camps and the country experienced a degree of free expression not seen since the 1920s.[27] On the foreign policy front, Khrushchev spearheaded a posture of "peaceful coexistence" with the West—histrionics notwithstand-ing.

For all that, as argued by Stephen Cohen: "Few political leaders have been less honored for the good they achieved than Nikita Khrushchev, who led the Soviet Union out of the terror-ridden wasteland of Stalinism.... Nor has his reputation fared well in the West, where he is remembered mainly as a blustering adversary who once tried to turn Cuba into a Soviet missile base" (47).

A rambunctious, off-the-cuff speaker, Khrushchev by the time of Iron Man's debut had long burnished the image of a loose cannon, as seen in inci-dents like the 1959 "kitchen debate" and an episode in which he banged his shoe on a table during a 1960 UN deliberation. His best-known public state-ment (outside the Soviet Union) was perceived by many in the West as a threat. Variations on the infamous phrase "We will bury you!" (My vas pokhoronim), which he first used in 1956, filled atomic-age U.S. citizens with dread. Never mind that the original statement in its entirety clarified Khrushchev's meaning: "Whether you like it or not, history is on our side, we will bury you!" The premiere was not dangling the prospect of nuclear annihilation; he was saying communism would outlive capitalism through peaceful means, as the human race learned the advantages of the former.[28]

Despite such political theater, Khrushchev led a crucial and brave reassessment of the Stalin era's excesses, starting with his "secret speech"[29] titled "On the Personality Cult and its Consequences," delivered at the 20th Communist Party Congress on February 25, 1956. Among the great historic speeches of the 20th century, its message proved a political firebomb:

> After Stalin's death, the Central Committee began to implement a policy
> of explaining concisely and consistently that it is impermissible and foreign
> to the spirit of Marxism-Leninism to elevate one person, to transform him

into a superman possessing supernatural characteristics, akin to those of a god....

We have to consider seriously and analyze correctly this matter in order that we may preclude any possibility of a repetition in any form whatever of what took place during the life of Stalin ... who practiced brutal violence, not only toward everything which opposed him, but also toward that which seemed, to his capricious and despotic character, contrary to his concepts....

We must abolish the cult of the individual decisively, once and for all; we must ... return to and actually practice in all our ideological work the most important theses of Marxist-Leninist science about the people as the creator of history and as the creator of all material and spiritual good of humanity... [We must] restore completely the Leninist principles of Soviet socialist democracy, expressed in the Constitution of the Soviet Union, to fight willfulness of individuals abusing their power. The evil caused by acts violating revolutionary socialist legality which have accumulated during a long time as a result of the negative influence of the cult of the individual has to be completely corrected [Khrushchev: 782–786].

As these excerpts from the "personality cult" speech show, Khrushchev faced down an entrenched neo–Stalinist wing in the communist party to, as he saw it, nudge the traumatized Soviet Union towards becoming a more humane and open society.[30] Such reforms proved an inspiration decades later to General Secretary Mikhail Gorbachev, whose Perestroika program in the 1980s eventually led to the collapse of the Soviet system itself (Taubman: 648–49).

We should not of course idealize Khrushchev as a champion of human rights; despite easing its worst aspects, he maintained a repressive undemocratic system and kept a stranglehold over Eastern Europe, most despicably in his brutal suppression of the Hungarian Uprising of late 1956 (inspired in part by his very speech!).[31] That said, the USSR under Khrushchev had much to celebrate, especially on the technology front (Tony Stark's home turf). From a "backward," agrarian country on the edge of Europe at the beginning of the 20th century, Russia by the 1950s had become a major industrialized nuclear power, a rival to the Western capitalist democracies—especially the USA. As noted, the launch of *Sputnik* in 1957 showcased Soviet science and exacerbated Cold War tensions; in 1961 the Red space program built on that success with Gagarin's breakthrough on the Vostok-1 rocket; and in 1963 Soviet cosmonaut Valentina Tereshkova became the first woman in space. (The U.S. had to wait a full 20 more years for its first female astronaut in space: Sally Ride, who carried out her mission in 1983.) These were all undeniable, extraordinary achievements of which the Soviet people (not just the state) were justly proud.[32]

Space race aside, in the 1950s and early 1960s the Soviets had to contend with a severe and chronic housing shortage, while climate fluctuations and inefficient farming methods led to widespread crop loss. The USSR increasingly imported staples like wheat, from places like the USA (Taubman: 516–17). Finally, Khrushchev courted nuclear armageddon (for real this time) with his embrace of the 1959 Cuban Revolution, which would ignite the Cuban Missile Crisis of October, 1962.[33]

By any measure, Nikita Khrushchev was a complex figure, whose tenure at the head of one of the two superpowers altered the history of his own nation and the world. In fact, by the time of his forced retirement, Khrushchev's reforms had sparked a process which would eventually lead (though he would have been horrified to know it) to the dissolution of the Soviet bloc in 1989, and the death of the USSR itself two years later.[34]

Not that a reader would hear anything about secret speeches or released prisoners in "Iron Man Faces The Crimson Dynamo!" *(Tales of Suspense* Vol. 1 #46, Oct. 1963, Lee/Heck). At the start of that tale, we see a dark-suited Premiere, flanked by armed guards, stride into a room. The caption reads: "Can you recognize the pudgy, scowling figure entering a strange laboratory just outside Moscow? If you don't, then you know nothing about the Cold War! For this stocky fellow is the 'Mr. Big' of the Iron Curtain!" (1). As Fellman points out, the caption snarkily chides any reader who would fail to recognize "Mr. Big" (the epithet vaguely recalls the Mafia) one year after the Cuban Missile Crisis. In any case, the ensuing portrait of Khrushchev—as scheming, dishonest, suspicious blowhard—says much more about U.S. preconceptions of Soviet leaders than about the man himself.

The Khrushchev of the story has come to see a demonstration of Professor Anton Vanko's Crimson Dynamo armor—but his chief concern seems keeping the genius scientist from threatening his own power: "How I hate this professor Vanko ... and *fear* him!" (1). The professor—who indeed despises the Premiere—goes through with his demonstration, at one point humiliating the "glorious leader" by electrically controlling a tank that traps "Khrushchev" against a wall.[35] Demeaned but also exhilarated by the power on display, the Premiere thinks, "[Vanko's] electric genius shall serve me well, before I ... eliminate him!" (4).

Of course, things don't turn out that way, and by story's end an enraged Khrushchev is tossing breakable objects at his staff, swearing, "Next time I shall *bury* Iron Man!" (13). The tale—not least in its depiction of the Soviet leader—paints the communist system as a never-ending struggle for control between equally vile officials, all awaiting the chance to backstab their way to greater power. The willful distortion of the "bury" quote as a direct, unambiguous threat to Iron Man, as well as Khrushchev's ill treatment of Black Widow's parents, typifies Cold War strategies to propagandize the worst possible image of the Reds: as scheming killers and blackmailers.[36] While that portrait would soften over the course of the 1960s, as noted, the frame of an East-West contest for supremacy remained in place; let us track that evolution in the representation of Russians in three early Iron Man stories.

Barbarians, Dynamos and Bull(sk)ies

We start with the earliest and most retrograde: the repugnant Red Barbarian, who debuted in "Trapped by the Red Barbarian" *(Tales of Suspense* Vol. 1 #42, June 1963, Lee/Heck). The absurd, laughable, revolting Barbarian (we never learn his real name)[37] wears a ridiculous heavy fur cape over a Red Army uniform (medals and all), while his office desk strains under the weight of what looks like a medieval feast: huge roasted legs and peas, ale or wine spilling from a flagon (he does offer a guest caviar at one point). But his most outrageous aspect: Neanderthal features, including a prominent forehead, buck teeth and hairy oversized hands. His surly personality breathes menace; he rules underlings by fear, yelling things like "I've got a good mind to have you *shot,* you blundering incompetent!" as he douses an officer with wine (6), fires randomly and knocks another soldier unconscious with a hambone. The Barbarian represents the most profoundly Russophobic of Iron Man's Cold War villains, his image recalling the racialized typage of World War II and Korean War comics.[38]

For all that, as argued by Fellman, "Trapped by the Red Barbarian" reflected this era's perception of Eastern European communists as a greater threat to the homeland than "less cosmopolitan" Asian ones, since the villain's spies infiltrate Stark Industries to steal nuclear weapons technology, almost succeeding.[39] Though it's hard to see how: from top to bottom, the whole communist organization seems a shambles: cowardly spies give up their secrets as soon as they are caught; the Barbarian's sadistic leadership style ("Fail in this mission, and I will nail your hide to the wall!" [7]) only terrifies his staff; mistrust runs so deep that the Barbarian has the Actor shot just as he was about to reveal Iron Man's secret identity. The Russians appear phylogenetically paranoid, anarchic thugs, working against their own purposes.

The Red Barbarian's "racialized" caveman features function as a visual marker in this regard, as an incarnation of the debased Slavic soul. As further noted by Costello, "The physical deformity of the communist villains in these stories implies that the political economic system they represent is not only ideologically repulsive but morally bankrupt" (65).[40] As such, that system deserves to lose the global superpower struggle.

Anton Vanko, described by Saunders as a "Russian version of Tony Stark" (108), represents a more worthy (and tasteful) opponent. As noted, the bald-pated Vanko first appears in "Iron Man Faces The Crimson Dynamo!," demonstrating his Crimson Dynamo armor to Khrushchev; he soon embarks on a mission of industrial wrecking in the USA, with Iron Man the ultimate target. Stark defeats the Red supervillain all too easily, in part by exploiting the paranoid distrust endemic in his society – "That gives me an idea! All commies are chronically *suspicious* of each other! Hmm…" (11)—playing Vanko a faked message from his leader ordering his liquidation (the story completely elides the fact that Khrushchev would be speaking in Russian, not English) (12). The Dynamo defects, saying, "I realize now that my scientific genius has been at the service of a savage, double-dealing system!" (13). Only casually does the story acknowledge that the scientist's defection is engineered through a piece of *capitalist* double-dealing. Stark thinks to himself, condescendingly: "Poor Vanko! He doesn't know he really heard *my* voice, not his leader's!" (ibid).

That lie slightly complicates (without in my opinion upending) Saunders' argument that Stark wins due to his and the USA's moral superiority, not necessarily the preeminence of U.S. technology—which reflects a core ambivalence toward that technology's capacity to save us from the Reds (109). (Though throughout the short battle Iron Man's tech clearly outmatches the Dynamo's.) In any case, Vanko *himself* clearly embraces his new home's ideology, offering to expose yet another Soviet spy ring as a measure of good faith. He is a good man now freed to carry out scientific research in accord with his conscience, to, as Stark tells him, "give your talent to a nation which *appreciates* men of genius … and allows them to work on projects to *aid* mankind … *not* to destroy others!" (13).

The Crimson Dynamo therefore represents a transitional figure: the rehabilitated Red. Among the first Marvel Eastern Europeans to transcend mere caricature, even his surname marks a more nuanced geopolitical reality behind the Iron Curtain than usually inferred in superhero comics. By giving him the name Vanko, a Ukrainian diminutive (a variation on Ivan, or John) rendered by some as "gracious gift,"[41] Lee and co-writer Robert Bernstein allude to the many different ethnicities of the USSR, as well as to old frictions between Ukrainians and Russians. In 1954 the Moscow leadership had handed over control of the Crimean Peninsula, home of the Black Sea Fleet, from the Russian Soviet Socialist Republic to the Ukrainian Soviet Socialist Republic, sparking simmering tensions (which boiled over in 2014).[42] Vanko's given name Anton[43] is also worth noting, for related reasons: it clearly references one of the best-known (and most Western-oriented) Russian writers, Anton

Chekhov—who as it happens is associated with the Crimean city of Yalta, where he spent much of his life. The Dynamo's character and identity are thus "deepened" by his name, all the more so once he crosses over to the free world.

He becomes a successful and proud U.S. immigrant, working late hours in the lab, as seen in "The Crimson Dynamo Strikes Again!" *(Tales of Suspense* Vol. 1 #52, Apr. 1964, Lee/Heck). The story gave Vanko the ultimate chance to prove his loyalty, as Soviet operatives the Black Widow and Boris infiltrate Stark Industries. The hulking Boris dons the Crimson Dynamo armor, and launches a sneak attack on an unsuspecting Iron Man. Through ingenuity and pluck, Stark outsmarts Boris, bringing the Dynamo to his knees. But for Vanko this is not enough. *"Finish him,* Iron Man, while you can! You *must* ... he will never give up!" he insists. *"Can't,* Vanko!" Stark replies. "We don't play that way! He's had enough!" Of course, the craven Boris renews his attack, uttering what was by now a Cold War cliché: *"That's* why we will bury you ... we're not as *trusting* as you!" (11). In the end, Vanko sacrifices himself to vanquish Boris with his laser light pistol (which also kills the shooter), proclaiming, "I would dare *anything* for this country, which has been so *good* to me!" (13).

In the high-stakes contest for world supremacy, we see why the USA is fated to win: its greater claim to righteousness—treating a foe decently, turning enemies into friends—transforms "weakness" into strength. Saunders' "morality" thesis actually works better here than in Vanko's first adventure; enacting the highest virtues of his adopted homeland, Vanko offers up his own life as proof of American moral superiority.

Stark's resolve—and the nation's—would again be tested (this time before the eyes of the entire world) by the Soviets' greatest challenger yet. Unfolding over three (12-page) installments in three 1965 issues, the battle royale between Iron Man and his ultimate Russian nemesis Titanium Man brought to a head as never before the issues of stereotyping and Cold War rivalry we have been discussing. The epic story, in fact, is a master class in how popular culture galvanizes, transmutes and reifies national ideology.

The tale begins in "If I Must Die, Let It Be with Honor!" *(Tales of Suspense* Vol. 1 #69, Sept. 1965, Lee/Heck), when Commissar Boris Bullski, sadistic boss of a "communist work camp not far from Siberia," orders a group of imprisoned scientists to build him a suit of hi-tech armor using the traitor Vanko's lab.[44] His greatest ambition: to single-handedly defeat "one of communism's greatest enemies!" and be crowned dictator. Bullski ("even the *Premiere* fears him!") cuts a redoubtable figure: bearded, cigar-chomping, scar across his left eye, his heavy-set body recalling the Kingpin's as he crushes metal pipes with his bare hands (3).

While still a black-hatted cartoon, Bullski appears human; the egregious, racism-tinged depiction of a Red Barbarian had faded by mid-decade. Yet once more the Soviet Union is depicted as a nation of brutal taskmasters lording over the weak: the scientists perform their work through a combination of fear and belief in Bullski's false promises of freedom.

Soon the commissar dons his Titanium Man suit, a huge green monstrosity which makes up for its technical inferiority with brute power, and issues his challenge. Though reluctant at first (the chest device that keeps him alive is malfunctioning), Stark gives in to patriotic entreaties like Pepper Potts': "Iron Man will *have* to fight him, boss ... or America might lose face in the eyes of the world!" (7). The champions meet in the "tiny, neutral nation of Alberia," whence flock thousands to witness the titanic clash. The event takes on a carnival atmosphere, with world-wide live television coverage (9).

Framing the showdown as a sort of Cold War superbowl (complete with pre-show and game analysis), Lee and Heck partake of sports imagery throughout: the warriors face off on a delimited "field" of action (a deserted World War II battle site); the bout has programmed "rest periods" after fifteen-minute "rounds"; Bullski watches newsreel footage of Iron Man in combat, like a football coach sizing up an opponent (4); fans cheer for their champion and boo the other guy; a caption even refers to them as "two superpowered heavyweights in the prize ring".[45] Such a representational strategy reflects the politicization of the Olympics, a time when "[p]ropagandists on both sides of the Iron Curtain [presented] the competition between Russian and American athletes as a portentous symbolic struggle between two ideological systems" (Guttmann: 554).

Furthermore, Heck's art emphasizes the physical distinctions between the antagonists—and not only the champions—as an emblem of their values: when the parties meet on the battlefield to agree to the strange contest's rules, the Titanium Man and his entourage appear more stout and squat (too much borscht, perhaps?), while on the opposing side Iron Man and his military handlers are depicted as more upright and slender. Also furthering the impression of American "lightness" and freedom on this page: the subsequent sequence of three panels that show Iron Man floating above the earthbound Russian villain, attacking him from the air (11).[46]

Of course, as a villain, Titanium Man cheats at the game: by illegally laying booby-traps, mines and hidden weapons at the site. Part two of the saga, "Fight On! For a World Is Watching!" *(Tales of Suspense* Vol. 1 #70, Oct. 1965, Lee/Heck), opens with Iron Man stumbling through the minefield, battered but determined. As throughout the storyline, Lee peppers the proceedings with Cold War repartee:

> TM: And now, while the whole world watches on television, I'll hand you the worst propaganda defeat the democracies have ever suffered! After this, none will ever doubt that communism alone can triumph!
> IM: Looks like you've got everything going for you, big man ... except one little detail ... I'm not beaten yet! [3].

The Hector-Achilles agon lurches on for several pages, with gawking crowds reacting to every twist as the advantage shifts back and forth. But while making them more or less evenly matched, the authors reduce the combatants to national stereotypes: Iron Man's armor, though lighter and smaller, is more sophisticated (US techno-faith); Titanium Man relies on greater bulk, brute strength, more crude weapons and "Communist" deviousness: feigning weakness to lure his foe close, he growls, *"Fool! I relied on your weak American compassion* to bring you within *striking* range!" (7).

The battle turns only when Stark's right-hand man Harry "Happy" Hogan enters the fray to deliver a top-secret "gizmo"—and gets cut down in the crossfire (11). With what he believes are Happy's last words ringing in his ears—"Just give that commie creep one for ... ol' Hap ...!"—Stark confronts his Red opponent with a new resolve (along with the superior technology Happy brought him) (12).

In the conclusion, "What Price Victory?" *(Tales of Suspense* Vol. 1 #71, Nov. 1965, Lee/Heck), Stark fights for his fallen friend, a modern-day Gilgamesh mourning his Enkidu, staring down the Bull(ski) of Heaven. It is an embarrassing rout. The once-fearsome Titanium Man, sworn "to show the world that communism is supreme" (1), tastes bitter defeat, outclassed by Iron Man's speed: "He is too *fast!* He evades my attack with the ease of a *Nijinski!*" (2)[47]; weighed down by his own flawed design: "Why did I make my armor so *bulky!* I cannot run away *fast* enough!" (3); astounded at U.S. technical might: "He has scientific weapons I never dreamed existed!" (4); and, finally, disgraced by his cowardice before the entire planet.

For his part, Stark mercilessly taunts: "Remember, comrade—the world is watching your every move on TV—watching me run rings around you!" (2); insults: "your clumsy tin overcoat" (4)[48]; infantilizes (shaking upside-down foe): "Now, now! We don't want you to get a *tummy-ache*, do we? Here, let me *burp* you!" (7); and lectures:

> You made the same mistake *all* tyrants and bullies make! You thought you'd just have to flex your muscles and show your strength, and your enemies

would fall by the wayside! Well, you picked the *wrong* enemy this time, mister! You made the worst mistake any Red can make—you challenged a foe who isn't *afraid* of you! (3).

In a flourish worthy of lucha libre, Stark concludes his public demolition by broadcasting his opponent's words of surrender and *unmasking* Bullski, live on television—the ultimate genre castration. Stranding the terrified Titanium Man on a high peak, Stark's tone is both magnanimous and mocking: "Don't worry! Lucky for *you,* I'm not a *Red!* I can't continue to attack a helpless enemy!" (8).

Be that as it may, the story's conclusion mirrors the real sports scandals of American-Russian relations. Despite the outcome, seen live by satellite all over the world, the Soviets immediately raise objections, accusing the USA of cheating. Long after Iron Man has left, the communist delegation protests, "But that other American entered the field of battle, bringing your champion a *weapon!* Everyone *saw* that!" U.S. Senator Harrington Byrd shoots back, "Have you *forgotten* about all the *illegal traps* your Titanium Man set for our boy? Remember—millions of people *saw* them on their own TV screens!" Response: "I, eh—will discuss it no longer! You Americans use *any* means to gain your own ends!" (10). The contretemps recalls allegations of rule-breaking that routinely sprang up regarding Olympic competition during the Cold War (see Guttmann: 556–557), as well as donnybrooks like the Kitchen Debate. (The presence of a U.S. senator and the fact that the mustachioed, presumably Russian official resembles Stalin [by then dead 12 years] enhance the connection.) But perhaps more than anything else the scene shows both sides bent on winning at all costs, even by (at the very least) bending the rules of the contest.

The Titanium Man saga culminates a progression in early Marvel comics from World War II-style racist caricature of Russians (Red Barbarian) to more measured portraits of individuals (Vanko/Crimson Dynamo; Romanova/Black Widow), all while retaining "superpower rivalry" as the predominant representational frame. As Wright argues, Iron Man's acceptance of the Reds' challenge rises to a matter of national pride, while his victory "underscore[s] America's determination to confront Communist aggression in whatever form it should take" (222).

Following Saunders, I see Bullski's vanquishing as only superficially (if indisputably) about technology and the USA's self-perception as the most technically advanced nation on earth (an identity, as noted, sorely tested during the early space race). The technology, rather, is an expression—confirmation—of an ineffable moral core, as is Happy's sacrifice for the team.

This is why one blogger's dismissive opinion of the story ("It's a clear

victory for ~~freedom and the American way~~ Iron Man, though perhaps the
only thing that was proven here was who was the better engineer and weapons
designer—Tony Stark, or a group of captured scientists" [Comicsfan]) falls
short; Happy's bravery trumps the "captured scientists" no less than Stark's
techne.

Cold War Olympic medals were not solely about speed and strength,
but virtue. Cold War superheroes, too, with all their blows and laser bolts,
fought not just to win, but in winning to show who was *right*. The contest
was all.

Conclusion: Repulsor Ray Diplomacy

> TM: *No!* You've *disgraced* me! You've made me *lose face!* Do you know what
>   they'll *do* to me?
> IM: Who? The leaders of the people's republic? The friends of the masses?
>   You can't be afraid of *them?!!* [TOS #71: 8].

The Cold War, what David Caute calls a "continuous pursuit of victory
by other means" (5), unfolded on many stages, many fields of action—but
perhaps no more crucial arena existed than the head space of countless East-
erners and Westerners. Alongside the proxy conflicts and espionage of the
real world, the Cold War was fought in the realm of the imagination. Hence
a "sophisticate and a scientist,"[49] a red and gold national hero, locked in battle
with a green (Red) giant on a million glowing screens, the masses registering
every blow with dread and hope. Every blow, but also every quip—a struggle
on a world stage fought with ideas no less than firepower. As Wright put it,
Iron Man "foils Communist agents and battles Soviet supervillains in symbolic Cold War contests of power and will" (222). He who shapes the symbols
frames the fight.

Decades later, with the Iron Curtain history, we still live with that symbolic burden: "Nearly 25 years after the Berlin Wall fell and marked the end
of the Cold War," writes the *New York Times,* "Hollywood's go-to villains
remain Russians" (Kurutz). Journalist and historian Anatol Lieven minces
fewer words on the matter than most: he diagnoses this ideological dead
weight as full-blown Russophobia—whose origins long predate the Soviets.
Indeed, one can trace a line of what Lieven calls an "essentialist or chauvin-
ist/historicist/racist element in critiques of Russia" as far back as the
Napoleonic Wars through the imperialist "Great Game" between Russia and
Great Britain,[50] from Gustav Doré's satirical *History of Holy Russia* (1854)[51]
to Iron Man's second encounter with Titanium Man, when he calls him a

"loud-mouthed, thick-skinned, empty-headed Volga boatman"[52] and beyond. And while Marvel, as I have argued, deserves credit for moving beyond the worst excesses of Red Barbarian–type caricature,[53] its commitment to the U.S. Cold War effort contributed to policies based on "bigotry, hysteria and nationalist lobbies" (Lieven): repulsor ray diplomacy.

In this era we devoured our four-color adventures with delight, thrilling at the greatest contest in human history—and we were always on the winning team. But, artificial moons stamped in Cyrillic buzzing high over our heads, we read too with fear.

NOTES

1. Salisbury.

2. That said, the reporter also emphasized that "their talk was straightforward and there was no hint of ill feeling in their fast and furious interchanges" (Salisbury).

3. The editors of that same volume, *Beyond the Cold War,* also emphasize rivalry when they define the conflict as one "between communism and capitalism with each side defending the virtuous features of its system while denouncing the other as its principal adversary" (3).

4. Though for a contrarian view on the Cold War's impact, at least on the thinking of most U.S. citizens, see Filene.

5. Also known as the United States Information Agency.

6. Writing as late as the 1980s, Cohen diagnosed the ongoing situation thusly: "the United States, unlike most nations, still has not fully acknowledged that, whether we like it or not, the Soviet Union has become a legitimate great power with interests and entitlements in world affairs comparable to our own" (20).

7. See Wright, chapter 5 for how Romance and War comics reflected Cold War thinking in the 1950s.

8. Gerbner quoting a psychologist: 31. His article examines images of Russians on U.S. television since 1976; he found that over half these characters were depicted as KGB agents (33).

9. The theory itself was first proposed by Henri Tajfel and John Turner in the 1970s.

10. For an application of Social Identity theory and such concepts as "confirmation bias" and "motivated reasoning" to current U.S. political culture, see Haidt.

11. Though see further in that chapter for a complication of the "naïve" hypothesis, through the concept of the modern subject's "cynical reason."

12. Genter notes that Marvel's 1950s return to fantasy was marked by "a conservative social agenda" (956).

13. See Wright: 123–127.

14. As Costello further notes, such a stance accorded with the strictures against government criticism promulgated by the Comics Code Authority (by this time barely a decade in existence) (69).

15. See Howe: 93–98 and Wright: 223 for more on Marvel's adoption of a "middle ground" approach to politics in the 1960s. As Costello described the turn: "While there is still a verbal commitment to American supremacy and Soviet inferiority, the clear distinctions became blurred, and the books begin to present these ideas in a cloudier context" (78).

16. As Lee explains, discussing his idea of Stark: "I could envision a Howard Hughes

type with almost unlimited wealth—a man with holdings and interests in every part of the world—envied by other males and sought after by glamorous females from every walk of life" (46).

17. See Genter: 965–969 for more on Stark and masculinity, as compared to more "effeminate" milksop scientist types of the Marvel Silver Age, such as Bruce Banner (963). Genter compares Stark favorably to such "macho" popular culture figures as Norman Mailer and Mickey Spillane. See also my own analysis of masculinity, the superhero body and disability in the early Silver Age (Alaniz: chapters 1 and 3).

18. That said: in another Marvel hallmark, the stories often complicated this surface image of Stark through, for example, the inability to consummate his love for Pepper Potts and the constant fear of death due to a failure of his armor. Peter Sanderson has pointed out the flight-worthy Iron Man was often depicted prone on the ground, batteries depleted (quoted in Genter: 968). Indeed, the pose resembles the repeated motif of X-Men leader Charles Xavier spilled from his wheelchair (see Alaniz: Chapter 5). For Ben Saunders, Stark's life-sustaining but fragile chest plate functions as "an unconscious emblem for the mixed feelings of the nation with regard to the effects of scientific and technological progress" (110).

19. Saunders argues that in the Cold War era technology took on a phantasmatic function in the U.S. collective psyche, as an "increasingly central concept around which fantasies of national identity coalesced but also a particularly fertile site for the projection of desire and her nervous twin, anxiety" (107).

20. Iron Man's archvillain was of course the Mandarin, whose Chinese heritage links him to some extent with the Sino-Soviet split of 1960, which merits its own study.

21. On the latter, see for example *Tales of Suspense* Vol. 1 (hereafter TOS) #42:12. As Saunders put it: "From our present historical distance, the glorious political simplicity of these early tales could almost be part of their charm, were it not for the frequent racial stereotyping of Iron Man's enemies from the various 'red' nations" (107).

22. Unless otherwise noted, all emphases and ellipses in the original comics.

23. "[L]etter from commieland" (TOS #69: 7); "commie colossus" (TOS #71: 3); "Does Kennedy tell Khrushchev?" (TOS #46: 12); "This is the *pay-off,* comrade!" (TOS #71: 5); "not bad for a mere *American,* huh?" and "Don't turn your back on *me,* Ivan!" (TOS #71: 3); "They don't build 'em so strong..." (TOS #42: 11).

24. "By Lenin's beard!" (TOS #42:12); "decadent capitalistic *innocence*" (TOS #71: 5); "replace even the leader himself!" (TOS #46: 9). This depiction of a supreme Russian will to power is reflected even in characters not explicitly identified but strongly hinted as Russian, e.g. Professor Gregor Shapanka aka Jack Frost, whose Russian-Jewish-derived name and "ruffled Anton Chekhov" appearance suggest his origins. In "Iron Man and the Icy Fingers of Jack Frost!" *(Tales of Suspense* Vol. 1 #45, Sept. 1963, Lee/Heck), the turncoat Stark Industries employee tries to rob transistor technology to fund his scheme to unlock the secret of eternal life (11). Shapanka/Jack Frost's super-cold powers, incidentally, cement the association of Russians with northern climes such as Siberia's.

25. Marvel's Silver Age representation of communism also recycled other formulae: the Widow's "normal-looking" parents, as well as the headscarf worn by her mother, recalls visual cues from publisher George A. Pflaum's "This Godless Communism," a series that ran in the Catholic journal *Treasure Chest of Fun and Fact* in 1961–62. As argued by Alexander Maxwell, "if Pflaum sought to instill fear of communism in his American audience, he also wanted Americans to sympathize with East Europeans suffering under communist rule" (194).

26. As the Widow makes clear, narrating the flashback: "I was taken to the Comrade *Leader,* just before his fall from power!" (TOS #64: 3). That would place the event in the fall of 1964; Khrushchev was ousted on October 14.

27. On prisoner releases, see Applebaum: 508–518. On greater freedom of expression in literature, see Taubman: 306–10; in cinema, see Woll: 9–13.

28. On the shoe-banging see Taubman: 475–76, on the "bury" remark see Taubman: 427–28. As David Caute explains: "When Nikita Khrushchev famously declared, 'We will bury you!,' he was predicting something akin to what happened in reverse thirty years later, in 1989–91: a moral and ideological collapse; our ballerinas will dance across your ruined stages, our paintings will hang from the peeling walls of your galleries, our books will occupy your library shelves, the Voice of America will broadcast Shostakovich, not Elvis Presley" (4).

29. The speech was closed to the public and not published in the press, but passed on to party members in special meetings throughout the country. It leaked to the rest of the world soon after (Hosking: 530).

30. See Hosking: 528–531. As Anne Applebaum wrote, the speech "shook the Soviet Union to its core. Never before had the Soviet leadership confessed to any crimes, let alone such a broad range of them" (508).

31. See Hosking: 531 and Johnson 1996: 253–255 for more on the link between Khrushchev's speech and the 1956 Hungarian uprising.

32. Along with the victory in World War II (which they call "The Great Patriotic War"), the achievements of the Soviet space program remain a major source of nostalgia and pride for many Russians up to the present day; at the age of 77, Cosmonaut Tereshkova served as a flag carrier at the opening ceremony of the 2014 Winter Olympics in Sochi.

33. For all the perceptions of Khrushchev as a fanatical figure, Alex Gillespie notes that throughout the Cuban Missile Crisis, President Kennedy regarded the Premiere as a rational actor, according to transcripts of White House recordings from the time (142).

34. Khrushchev was replaced by Leonid Brezhnev (1906–1982), General Secretary of the USSR, a conservative and admirer of Stalin. He immediately set about undoing most of the liberal policies of the Thaw, but did not return the country to full-blown Stalinism. As Khrushchev summed up his reforms: "I've done the main thing. Could anyone have dreamed of telling Stalin that he didn't suit us anymore and suggesting he retire? Not even a wet spot would have remained where we had been standing. Now everything is different. The fear is gone, and we can talk as equals. That's my contribution" (Taubman: 13).

35. The scene is perhaps an unintended parody of the famous opening to the Russian World War II film *Ballad of a Soldier* (directed by Grigory Chukhrai, 1959), in which a Red Army soldier is chased by a German tank.

36. In some rare instances, a more complex image slides through. In another early Iron Man story, the villainous Actor impersonates Khrushchev, saying, "Who then should visit you … *Stalin's* ghost?" (TOS #42: 6). The line, superficially a throw-away, could be read to hint at Khrushchev's role in exorcising the late dictator's "ghost" through his Destalinization program.

37. Though a 21st-century retcon established his alter ego as Andre Rostov. See the "Longest Winter" storyline in *Winter Soldier* Vol. 1 #s 1–5 (2012).

38. As Costello puts it: "The visual representation of the communist enemies reinforced the assertion of the moral superiority of America, which was also very similar to the racial stereotyping common to World War II comic books" (63).

39. Fellman links the "spies in our midst" subplot to Julius and Ethel Rosenberg, executed ten years before in 1953.

40. The Red Barbarian bears comparison with another deformed Russian communist villain, the Gargoyle aka Yuri Topolov (debuted in *The Incredible Hulk* Vol. 1 #1, May 1962, Lee/Kirby), whose political reformation is accompanied by the restoration of his "normal" human physique. For more on physical deformity and Silver Age Marvel villains, see Alaniz: chapter 2.

41. On the meaning see http://www.20000-names.com/origin_of_baby_names/etymology_V_male/meaning_of_the_name_vanko.htm and http://www.sheknows.com/baby-names/name/vanko. The use of Vanko as a surname is odd, not unlike calling someone "Anton Johnny."

42. See Taubman: 186 and Thompson: 357 for more on the Crimea question.

43. Vanko is not referred to by this name in his debut appearance, though the Marvel Comics Grand Database lists it so in its entry on the issue.

44. The late Vanko's technology would be utilized by numerous villains over the years, such as Milo Masaryk, the Czechoslovak national better known as the Unicorn (TOS #56, Aug. 1964).

45. The caption appears in part two (TOS #70: 9).

46. The inability of Russian villains to fly (in an era when the U.S. was losing the space race) remained a constant, as did the motif of "stout" Slavic males throughout the series; both Crimson Dynamo and Titanium Man wear bulky, heavy armor that contrasts with Iron Man's sleek, body-hugging evolved suit. Moreover the men appear either bullet-headed (Khrushchev, Vanko) or overly hirsute (Red Barbarian, Bullski), mirroring the hair patterns of successive Soviet leaders.

47. Vaslav Nijinski (1889–1950), Russian-Polish ballet dancer.

48. We may read this as a reference to Nikolai Gogol's short story "The Overcoat" (1842), whose nebbish hero Akaki Akakievich Bashmachkin undergoes a nigh magical transformation when donning the title garment, only to have it stolen through violence—his ultimate unmanning.

49. TOS #39: 3.

50. As John Howes Gleason wrote in his landmark 1950 study of Russophobia:
Great Britain and Russia emerged from the Napoleonic wars as the preeminent powers in the European world.... Likewise they alone controlled significant extra–European territories. If the concept of the balance of power had any force in shaping events—the whole history of international relations seems to suggest that is inherent in a system of sovereign states—they were inescapably cast as rivals (289).

51. David Kunzle calls it "derisively distorted but remarkably comprehensive history" (272).

52. Lee/Colan: 9.

53. US popular culture as a whole was moving away from such depictions as well, as seen in the television spy series *The Man From U.N.C.L.E.*, which featured a charismatic Russian spy, Ilya Kuryakin (David McCallum), as one of the main characters. It ran from 1964 to 1968.

Works Cited

Ackerman, Spencer. "Iron Man Versus the Imperialists." *The American Prospect* (May 15, 2008). http://prospect.org/article/iron-man-versus-imperialists.

Alaniz, José. *Death, Disability and the Superhero: The Silver Age and Beyond.* Jackson: University Press of Mississippi, 2014.

Caute, David. *The Dancer Defects: The Struggle for Cultural Supremacy During the Cold War.* Oxford: Oxford University Press, 2003.

Cohen, Stephen F. *Sovieticus: American Perceptions and Soviet Realities.* New York: W.W. Norton, 1986.

Comicsfan. "The Biggest Loser." *The Peerless Power of Comics!* (April 2, 2013). http://peerlesspower.blogspot.com/2013/04/the-biggest-loser.html.

Costello, Matthew J. *Secret Identity Crisis: Comic Books and the Unmasking of Cold War America.* New York: Continuum, 2009.

Dennis, Everette E. "Images of the Soviet Union in the United States: Some Impression-sand an Agenda for Research." In *Beyond the Cold War: Soviet and American Media Images*, edited by Everette E.Dennis, George Gerbner and Yassen N. Zassoursky. Newbury Park: Sage, 1991: 46–54.

Fellman, Paul. "Iron Man: America's Cold War Champion and Charm Against the Communist Menace." *Voces Novae: Chapman University Historical Review*. Vol. 1, No. 2 (2009). http://journals.chapman.edu/ojs/index.php/VocesNovae/article/view/37/126.

Filene, Peter. "'Cold War Culture' Doesn't Say It All." In *Rethinking Cold War Culture*, edited by Peter J. Kuznick and James Gilbert. Washington: Smithsonian Institution Press, 2001: 156–174.

Genter, Robert. "'With Great Power Comes Great Responsibility': Cold War Culture and the Birth of Marvel Comics." *The Journal of Popular Culture*. Vol. 40, No. 6 (2007): 953–978.

Gerbner, George. "The Image of Russians in American Media and The 'New Epoch.'" In *Beyond the Cold War: Soviet and American Media Images*, edited by Everette E. Dennis, George Gerbner and Yassen N. Zassoursky. Newbury Park: Sage, 1991: 31–35.

Gillespie, Alex. *Trust and Conflict: Representation, Culture and Dialogue*. Ed. Ivana Marková and Gillespie. Hove, East Sussex: Routledge, 2012.

Guttmann, Allen. "The Cold War and the Olympics." *International Journal*. Vol. 43, No. 4 (Autumn, 1988): 554–568.

Haidt, Jonathan. *The Righteous Mind: Why Good People Are Divided by Politics and Religion*. New York: Pantheon Books, 2012.

Hajdu, David. *The Ten-Cent Plague: The Great Comic-Book Scare and How It Changed America*. New York: Farrar, Straus and Giroux, 2008.

Harper, John L. *The Cold War*. Oxford: Oxford University Press, 2011.

Hogg, Michael A. and Dominic Abrams. *Social Identifications: A Social Psychology of Intergroup Relations and Group Processes*. London: Routledge, 1988.

Hosking, Geoffrey A. *Russia and the Russians: A History*. Cambridge, MA: Belknap Press of Harvard University Press, 2001.

Johnson, Jeffrey K. *Super-history: Comic Book Superheroes and American Society, 1938 to the Present*. Jefferson, NC: McFarland, 2012.

Johnson, Lonnie. *Central Europe: Enemies, Neighbors, Friends*. New York: Oxford University Press, 1996.

Khrushchev, Nikita Sergeyevich. "The Personality Cult and Its Consequences" [February 24–25, 1956]. *The World's Great Speeches*, 4th Ed. Ed. Lewis Copeland et. al. New York: Dover, 1999: 782–786.

"Khrushchev-Nixon Debate." (July 24, 1959). *CNN Cold War*. http://astro.temple.edu/~rimmerma/Khrushchev_Nixon_debate.htm.

Kunzle, David. "Gustave Dore's History of Holy Russia: Anti-Russian Propaganda from the Crimean War to the Cold War." *Russian Review*. Vol. 42, No. 3 (1983): 271–299.

Kurutz, Steven. "Russians: Still the Go-To Bad Guys." *The New York Times* (January 17, 2014).

Lee, Stan. *Son of Origins of Marvel Comics*. New York: Simon Schuster, 1975.

_____, and Don Heck. "The Crimson Dynamo Strikes Again!" *Tales of Suspense*. Vol. 1, No. 52 (April, 1964).

_____."Fight On! For A World Is Watching!" *Tales of Suspense*. Vol. 1, No. 70 (October, 1965).

_____. "Hawkeye and The New Black Widow Strike Again!" *Tales of Suspense*. Vol. 1, No. 64 (April, 1965).

_____.If I Must Die, Let It Be With Honor!" *Tales of Suspense*. Vol. 1, No. 69 (September, 1965).

_____. "Iron Man Faces The Crimson Dynamo!" *Tales of Suspense*. Vol. 1, No. 46 (October, 1963).

_____. "Iron Man is Born!" *Tales of Suspense*. Vol. 1, No. 39 (March, 1963).

_____. "Trapped by the Red Barbarian." *Tales of Suspense*. Vol. 1, No. 42 (June, 1963).

_____. "What Price Victory?" *Tales of Suspense*. Vol. 1, No. 71 (November, 1965).

Lee, Stan and Gene Colan. "By Force of Arms!" *Tales of Suspense* Vol. 1, No. 82 (October, 1966).

Lieven, Anatol. "Against Russophobia." *World Policy Journal*. Vol. 17, No. 4 (2000/01): 25–32. http://carnegieendowment.org/2001/01/01/against-russophobia.

Mal'kov, Viktor Leonidovich. *Rossiia i SShA v XX veke*. Moscow: Nauka, 2009.

Maxwell, Alexander. "East Europeans in the Cold War Comic *This Godless Communism*." In *Comic Books and the Cold War, 1946–1962: Essays on Graphic Treatment of Communism, the Code and Social Concerns*, edited by Chris York and Rafiel York. Jefferson, NC and London: McFarland & Co., 2012: 190–203.

May, Lary. "Movie Star Politics: The Screen Actor's Guild, Cultural Conversion and the Hollywood Red Scare." In *Recasting America: Culture and Politics in the Age of Cold War*. Chicago: University of Chicago Press, 1989: 125–153.

Painter, David S. *The Cold War: An International History*. London: Routledge, 1999.

Ryan, David. "Mapping Containment: The Cultural Construction of the Cold War." In *American Cold War Culture*, edited by Douglas Field. Edinburgh: Edinburgh University Press, 2005: 50–68.

Salisbury, Harrison E. "Nixon and Khrushchev Argue In Public As U.S. Exhibit Opens; Accuse Each Other Of Threats." *The New York Times* (July 24, 1959). http://www.nytimes.com/learning/general/onthisday/big/0724.html.

Saunders, Ben. *Do the Gods Wear Capes?: Spirituality, Fantasy, and Superheroes*. London: Continuum, 2011.

Schwartz, Richard A. *Cold War Culture: Media and the Arts, 1945–1990*. New York: Facts on File, 1998.

Sibley, Katherine A. S. *The Cold War*. Westport, Conn: Greenwood Press, 1998.

Taubman, William. *Khrushchev: The Man and His Era*. New York: Norton, 2003.

Thompson, John M. *Russia and the Soviet Union: An Historical Introduction from the Kievan State to the Present*. Boulder, CO: Westview Press, 2009.

Whitfield, Stephen J. *The Culture of the Cold War*. Baltimore: Johns Hopkins University Press, 1991.

Woll, Josephine. *Real Images: Soviet Cinema and the Thaw*. London: I.B. Tauris, 2000.

Wright, Bradford W. *Comic Book Nation: The Transformation of Youth Culture in America*. Baltimore: Johns Hopkins University Press, 2001.

Žižek, Slavoj. *The Sublime Object of Ideology*. London: Verso, 1989.

Ike's Nightmare

Iron Man and the Military-Industrial Complex

WILL COOLEY *and* MARK C. ROGERS

On January 17, 1961, President Dwight D. Eisenhower gave his farewell address. In it, he stated that the "military establishment" was a "vital element in keeping the peace." However, Eisenhower also cautioned that Americans must guard against the "unwarranted influence" of the military-industrial complex, asserting that it could endanger civil liberties and democracy (Eisenhower). Eisenhower was a staunch anti-communist and a war hero, and he delivered this speech during the Cold War. He stressed legitimate concerns over the menace of communist imperialism, but paid more attention to the peril of an unchecked defense industry.

Two years later, Marvel Comics introduced Iron Man, a superhero who personified the military-industrial complex. In the comics, Tony Stark, an engineer and industrialist, uses his Iron Man suit to battle an assortment of villains, including many Communists. Stan Lee, the co-creator of Iron Man with Jack Kirby,[1] based the character on the business magnate/engineer Howard Hughes, and the comic advocated a fusion of business and technology as the recipe for a Cold War victory (Genter 966–967).

Throughout the 1960s, as Iron Man defeated foes such as the Red Dynamo, Titanium Man, and the Unicorn, Stark's expertise and the Iron Man suit bested communist science and technology. The comic exemplifies how, despite Eisenhower's counsel, Americans thought that the military-industrial complex's technological innovations were an aggressive yet antiseptic means to battle communism and establish global hegemony. The disastrous Vietnam

War proved otherwise, but for the real-life Tony Starks, the war was a profit-churning boon. General Electric's prime defense contracts, for instance, nearly doubled between 1958 and 1968, to $1.5 billion. By 1969, military-industrial complex spending accounted for approximately 45 percent of total federal outlays (Kaufman 10–11, 1969).

The American defense industry developed after World War II as a response to Cold War threats. In previous eras, industries converted to war production and then reverted to producing goods for the civilian economy. During the Cold War, however, national defense proponents insisted that the battle against communism and the lethality and sophistication of modern weapons necessitated industries that focused solely on defense. Detractors often charged that the military-industrial complex was a creation of right-wing politicians and business interests, but it actually owed much of its formation to Cold War liberals. In July 1958, the Committee for Economic Development, a corporate-liberal group, called for higher defense spending and more "flexible response capability" (Pursell 11). John F. Kennedy, the standard-bearer for muscular liberalism, made effective (though specious) claims about a "missile gap" in his campaign for the presidency in 1960 (Raymond 1 1960). Even many of the critics of the military-industrial complex assumed its development was irreversible, and that it was integral to the country (Hitch 132–34). The military-industrial complex was not a conspiracy, nor was it monolithic. It was, however, massive. By 1967, businesses that filled military orders were the largest producers of goods and services in the country; the defense industry and armed forces employed about 10 percent of the labor force. As Senator William Fulbright noted, the $75 billion defense budget was "a giant concentration of socialism" in the free-enterprise economy (Fulbright 174). For corporations, military contracts were more profitable, less competitive, and more easily gained through lobbying and the incestuous relationship between public and private interests.

American policymakers generally ignored President Eisenhower's warnings on the seductions of military strength and eagerly poured more resources into the defense budget. Corporate liberals thought defense spending would spur domestic economic growth while vigorously containing communism abroad. The Soviet Union's 1957 launch of Sputnik had heightened fears that the United States was falling behind technologically. The Committee for Economic Development argued that the country needed to be prepared for anything, because of a "frail capacity to foresee the future." When it came to keeping the country safe, "We can afford what we have to afford" (Committee 200). This rhetoric tapped into both Cold

War paranoia and ethnocentric bravado; Americans would surpass Soviet technology because they would spend whatever was necessary to beat them.

Tony Stark/Iron Man embodied these liberal dreams of an effective and benevolent military-industrial complex. Stark not only produces armaments, he becomes a remarkably effective American weapon in his Iron Man suit, conveying that the military-industrial complex was essential to defeating communism (Lee, "Iron Man Faces..." 5). As one friendly politician in the comic states, Tony Stark can keep the identity of Iron Man secret "so long as you continue to produce our weapons" (Lee, "The Monstrous Menace..." 2). Iron Man, with all of his gadgetry, symbolizes an exceptionally resilient and adept America that prevails against danger by projecting this strength at home and abroad. While scholars have examined how America's political culture propelled the country into Vietnam (Baritz, Scanlon), this study shows how popular culture convinced Americans that the war was a noble imperative to preserve freedom. Iron Man's appearances in the *Tales of Suspense* and *Iron Man* comic books not only echoed the conviction that technology would win the Cold War, it also helped produce this confidence by showing readers the might and necessity of the military-industrial complex.

Iron Man is unquestionably a product of the Cold War. Tony Stark, while battling Communists in Vietnam, crafts his suit after an accident. As historian Bradford Wright notes, Iron Man comic books' "portrayal of the Vietnam conflict is not only childishly simplistic, but ethnocentric as well" (Wright, "Vietnam War and..." 442). Americans were generally oblivious to the conditions in countries where they tried to construct pro–Western regimes; not surprisingly, the comic failed to explore the complexities of hot wars in the developing world. Iron Man's communist foes are one-dimensionally venal, treacherous and cruel. In step with the era's messianic idealism, Iron Man considers it his duty to rescue peasants from the clutches of these tyrants. After deciding to intervene in a Caribbean country, Iron Man declares that the country's peasants are "listless, lifeless men, their faces without hope, their stances without pride. They carry the fruits of a land no longer theirs." He must overthrow the dictator enslaving these people in a "manufactured utopia," because "a nation that has lost its will need not take long to regain it ... once it is shown the way" (Gold 5–7). Iron Man plunges into foreign affairs with swagger and self-assurance, supremely certain that American intercession could repair nearly any situation. "There was nothing we could not do because we were Americans," the marine and journalist Philip Caputo recalled of the era, "and for the same reason, whatever we did was right" (Caputo 66).

Indeed, Iron Man crusades for capitalism, democracy, and freedom. *Iron Man* writers dub him "the fighting-mad champion of liberty" (Lee, "Victory" 7), and portray Stark as possessing the best qualities of the modern American man: tolerance, ingenuity, broadmindedness, and the profit motive. As Lee recalled, most Marvel writers and artists were "young, idealistic, and passionately liberal." The company did not have a party line, but insisted on accepting differences and seeking peaceful outcomes. "The only philosophies that have no place at Marvel," Lee insisted, "are those preaching war and bigotry." He envisioned Stark as "a playboy, a tycoon, a man's man" (Lee, *Son of Origins*, 45–46). Stark is a capitalist, but hardly rapacious. Instead, he is a liberal's ideal: a benevolent boss, environmentalist, and hard-working scientist as concerned with enhancing mankind as he is with the bottom line. While some critics in the comic cast doubt on the benefits of Stark Industries, they are usually revealed to be malevolent or naïve; the writers make clear that Stark is above reproach. In a 1967 issue, "the world-renowned millionaire inventor-manufacturer" labors "fearlessly, tirelessly" to harness atomic power. "If I succeed it'll be a great day for science and progress," Stark declares, as "mankind will be able to take another step forward in the advancement of human knowledge" (Lee, "Crisis..." 3).

Lee and Kirby's Iron Man differs from many of the other comics of Marvel's 1960s revival in its positive outlook on science and technology. The risks and possible consequences of science, particularly nuclear weapons, play a prevalent role in the origins and early stories of the Fantastic Four, Spider-Man, the X-Men, and the Hulk. Science is a double-edged sword for many Silver Age Marvel Heroes. For both Bruce Banner (the Hulk) and Ben Grimm (the Thing), science gives them their extraordinary powers but strips them of their humanity. While Tony Stark must wear the Iron Man chest piece to keep his heart beating (until 1969), he remains Tony Stark, promethean warrior/scientist.

Though Iron Man frequently extols the "American Way," his antagonists are not just Communists, but government oversight and the free press, two vital aspects of a functioning democracy. Elected officials repeatedly summon Stark to congressional hearings to question him on his defense contracts. In line with the paranoia of the Cold War era, they frequently accuse him of disloyalty. While the comic claims that one of the primary failings of the Communists is that they are "chronically suspicious of each other" (Lee and Berns, "Iron Man Faces..." 11), the irony is that *Tales of Suspense* and *Iron Man* are rife with distrust over allegiances and identities. Even his closest friends, Pepper Potts and Happy Hogan, express suspicions over Iron Man's motives (Lee, "Suspected of Murder!" 4–5).

In one histrionic display, Senator Harrington Byrd, one of Stark's main adversaries, cancels his contracts. "This is a grave moment in our nation's history! A time for patriotism.... For dedication to the cause of freedom!" the infuriated politician exclaims. "There must be no special privileges for self-seeking opportunists like Stark, who flout their country's laws!" (Lee, "Ultimo Lives!" 12). In the actual Washington D.C., politicians such as senators Fulbright and William Proxmire raised legitimate concerns over the largess and clout of the military-industrial complex. Proxmire forthrightly questioned the wisdom of the "blank check" for the military and drew attention to the cozy relationships between the military and the industries that supplied it (Proxmire 48, 62). In contrast, the government officials in *Iron Man* are not responsible watchdogs, but bloviating nuisances inhibiting Stark's brilliance.

The comic also paints the press as an irresponsible irritant. Stark Industries' scientific breakthroughs must be safeguarded from enemies, but media reports often unwittingly undermine any advantages the United States' defense industry enjoys. After the media reports on a new weapon, thereby informing the Communists, an exasperated Stark complains "Those characters are like shadows!" (Lee and Korok, 3), indicating that journalists are more akin to domestic spies than guardians of a transparent society. In another telling case, blundering reporters make Stark's nemesis the Mandarin aware of his whereabouts, hampering Iron Man's ability to keep the world safe (Lee, "The Death of..." 7).

This mistrust of journalism was consistent with the divide in American public opinion about the media during the Cold War. Some extolled the press for putting a check on the power of corporations and the government, while others, including many politicians and military officers, regarded the media as unwitting Soviet dupes at best and a traitorous fifth column at worst. According to the Americans running and supporting the Vietnam War, the press put American interests and lives at risk (Hallin 3–4, 9; Hammond ix, 292). In *Iron Man*, reporters harry Stark, until he finally buys his own newspaper to kill unflattering stories (Goodwin, "Once More..." ;. Goodwin, "Unmasked!"). As with real world corporate titans, Stark's money buys him the best press available.

While the government and the media question Stark's loyalties and competence, the comic emphasizes that Stark's efforts are selfless and in the best interest of the country. Any subterfuge he undertakes is merely to keep his Iron Man identity a secret and to shield the public from dangers it cannot handle. The writers depict Stark as an underappreciated genius, suggesting that Americans should have more admiration for its technocratic and business elites. In the Marvel Universe, Tony Stark's clandestine activities are necessary because he sees what elected officials and the unwitting public cannot. Similar to most superheroes who lauded Americanism, philosopher Andrew Terjesen notes, Iron Man deems checks and balances an annoyance and acts as a lone avenger (Terjesen 108). While Eisenhower warned that the military-industrial complex potentially imperiled liberty and democracy, *Iron Man* implies that society would be better off if munificent industrialists such as Stark had more of a free hand. Democracy might be under attack, but the threats are too great for democracy to handle.

The comic maintains that Stark should be above oversight because his pioneering technologies will contain and ultimately defeat the Communists. In his first appearance in print in 1963, Tony Stark demonstrates his weaponry to a military official and asks, "Now do you believe that the transistors I've invented are capable of solving your problem in Vietnam?" South Vietnamese soldiers are outnumbered and cannot transport heavy artillery through the dense jungle, but Stark's transistors give the South Vietnamese the advantage. As the enemy retreats, a Vietnamese soldier credits the weaponsmaker. "Stark, your weapons are everything we hoped for!" (Lee and Lieber, 2). In the following issue, Stark invents roller skates that "enable an entire infantry division to race down a highway at 60 miles an hour" which will "revolutionize troop movements." Stark modestly notes that he is "just a scientist who realizes that the boundaries of science are infinite" (Lee and Berns, "…Gargantus" 2). Vietnam was still an advisors' war in 1963; Stark, and his inventions, are the answer to the vulnerability of the free world. Naysayers need to let him do his work. In the actual Pentagon, military experts contended that the conflict would be a short one. Secretary of Defense Robert McNamara and General Maxwell Taylor visited Vietnam in the same year and deduced that "the major part of the U.S. military task can be completed by the end of 1965" (Lederer 32). With American potency and know-how, Vietnam was supposed to be a cakewalk.

The intricacies of the Cold War in places such as Vietnam befuddled Americans, but *Iron Man* simplified it by turning it into a personal battle between dueling titans. Iron Man's made-for-television battles against his communist nemesis, Titanium Man, established American pre-eminence for readers. Titanium Man proves a worthy opponent, but Iron Man vanquishes him as Americans cheer wildly. During one encounter, the comic shows President Lyndon B. Johnson and McNamara watching excitedly. "If only the day would come when force is no longer necessary—when men would reason together instead!" the President states. "But, until such a time, we should be thankful that power such as Iron Man's exists—and can be used in behalf of freedom!" McNamara agrees, exclaiming "He's like a human fighting machine—irresistible—unstoppable—invincible!!" (Lee, "Victory" 7). Iron Man epitomized the cyborg fantasies of defense experts such as McNamara as a sophisticated instrument that triumphs in battle without spilling any American blood.[2] As the U.S. deepens its commitments in Vietnam, soldiers shower compliments on Stark and Iron Man for helping them to victory. One GI remarks that Stark is a "genius," while a colonel says "I wish Stark himself were here, so we could tell him how much his help in weaponry has meant to us" (Lee, "Within the Vastness..." 2–3). The baffled Viet Cong imagine Iron Man is "some sort of Demon," and Iron Man quips "now it's time to convince 'em that they're right" (5). Despite growing reservations about the progress, aims, and ethics of the war in Vietnam, Iron Man not only fully champions the conflict, but supplies the high-tech dominance needed to win it.

Americans had logical reasons to think that technology and the military-industrial complex made their fighting force nearly invincible. During the Great War, the War Industries Board fostered cooperation between business and the military. Historian Stuart W. Leslie notes that "wartime successes in submarine detection, radio signaling, artillery range finding, and chemical weapons confirmed the confidence both scientists and industrialists had in the new alliance of science, government, and big business" (Leslie 4). World War II brought forth more technical wonders that pushed the Allies to victory, such as radar, the proximity fuse, solid fuel rockets, and the atomic bomb. Although Eisenhower later criticized the military-industrial complex, as a general he helped foster it by planning collaboration among scientists, business, and the armed forces as the United States transitioned into the Cold War (Leslie 7). The Cold War American mood was simultaneously anxious and overconfident. Americans worried that the Soviets were prevailing in the technology contest, but also feared that the arms race would lead to annihilation through nuclear war. They fretted about a "missile gap," yet assumed their armed forces could not be bested in a fair fight, especially against ragtag insurgents in Indochina. For comic readers, Tony Stark/Iron Man soothed their unease by advancing scientific knowledge and using this expertise to subdue the nation's enemies.

On the ground in the real Vietnam, the military-industrial complex's high-tech capacities awed policymakers and soldiers, fueling the country's confidence. Eager military officers considered the conflict a testing ground for new equipment and tactics (Shoup 101). An information officer told the journalist Michael Herr that the battles in Vietnam "showed what you can do if you had the know-how and the hardware" (Herr 2). Whereas once stopping communism in Vietnam had been a matter of intelligence and soft power, by the mid–1960s it had fallen into the "hard hands of firepower freaks out to eat the country whole, and with no fine touches either, leaving the spooks on the beach" (Herr 53). The American fighting man definitely had unprecedented power at his command.

Vietnam was history's most technologically advanced war, and soldiers marveled at the destructive power at their fingertips. "Simply by speaking a few words into a two-way radio, I had performed magical feats of destruction," Caputo wrote. "Summoned by my voice, jet fighters appeared in the sky to loose their lethal droppings on villages and men. High-explosive bombs blasted houses to fragments, napalm sucked air from lungs and turned human flesh into ashes" (Caputo 3–4). This god-like authority reinforced the righteousness of the mission, lending the clout of power to a messianic faith in saving Vietnam.

The weaponry made some commanders giddy, sometimes even reaching erotic levels. A captain, after admiring gunships hover overhead, remarked, "That's sex. That's pure sex" (Herr 170). At times, the war's aims were lost amongst the spectacle produced by American armaments. After one operation, an officer asked a journalist, "What I want to know is: Did you get a feeling of the tremendous firepower we were able to bring to bear, and the precise coordination? The infantry man today has six times the firepower of his Korean counterpart." Similar to Iron Man's assertion that his force was bringing peace, the officer also maintained that his soldiers had "diverse talents," as "this isn't a war for territory, it's a war for the hearts and minds of the people" (Schell 97). As with the war's managers, the officer apparently did not grasp that mass killing and flattening villages did not charm the Vietnamese. GI's regularly observed that they might enter a friendly village, but their tactics ensured that by the time they left residents backed the Viet Cong (Gibson 145).

The admiration for overwhelming power was not just a matter of soldiers with expensive and deadly toys. The entire strategy in Vietnam involved incapacitating guerrilla warriors through prodigious force. If the U.S. military could simply lure the North Vietnamese into a set-piece battle such as at Khe Sanh, and do battle on conventional terms—"fighting for once like men," journalist Michael Herr noted—then American soldiers could use their "power and precision and exquisitely geared clout" to kill wholesale, and "if we killed enough of him, maybe he would go away" (Herr 106, 113–114). The Pentagon was convinced that technology and military might could overcome any logistical and political advantages held by the Vietnamese. Tony Stark's "disintegrator ray" and Iron Man's suit of armor were not all that far-fetched considering the Pentagon ordered production of the "Snake Eye," a low-drag bomb, "Sad Eye," an air-launched cluster bomb, "Wet Eye," a chemical bomb, and "Fire Eye," a bomb that delivered a burning agent (Melman 152–3). Arms manufacturers bought into their own rhetoric, believing that firepower—the demonic magic—was beyond the enemy's imagination and prowess. The resulting atrocities of war revealed how awe-inspiring force masked inherent weaknesses in strategy, vision, and honesty.

Eerily, Eisenhower's farewell address foretold this faith in invasive, technological answers to every predicament. "Crises there will continue to be," he stated. "In meeting them, whether foreign or domestic, great or small, there is a recurring temptation to feel that some spectacular and costly action could become the miraculous solution to all current difficulties." The "huge increase in newer elements of our defense" (Eisenhower) not only failed to pacify the Vietnamese, but probably made chances for success even more remote. The United States had a decided advantage in armaments and capabilities, but it applied conventional tactics to a guerrilla war. The sheer ferocity of its military equipment and the top brass's body count strategy were ultimately counterproductive (Turse 47–48; Gibson 181–183).

Relatedly, *Iron Man* writers stubbornly refused to acknowledge the possible drawbacks of firepower. Instead, they pinned the mass destruction of the Vietnamese countryside on communist malfeasance. In issues 92–94 of *Tales of Suspense* (1967), Iron Man returns to Vietnam to square off with Half-Face, "the commies answer to Tony Stark" (Lee, "Within the Vastness…" 2–3). Half-Face has fooled the peasants into thinking he was aiding them, but his plan was to destroy their village and make it appear it was the work of American bombers. "The entire world will be stunned and shocked," Half-Face chortles. "It will be our greatest propaganda victory!" (Lee, "The Golden Gladiator…" 12). Iron Man foils the plot and saves the villagers, and one thanks him by remarking that "If the American should fall … there will be no safety for us anywhere.… We can only wait … and place our faith in him who is known as … Iron Man" (Lee, "The Tragedy and…" 9). In the comic, the Vietnamese Communists are soulless and calculating, while the only goal of the American armed forces is to protect the appreciative peasantry.

In Vietnam, however, it was the United States that was "destroying the village to save it." The nation of South Vietnam existed only on paper, as the Vietnamese had long been one unified people, an identity forged in part through a thousand-year tradition of repelling invaders (Lederer 45). The U.S. had little to offer the majority of the Vietnamese people, who generally favored Ho Chi Minh and saw Yankees as just another colonialist invader. Lacking credible allies, the U.S. military used drastic means to pacify resist-

ance such as Operation Cedar Falls. To quell the Viet Cong in the Iron Triangle in 1967, the military leveled villages, obliterating every home and building and bulldozing all the farmers' fields (Schell 131–132). The military
relocated villagers to refugee camps with signs announcing "WELCOME TO
FREEDOM AND DEMOCRACY" and "WELCOME TO THE RECEPTION CEN-
TER FOR REFUGEES FLEEING COMMUNISM" (94). In theory, the operation
would deprive the Viet Cong of cover and supplies, and expose them to American military capability. "From now on, anything that moves around here is
going to be automatically considered V.C. and bombed or fired on," a captain
stated. "The whole jungle is going to become a Free Zone. These villages here
are all considered hostile villages" (Schell 70–1). Just two days after the end
of Operation Cedar Falls the Viet Cong moved back into the area. The maneu-
ver not only produced a substantial refugee population, it also turned local
Vietnamese against the United States. Belatedly, many Americans started
conveying serious skepticism over the war's aims and strategies. "The sad
and terrible truth of the decision to blow up South Vietnam's cities in order
to defend them," journalist Tom Wicker reported in the *New York Times* during the Tet Offensive a year later, "is that neither Washington nor Saigon has
anything to rely on but firepower" (Wicker, 1968, 46). Iron Man, once a symbol of what would lead to victory in Southeast Asia, gradually represented
the country's arrogant overkill. Critics made the connection between the
comic and the bloodshed in Vietnam, and urged writers to see the error of
their ways. "I hope you realize that Tony Stark is going to have to do some
pretty big re-structuring of his life to avoid being classified as an enemy of
the people," a reader wrote in a 1971 letter column. "Among other things, he'll
have to stop supplying the government with weapons" ("Sock it to Shell Head,"
Jan., 1971). In the Marvel Universe, the enemies had always been unambiguous. Vietnam blurred those distinctions.

The odds that the United States could invent and prop up the imaginary
state of South Vietnam were long to begin with, but they were further undermined by the destructiveness of unceasing bombing raids, napalm, and
ruinous tactics such as Operation Cedar Falls. By end of war, there were an
estimated 21 million bomb craters in South Vietnam, planes sprayed 18 million gallons of herbicide containing dioxins on some 6 million acres, and
bulldozers flattened 1200 square miles of land (Gibson 225). The war subjected Vietnamese civilians to a cycle of suffering, and as historian Nick Turse
convincingly reveals, this misery was "the inevitable outcome of deliberate
policies, dictated at the highest levels of the military" (Turse 6). Blinkered
by Cold War Manichaeism, though, *Iron Man*'s writers maintained that Americans were saviors for grateful peasants. Stan Lee claimed that preaching war

was taboo at Marvel, and *Iron Man* writers seemed to regard Vietnam as more of a humanitarian operation than a bloody, merciless struggle. "Most of us genuinely felt that the conflict in that tortured land really was a simple matter of good versus evil and that the American military action against the Viet Cong was tantamount to St. George's battle against the dragon," a repentant Stan Lee later admitted (Lee 45). Lee, like many other Americans, could not imagine the United States as the dragon—the empire—but only as the plucky underdog rescuing appreciative, helpless Third-World peoples. As historian Robert Genter observes, Marvel's creators were slow to educate themselves on the nuances of the Cold War, as their superheroes remained committed to fighting long after many readers had misgivings or were openly protesting (Genter, 974). "Can't you see what your schemes of conquest cost?" Iron Man asks the Mandarin in 1969. "Does anyone else have to die before you abandon your insane goals?" (Goodwin, "Unmasked!" 18). The irony of a munitions magnate actively involved in increasing body counts in Vietnam posing this question was apparently lost on the writers.

Meanwhile, some of the military-industrial complex's functionaries began to question its efficacy and morality. In January 1969, M.I.T. faculty members went on strike to resist the Defense Department's abuses of science and to encourage the university to lessen its reliance on military funding (Sullivan *New York Times*, 1). A survey of scientists involved in weapons-making found that the majority were critical of their labors, with some actively turning against the Vietnam War (Schevitz 143). One engineer at the Stanford Research Institute enjoyed his project analytically, but when he found himself at his desk examining a map of North Vietnam searching for optimal bombing routes, "I just could not, in clear conscience, continue to work on the project. I had to take a stand either for or against the war at this point" (Schevitz, 44–45). For many military officers and enlisted soldiers, the Vietnamese jungle was not a proving ground, but an untamable nightmare. For all of the "good gear," journalist Michael Herr noted, the Viet Cong offensives instilled "incalculable" terror in GI's (Herr 246). As one soldier recalled, he first supposed that the military endowed him with enhanced armaments to protect him from harm's way. Over time, however, he realized that his body was just part of the impersonal war machine. "You are only another piece of equipment, like a tank or the M-16 you carry, and your loss would be counted and calculated only in those terms" (Pratt 652).

Additionally, soldiers often had difficulty reconciling the damage they did to others, despite the fact that military trainers did their best to suppress these feelings. Most marines, Philip Caputo noted, could not get over the shock at seeing "the mutilation caused by modern weapons." *Iron Man* and the weaponsmakers promised a vision of an invincible fighting machine, but battle carnage revealed that the human body was "only a fragile case stuffed full of disgusting matter" (Caputo 121). Iron Man was a comic-book super-hero, but his forays into real-world situations encouraged the vision of the indestructible American fighting man clad in armor and virtue. Yet instead of a fantastical triumph, young men were plunged into an ordeal with steep human costs.

In 1971, Tony Stark began to have his own qualms over Vietnam. Pro-testers descend on Stark Industries, chanting it is a "death factory" (Friedrich, "Beneath the Armor…" 11–13). Initially Stark states that the militants are in the wrong, and that "for every person killed because he encountered Iron Man—a hundred more have lived!" In a revisionist retelling of Iron Man's origins, Stark claims that his weapons were meant to shorten the war, and that Stark has always been a "reluctant" solider for "human dignity" (Thomas 19–21). However, the critiques and subsequent self-reflection continue, and Stark decides he needs to diversify his holdings and de-emphasize munitions manufacturing. By 1973, he advocates sharing technology with the once-loathed Communists "if it makes the prospect of world peace stronger—and us, therefore, much safer!" (Gerber and Friedrich 13). This proves inadequate, as a wounded and vulnerable woman rejects his "suave charm" because, as her nurse states, "she detests a man whose fortune rests on the inventive sav-agery of Stark Industries munitions. No amount of well-publicized 're-ordered priorities' will wash away the Asian blood your weapons shed—not merely once or twice—but for a decade, Mister Stark" (Friedrich, "Cry Marauder!" 7). This denunciation is the final straw, as his business undermines his mas-culine wiles. Three issues later Stark repudiates defense contracts (Friedrich, "Enter: Dr. Spectrum" 6).

As the United States' involvement in Vietnam wound down in 1974, Iron Man was attempting to liberate an American prisoner-of-war. Unlike future avengers in the *Missing in Action* and *Rambo* films, Iron Man's trip is pure disillu-sionment, as his previous allies in the South Vietnamese Army are now the vio-lent oppressors of the peasantry (Friedrich, "Night…" 5). Stark (disingenuously) claims he always had apprehensions about Vietnam, and harbors deep guilt. "[American soldiers] were out here because a weapon I'd built gave them the promise of a faster kill, a well-oiled war," he says. "This is all my fault" (Mantlo 11). The writers seek to partially redeem Stark by describing his shame, agony, and soul searching. This reflected how many Americans responded to the national humbling in Southeast Asia. Unable to deal with the defeat in Viet-nam and the damage and bloodshed they caused, the writer Tom Engelhardt explains that Americans hastily reimagined themselves not as victimizers, but as victims of a quagmire (Engelhardt 199–200). In addition, Stark, and America, have seen the light and will not repeat their mistakes, as Tony transforms his operations from military hardware to alternative energy and space exploration. Proudly, he tells his former critic and current love interest Roxie Gilbert, "I may have been a 'war-mongering weapons maker' for far too long a time, Roxie—but I've always cared about the people" (Wein, 8). *Iron Man* suggests that even if the country blundered in Vietnam, the postwar recovery entailed insisting that its heart was always in the right place.

Popular culture does indeed deserve a share of the blame for the disaster in Vietnam. Film, television, and comic books advanced the mythos that the United States was destined to guide the world toward a liberal-democratic order through force. Young men pictured themselves as John Wayne– and Audie Murphy–style heroes, battling imaginary enemies in distant locations. After playing war, veteran Ron Kovic remembered, "we'd walk out of the woods like the heroes we knew we would become when we were men" (Kovic 55). The effect of the comics industry is hard to gauge, but it certainly socialized youth, particularly young men, in the post–World War II era (Szasz 135). Marvel Comics were tremendously popular with young men in the 1960s. Fans sent bundles of letters to the company and Stan Lee spoke at colleges across the country (Braun 32, 1971). Comic books, Tom Engelhardt writes, were "the reading matter of choice for the young men who went to war for America" in Korea and Vietnam (Engelhardt 97). Readers, who took their critiques of the comic seriously, initially reveled in Stark's aggressiveness, with one calling him "America's greatest man" (Mails of Suspense). Americans frequently viewed and expressed themselves through the lens of popular culture, showing its influence in shaping their politics.

By the late 1960s, young anti-war Americans lodged protests against the military-industrial complex; some readers viewed the formerly-heroic Tony Stark as part of the problem in Southeast Asia. At the University of Illinois, students decried the school's links to the Dow Chemical Company, the makers of napalm. According to the Committee to End the War in Vietnam, "The use of this genocidal weapon reveals only too clearly the nature of the war in Vietnam: it is a war against the entire Vietnamese people" ("Dow Is Back Again," Feb. 19, 1968). Demonstrators also targeted the presence of General Electric recruiters on campus. As a student wrote in the *Daily Illini*, General Electric "makes weapons systems and communications devices to keep the empire and shoot down people when they rise up, as in Vietnam" (Horwitz, 11). Additionally, activists turned their ire toward popular culture, arguing that it was part of the military-industrial-media complex buttressing the war. As the casualties mounted, some readers urged Stark to forgo defense contracts. "When are you going to admit that Tony Stark produces devices to kill people?" a critic asked. "He needs to start converting from military to civilian uses" ("Sock it to Shellhead," Jun. 1971). Another respondent told *Iron Man* writers that Tony Stark would be "much more respected and admired if he would give up being a merchant of death" ("Sock it to Shellhead," Mar. 1971). Tony Stark had once been a hero, a maverick scientist that bucked government bureaucrats while battling dangers to America. By 1973, though, his claims that he was "fighting for humanity! Trying to save lives instead of ending them!" were pitiful, self-serving pleas rather than rallying cries for freedom and democracy (Gerber 5). Stark was a beaten man, headed for an alcoholic spiral.

The military-industrial complex, however, was here to stay. The occasional weaponsmaker may have seen the light, but the profits were too immense for corporations to pass up. As Stuart Leslie observes, the damage was not only in taxpayer dollars to a bloated industry, but "in terms of our scientific community's diminished capacity to comprehend and manipulate the world for other than military ends" (Leslie 9). In *Iron Man*, Stark seamlessly transitions to socially beneficial production, but in reality most military research and manufacturing is too specialized to correlate to the civilian sector (Leslie 254–256). As Eisenhower warned, "partly because of the huge costs involved, a government contract becomes virtually a substitute for intellectual curiosity" (Eisenhower). Contractors and top military brass were not conspiratorial puppet masters directing American foreign policy, but they contributed to scientific myopia and to the government's disregard for addressing disagreements with means other than force. Even more troubling, James Gibson notes, was that elites thought that the United States possessed more knowledge and virtue than other countries, giving them moral license to use their destructive technology as they saw fit (Gibson 15). In the view of American policymakers, might made right.

Even after being humbled in Vietnam, the military-industrial complex continued to affect not only the economy, but the nation's mindset. Inflated by virtually risk-free contracts, it steadily penetrated into the country's tenets and politics, manufacturing weaponry and military equipment in preparation for endless conflicts. In *Iron Man*, Tony Stark wallows in self-pity over his arms manufacturing, succumbs to alcoholism, and even attempts to disable his munitions. Yet Stark, like his country, never fully abandoned the faith that the armed forces not only kept the United States safe, but should be deployed to make the world in its image. The nostalgia for the conflation of American righteousness and power, critic Ty Hawkins argues, overcame any lessons imparted by the Vietnam War (Hawkins, 111).

Stark and his real-world elite contemporaries often saw the complications of far-flung military involvements, but they decided to try to control the situations rather than fundamentally rethinking the consensus creed of intervention. The challenges changed over time, but American decision-makers, wedded to the military-industrial complex, came back to the same solutions: a global military presence, projecting power through an ever-expanding defense budget, and imposing change on recalcitrant countries (Bacevich 225). "If we have to use force, it is because we are America," Secretary of State Madeleine Albright stated in 1998. "We are the indispensable nation. We stand tall. We see further into the future" (Herbert, *New York Times*, 1998). The Cold War had ended, but few experts proposed that the military return to being small and only temporarily expanded.

Iron Man reached new heights of popularity in the rebooted era of aggressiveness during the War on Terror, demonstrating the wonders of weaponry in three highly profitable films. The first film included cursory examinations of the responsibilities of weaponsmakers such as Stark, but concluded that the world was only in danger if these marvelous armaments fell into the wrong hands—never considering whether American military interventions were justified and advisable. The United States was again thwarted in their elaborate nation-building exercises in Iraq and Afghanistan, yet Americans continued to be dazzled by the "shock and awe" of the military-industrial complex. As Philip Caputo lamented, "every generation is doomed to fight its war, to endure the same old experiences, suffer the same loss of the same old illusions and learn the same old lessons on its own" (Caputo 77). Iron Man, created to reassure Americans of the dominance of technological ingenuity and their unlimited capacity to spread liberty, continued to lumber onward.

NOTES

1. Though the first appearance of Tony Stark/Iron Man was scripted by Larry Lieber and drawn by Don Heck, Lee and Kirby conceptualized and designed the character.

2. Robert McNamara, Secretary of Defense from 1961 to 1968, was a chief architect of military strategy in Vietnam. He advocated technological innovations such as the "electronic battlefield," designed to prevent Communist infiltration into South Vietnam.

WORKS CITED

Bacevich, Andrew J. *Washington Rules: America's Path to Permanent War*. New York: Metropolitan, 2010.

Baritz, Loren. *Backfire: A History of How American Culture Led Us into Vietnam and Made Us Fight the Way We Did*. New York: W. Morrow, 1985.

Braun, Saul. "Shazam! Here Comes Captain Relevant." *New York Times* 2 May 1971: 32+.

Caputo, Philip. *A Rumor of War*. New York: Ballantine Books, 1977.

Committee for Economic Development. "Problem of National Security." In *The Military-Industrial Complex*, edited by Carroll W. Pursell. New York: Harper & Row, 1972. 198–203.

Committee to End the War in Vietnam. "Dow is Back Again." 19 February 1968. University of Illinois Student Life and Culture Archives, RS 41/6/840, Box 12.

Eisenhower, Dwight. *Text of the Address by President Eisenhower. The Farewell Address.* Eisenhower Presidential Library, 17 January 1961. http://www.eisenhower.archives. gov/research/online_documents/farewell_address/1961_01_17_Press_Release.pdf. Accessed 10 May 2014. Web.

Engelhardt, Tom. *The End of Victory Culture: Cold War America and the Disillusioning of a Generation*. New York, NY: Basic, 1995.

Friedrich, Gary (w) and George Tuska (a). "Beneath the Armor Beats a Heart." *Iron Man* #45 (Mar. 1972) New York: Marvel Comics.

Friedrich, Mike (w) and George Tuska (a). "Cry Marauder!" *Iron Man* 60 (Jul. 1973) New York: Marvel Comics.

_____. "Enter: Dr. Spectrum." *Iron Man* #63 (Oct. 1973) New York: Marvel Comics.

_____. "Night of the Rising Sun!" *Iron Man* #68 (Jun. 1974) New York: Marvel Comics.

Fulbright, William. "The War and Its Effects: The Military-Industrial-Academic Complex." In *Super-state Readings in the Military-industrial Complex*, edited by Herbert I. Schiller and Joseph Dexter Phillips. Chicago: University of Illinois Press, 1970. 173–78.

Genter, Robert. "'With Great Power Comes Great Responsibility': Cold War Culture and the Birth of Marvel Comics." *Journal of Popular Culture* 40.6 (2007): 953–78.

Gerber, Steve (w) and George Tuska (a). "Strike!" *Iron Man* #68 (Apr. 1973) New York: Marvel Comics.

Gerber, Steve with Mike Friedrich (w) and George Tuska (a). "Mandarin and the Unicorn: Double-Death!" *Iron Man* #58 (May 1973) New York: Marvel Comics.

Gibson, James William. *The Perfect War: Technowar in Vietnam*. Boston: The Atlantic Monthly Press, 1986.

Gold, Mimi (w) and Don Heck (a). "Save the People, Save the Country." *Iron Man* #29 (Sep. 70) New York: Marvel Comics.

Goodwin, Archie (w) and George Tuska (a). "Once More... The Mandarin!" *Iron Man* #10 (Apr. 1969) New York: Marvel Comics.

_____. "Unmasked!" *Iron Man* #11 (Mar. 1969) New York: Marvel Comics.

Hallin, Daniel C. *The "Uncensored War": The Media and Vietnam*. New York: Oxford University Press, 1986.

Hammond, William M. *Reporting Vietnam: Media and Military at War*. Lawrence: University of Kansas Press, 1998.

Hawkins, Ty. *Reading Vietnam amid the War on Terror*. New York: Palgrave Macmillan, 2012.

Herbert, Bob. "War Games." *New York Times*. 22 February 1998: 138.

Herr, Michael. *Dispatches*. New York: Avon Books, 1978.

Hitch, Charles. "The Defense Sector: Its Impact on American Business." In *Super-state Readings in the Military-industrial Complex*, edited by Herbert I. Schiller and Joseph Dexter Phillips. Chicago: University of Illinois Press, 1970. 131–155.

Horwitz, Steven. "General Electric." *Daily Illini*. 3 March 1970: 11.

Kaufman, Richard F. "As Eisenhower Was Saying ... We Must Guard Against Unwarranted Influence by the Military-Industrial Complex.'" *New York Times*. 22 June 1969.

Kovic, Ron. *Born on the Fourth of July*. New York: Simon and Schuster, 1976.

Lederer, William J. *Our Own Worst Enemy*. Greenwich, CT: Fawcett Publications, 1968.

Lee, Stan. *Son of Origins of Marvel Comics.* New York: Simon and Schuster, 1975.

_____ (w), and Don Heck (a). "The Death of Tony Stark!" *Tales of Suspense* #61 (Jan. 1965) New York: Marvel Comics.

_____. "Suspected of Murder!" *Tales of Suspense* #60 (Dec. 1964) New York: Marvel Comics.

Lee, Stan (w) and Gene Colan (a). "Crisis at the Earth's Core!" *Tales of Suspense* #87 (Mar. 1967) New York: Marvel Comics.

_____. "The Golden Gladiator and the Giant!" *Tales of Suspense* #93 (Sep. 1967) New York: Marvel Comics.

_____. "The Monstrous Menace of the Mysterious Melter!" *Tales of Suspense* #89 (May 1967) New York: Marvel Comics.

_____. "The Tragedy and the Triumph!" *Tales of Suspense* #94 (Oct. 1967) New York: Marvel Comics.

_____. "Victory." *Tales of Suspense* #83 (Nov. 1966) New York: Marvel Comics.

_____. "Within the Vastness of Viet Nam!" *Tales of Suspense* #92 (Aug. 1967) New York: Marvel Comics.

Lee, Stan (w) and Gene Colan (as Adam Austin) (a). "Ultimo Lives!" *Tales of Suspense* #77 (May 1966) New York: Marvel Comics.

Lee, Stan with Larry Lieber (w) and Don Heck (a). "Iron Man Is Born!" *Tales of Suspense* #39 (Mar. 1963) New York: Marvel Comics.

Lee Stan with N. Korok (w) and Don Heck (a). "The Black Widow Strikes Again!" *Tales of Suspense* #53 (May 1964) New York: Marvel Comics.

Lee, Stan with R. Berns (w) and Jack Kirby (a). "Iron Man Faces the Crimson Dynamo!" *Tales of Suspense* #46 (Oct. 1963) New York: Marvel Comics.

_____. "Iron Man versus Gargantus!" *Tales of Suspense* #40 (Apr. 1963) New York: Marvel Comics.

Leslie, Stuart W. *The Cold War and American Science: The Military-industrial-academic Complex at MIT and Stanford.* New York: Columbia University Press, 1993.

Mantlo, Bill (w) and George Tuska (a). "Long Time Gone." *Iron Man* #78 (Sep. 1975) New York: Marvel Comics.

Melman, Seymour. *Pentagon Capitalism: The Political Economy of War.* New York: McGraw-Hill, 1970.

Pratt, John Clark. *Vietnam Voices: Perspectives on the War Years, 1941–1982.* New York: Penguin, 1984.

Proxmire, William. "Blank Check for the Military." In *Super-state Readings in the Military-industrial Complex,* edited by Herbert I. Schiller and Joseph Dexter Phillips. Chicago: University Press of Illinois, 1970. 46–64.

Pursell, Carroll. "Introduction." *The Military-industrial Complex.* New York: Harper & Row, 1972. 1–12.

Raymond, Jack. "Kennedy Favors Pentagon Shift and Plane Alert: Calls for More Missiles." *New York Times* 24 Oct. 1960: 1.

Scanlon, Sandra. *The Pro-War Movement: Domestic Support for the Vietnam War and the Making of Modern American Conservatism.* Amherst: University of Massachusetts Press, 2013.

Schell, Jonathan. *The Village of Ben Suc.* New York: Knopf, 1967.

Schevitz, Jeffrey M. *The Weaponsmakers.* Cambridge, MA: Schenkman, 1979.

"Scientists at M.I.T. Plan One-Day Strike." *New York Times* 24 Jan. 1969: 73.

Shoup, David. "The New American Militarism." In *Super-state Readings in the Military-industrial Complex.* Eds. Herbert I. Schiller and Joseph Dexter Phillips. Chicago: University of Illinois Press, 1970. 93–104.

"Sock It to Shellhead." *Iron Man* #35 (Jan. 1971). New York: Marvel Comics.

"Sock It to Shellhead." *Iron Man* #35 (Mar. 1971). New York: Marvel Comics.

"Sock It to Shellhead." *Iron Man #38* (Jun. 1971). New York: Marvel Comics.

Sullivan, Walter. "Strike to Protest 'Misuse' of Science." *New York Times.* 6 Feb. 1969: 1.

Szasz, Ferenc Morton. *Atomic Comics: Cartoonists Confront the Nuclear World.* Reno: University of Nevada, 2012.

Terjesen, Andrew. "Tony Stark and 'The Gospel of Wealth." In *Iron Man and Philosophy: Facing the Stark Reality,* edited by Mark D. White. Hoboken, NJ: John Wiley & Sons, 2010. 97–114.

Thomas, Roy (w) and Barry Windsor-Smith (a)."Why Must There Be an Iron Man?" *Iron Man #47* (Jun. 1972) New York: Marvel Comics.

Turse, Nick. *Kill Anything That Moves: The Real American War in Vietnam.* New York: Metropolitan /Henry Holt, 2013.

Wein, Len (w) and Herb Trimpe (a). "Plunder of the Apes!" *Iron Man #82* (Jan. 1976) New York: Marvel Comics.

Wicker, Tom. "In the Nation: Firepower vs. South Vietnam." *New York Times.* 20 Feb. 1968: 46.

Wright, Bradford W. *Comic Book Nation: The Transformation of Youth Culture in America.* Baltimore: Johns Hopkins University Press, 2001.

_____. "The Vietnam War and Comic Books." In *The Vietnam War: Handbook of the Literature and Research,* edited by James Stuart Olson. Westport, CT: Greenwood, 1993. 427–54.

Socking It to Shell-Head

How Fan Mail Saved
a Hero from the
Military-Industrial Complex

CHARLES HENEBRY

Born in the jungles of Indochina more than a year before the Gulf of Tonkin incident made Vietnam a household word, Iron Man was conceived from the start as a Cold Warrior. His alter-ego, Tony Stark, played a crucial role in this formulation. Unlike Marvel's other science nerds, Peter Parker and Bruce Banner, Stark was a winner in the game of life, a handsome devil as well as a genius inventor. Just as Iron Man embodied America's nimble prowess in technology, Tony Stark embodied the nation's entrepreneurial spirit. So from March 1963 through October 1967, Iron Man fought a series of brutal bullies who sought to enslave humanity under the mantle of International Communism. But in the late 60s this formula broke down. The Vietnam War had become deeply unpopular in some quarters, especially on college campuses, where many of Marvel's most fervent readers lived. What's more, though, the war was increasingly being blamed on the "military-industrial complex," envisioned as a shadowy network of vested interests that dealt in death and dismemberment for the sake of corporate profits. And this otherwise faceless abstraction found a ready-made personification in Tony Stark.

In a process that lasted over eight years, Marvel struggled to bring Tony Stark and Iron Man in line with the progressive politics of the late 60s and early 70s. The transition began with the comic's sudden shift away from geopolitical stories in late 1967 and ended with the transformation of Stark Industries into Stark International, a company working on ecology, world food production, and space exploration. As we shall see, the process was made possible by the ingenuity of Marvel's artists and writers, but it was driven in considerable part by fans. Their letters, preserved in the letters columns of *Tales of Suspense* and *Iron Man,* pestered the comic's creators with complaints and unsolicited advice, much of it mutually contradictory. And, as Marvel's editors liked to claim in their responses, they listened to their readers.

Before exploring this change, however, I should perhaps dispense with a different version of the character's origins with which readers may already be familiar. For at least the past decade, Stan Lee has been describing Iron Man as a deliberate effort to tweak the liberal sensibilities of his readers.[1] Lee claims that, coming off the success of the first wave of Marvel superhero titles, he set himself the challenge of seeing whether he could make teenage readers who "had no use for industrialists" and who "despised what they called the military/industrial complex" become fans of a hero who was modeled after Howard Hughes (Lee 160). Lee's account badly compresses the 1960s, transplanting the antiwar sentiment of the decade's final years onto the earlier period of broad national consensus. The error is of a sort frequently encountered in oral histories, but in this case the error is not wholly innocent. As we shall see, Tony Stark did indeed become a lightning rod for criticism from antiwar radicals, but Stan Lee had not sought out that controversy; to the contrary, it alienated him, leading him to hand *Iron Man* over to another writer years before other titles. That subordinate and his many successors undertook the challenge of winning back those readers as fans, not Stan Lee.

The one clear truth in Stan Lee's account is that he based the character of Tony Stark on Howard Hughes, the billionaire genius and playboy industrialist who figured prominently in the cultural imagination in the 1930s and 40s, when Lee was in his teens and early twenties. By the 1960s, Hughes had dropped from public view, the victim of mental disorders, but this only magnified his mystique in some quarters. *Life* magazine ran a lengthy profile of Hughes in its September 7, 1962 issue, mere months before Stan Lee and Don Heck must have begun work on the first Iron Man story, published in *Tales of Suspense* #39 and dated March 1963. *Life's* headline and subheads presented Hughes as a mystery—"Riddle of an Embattled Phantom" (20–21); "A Playboy who turned into a secretive, besieged and lonely man" (24–25)—a mystery to which Stan Lee's Iron Man offered one possible, if fantastical, solution: a millionaire isolated by the very armor that kept his heart beating. One photograph from *Life's* profile stands out: Hughes sitting at the controls of one of his company's airplanes (23). It's easy to imagine that this image served Don Heck as a point of departure for his visual characterization: tall forehead, straight hair combed back, dark, soulful eyes, thin aquiline nose, neatly trimmed mustache, lips twisted coyly in a hint of a smile—the photograph is the spitting image of Tony Stark.[2]

But if Hughes embodied the romance of aerospace in the 1940s and 50s, the 1960s witnessed a new phase in America's love affair with vertical movement. In an address at Rice University in September 1962, President Kennedy challenged the nation to respond to Russia's recent ventures in space by putting a man on the moon by the end of the decade: "For the eyes of the world now look into space, to the moon and to the planets beyond, and we have vowed that we shall not see it governed by a hostile flag of conquest, but by a banner of freedom and peace." Kennedy's phrasing helped set the terms for what would become known as the "Space Race": a contest pitting free enterprise against central planning, a struggle whose outcome mattered for both pragmatic and symbolic reasons.

In the course of Iron Man's five-year run in *Tales of Suspense* from 1963 to 1968, Stan Lee repeatedly enacted this Cold War struggle by pitting Iron Man against products of the Soviet war machine, from the Crimson Dynamo to the Unicorn and the Black Widow. The most symbolically resonant of these was Titanium Man, a powered armor suit conceived and worn by the ambitious Comrade Bullski. Commissar of a Siberian prison camp, Bullski aimed to outdo Iron Man in every respect: size, strength, and durability. Standing head-and-shoulders taller and at least a foot broader than Iron Man, pitting Soviet might against American ingenuity, the green behemoth called to mind the Vostok rockets that towered over their early–60s American rivals, the Atlas and the Titan. What's more, Titanium Man embodied the fearful threat of an economy under totalitarian control: a physical bully willing to squander the talents of a cadre of prisoner-scientists in the hope of advancing his personal standing. By contrast, Stark's work as a military contractor was dogged at every turn by government officials exercising oversight, chief among them Senator Byrd, whose efforts to call Stark to account before a Senate subcommittee were a recurring subplot in the latter half of Iron Man's run in *Tales of Suspense*. Byrd's energetic pursuit of Stark had an interesting double valence. On the one hand, he presented an enormous distraction, impeding Stark from the performance of more important duties; on the other hand, as Stark commented in an aside, "The Senator's a dedicated man, doing his job as he sees it!" (Hartley, "If a Man...," *Tales of Suspense* #68, 12). Byrd's vigilance was a handicap that Stark willingly suffered to keep the nation free from tyranny.

Conceived in close parallel to the Space Race, the first two battles between Iron Man and Titanium Man were televised to a world audience, proxy fights in a larger Cold War struggle. The first, staged by mutual agree-

ment on a barren old battlefield of Central Europe, presented the two con-
testants as armored "knights" fighting as national champions in the manner
of David and Goliath. At the contest's start they stood facing one another,
each backed by a trio of high-ranking military personnel (Heck, pencils,"If
I Must Die...," *Tales of Suspense* #68, 11). In the neutral space separating the
champions stood a panel of three judges dressed quaintly in the national cos-
tumes of several different European countries, as if to suggest that the fate
of Europe hung in the balance. Their second showdown followed a year latter,
in issues published in the fall of 1966. Taken by surprise on his way to testify
before Byrd's committee, Iron Man duked it out with his adversary in the
skies over Washington, the Capitol dome providing a dramatic backdrop for
their midair battle—as well as a nagging reminder of the Senate hearing that
Stark was supposed to be attending (Colan, pencils, "By Force...," *Tales of
Suspense* #82, 1). The fight got picked up by the national media, with one crucial panel presenting President Johnson's reaction to the televised fight: "If
only the day would come when force is no longer necessary, when men would
reason together, instead! But, until such a time, we should be thankful that
power such as Iron Man's exists—and can be used in behalf of freedom!"
(Lee, "Victory," *Tales of Suspense* #83, 7).[3]

Iron Man's struggles against the Mandarin in this period referenced
Communist China, but whereas the Crimson Dynamo and Titanium Man were
both personifications of Soviet power, the Mandarin lay squarely within the
"Yellow Peril" tradition of Fu Manchu. Claiming descent from Ghengis Khan
and dwelling in a hidden mountain fortress, the Mandarin was the skillful
puppeteer behind Mao's Red Army. Judging from the frequency of his appearances, the character was a hit, but he was also an oddly fanciful anachronism
by contrast to the Soviet scientist who became the Crimson Dynamo or the
prison camp warden who became Titanium Man. In this sense, the Mandarin
stood as testament to America's continuing refusal to come to grips with China
as a Communist state in the 1960s. Interestingly, Lee presented Iron Man's
Vietnamese villains in a manner far more similar to the hero's Russian antagonists than to his Chinese nemesis: Wong Chu of *ToS*#39 is a tyrannical bully
from the same mold as Comrade Bullski, while Half-Face of *ToS*#92–94 is a
deluded super-scientist akin to Professor Vanko, the Crimson Dynamo. Indeed,
like Vanko, Half-Face is ultimately redeemed. Inspired by Iron Man's valiant
defense of a peaceful village from the depredations of Titanium Man, Half-
Face turns away from the cold-hearted dictates of the Party (Lee, "The Golden
Gladiator...", *Tales of Suspense* #93, 8) and embraces the universal human values of family and freedom (Lee, "The Tragedy...," *Tales of Suspense* #94, 12).

The extent of Iron Man's engagement with Cold War politics can also be measured by the frequency with which caricatures of Communist leaders appeared in the pages of *Tales of Suspense*. Don Heck drew Khrushchev's likeness into issues 41, 42, 46, 52, 53, and 64, and Stan Lee had Professor Vanko quote his most famous line, "We will bury you," in *Tales of Suspense* #52 (Apr. 1964). Khrushchev fell from power in October 1964; the fact that his final appearance (dated April 1965) was drawn and scripted months later suggests the hold of this colorful leader on the American imagination; his successor, Leonid Brezhnev, never rated an appearance. But Fidel Castro did, drawn by Gene Colan in *Tales of Suspense* #91 (Jul. 1967). Just as with President Johnson, and in keeping with a tradition stretching back to Hitler's appearances in *Superman* during World War II, Lee played these references coyly, never naming the leaders, but Marvel's artists left no room for doubt as to their identity.

The final issues of *Tales of Suspense*, however, marked a dramatic shift away from Cold War politics. Following Iron Man's encounter with Half-Face and Titanium Man in *Tales of Suspense* #92–94, the comic entered a long stretch of essentially apolitical stories spanning the transition from *Tales of Suspense* to *The Invincible Iron Man*: a full 18 issues from *Tales of Suspense* #95 (Nov. 1965) through *The Invincible Iron Man* #13 (May 1969). Early issues in this period borrowed villains from other Marvel titles, underlining the turn away from Iron Man's past: the Grey Gargoyle from *Thor,* the Maggia crime organization from *The Avengers,* and the high-tech terrorist organization A.I.M. from Nick Fury's run in the back pages of *Strange Tales*. Coming on the heels of Iron Man's success in winning over the hearts and minds of Vietnamese peasants in *Tales of Suspense* #92–94, his multi-issue struggle to escape the clutches of the Maggia and A.I.M. marked a wholesale disengagement from reality, moving from fantasizing about success in South Asia to a James Bond fantasia of secret organizations equipped with wondrous devices but no motivation beyond the cripplingly vague "world domination."

Later issues in this period saw the reintroduction of Iron Man's classic Cold War villains rewritten as independent actors. In *The Invincible Iron Man* #4, the Unicorn permanently parted ways with his Soviet masters after overcoming their brainwashing and destroying their laboratory. In issue 6 (Oct. 1968), the Crusher, once an ambitious scientist from Communist Cuba, dug his way out of a trap set fourteen issues earlier and promptly forsook all prior allegiance with a vow of vengeance: "This time I act not on the whim of some scheming dictator, but on my own surging, unstoppable need for revenge!" (Goodwin, "Vengeance..."). The Mandarin, in issue 9 (Jan. 1969), moved his base of operations from the mountains of Communist China to an oriental antiques dealership in Manhattan. In each case, the reworked villain had a personal, rather than a geopolitical, sphere of reference. Notably, two villains most closely associated with Iron Man's Cold War past, the Crimson Dynamo and Titanium Man, did not appear at all in this period.

Iron Man's vacation from geopolitics was the more striking because it ran from November 1967 to May 1969, a period of political unrest and upheaval in American society, much of it centered on Vietnam. In March 1968, Lyndon Johnson unexpectedly withdrew from his reelection campaign after losses in the primaries suggested the unpopularity of his Vietnam policy; that same spring, student protesters occupied or firebombed the administration buildings of Columbia, Berkeley, Cornell, U Michigan, and U Wisconsin; and in August the Democratic National Convention was the scene of brutal clashes between the Chicago police and antiwar protesters (Heineman 182–183).

The radicalization of American youth left its mark on the letters pages that ran in *Tales of Suspense* and *The Invincible Iron Man*. In the "Mails of Suspense" column that ran in *Tales of Suspense* #96 (Dec. 1967), William Martin of the Columbia University graduate school expressed his "thorough disgust" with the "base propaganda" of the Half-Face story. In joking reference to the fashionable trend among radicals of burning their draft cards, Martin threatened to mail Marvel the ashes of his M.M.M.S. card.[4] Five months later, Chris Barth of Ambler, Pennsylvania, inaugurated the "Sock It to Shell-Head" letters column in *The Invincible Iron Man* #1 (Jan. 1969) by calling Tony Stark a "sadistic hatemonger," reasoning that "anyone who turns out disintegration rays and stun machines and a cobalt weapon against which there can be no defense has got to be all bad.... Really, is that any way for a hero in a Marvel mag to act? What's he trying to do, destroy the world? Let him invent something peaceful like an atomic-powered guitar."

Martin's and Barth's letters represented a marked shift in reader sentiment. Back in *Tales of Suspense* #66 (June 1965), Jerry Pritchett of Danville, Virginia, had asked the comic's creative team to focus less on personal problems and "ordinary costumed villains" so that Iron Man could concern himself solely with the threat of Communism. Letters in issues 71 and 72 (Nov. and Dec. 1965) called for replacing the World War II–era Captain America stories then running in the back of *Tales of Suspense* with stories pitting the hero against modern-day Communist threats. Anti-communist sentiment may not have been universal in 1965 (Stan Lee replied in *Tales of Suspense* #71 [Nov. 1965] that "Some Marvelophiles want us to keep Cap out of Viet Nam"), but judging from the letters selected for publication, it represented the dominant strain of thought. Indeed, the story of Half-Face to which William Martin so strenuously objected had evidently been created in response to reader demand for a story that would return the hero to his place of origin:

> NEXT ISH: We had to do it! It would take a week just to count all the letters we've received demanding that we present an adventure of Shell-Head in Viet Nam! We held off as long as we could, waiting till we had the perfect yarn—one that would do justice to the scope and power of the subject matter—and now we think we've got it! ["Mails of Suspense," *Tales of Suspense* #91].

Lee was able to run a favorable critique in *Tales of Suspense* #97 (Jan. 1968) from Ronald Williams, a soldier serving in Vietnam, but if William Martin's wholly negative assessment in *Tales of Suspense* #96 (Dec. 1967) is at all representative of the letters Marvel received in response to its "perfect yarn," it's easy to understand the character's sharp turn away from political stories in the issues that followed.

Marvel historian Sean Howe has suggested that the unhappy memory of the 1954 Kefauver hearings gave Stan Lee a strong aversion to political expression in comics (94–95). But, especially on Iron Man, Lee's work in the early and middle sixties wasn't apolitical so much as unobjectionably mainstream, an expression of the "Ideology of the Liberal Consensus" described by Geoffrey Hodgson: "Confident to the verge of complacency about the perfectibility of American society, anxious to the point of paranoia about the threat of communism—those were the two faces of the consensus mood" (75). Hodgson's characterization of the political climate might easily be mistaken for a description of any number of Iron Man stories from *Tales of Suspense*. As that consensus broke down in the late 1960s, however, Stan Lee was left with no middle ground on which to position his fictional Cold Warrior. The problem was especially acute given Marvel's popularity with college-age readers.[5] For in fact college students were in 1968 anything but unanimous in their views on the war. As detailed by Kenneth Heineman, antiwar radicals may have dominated campus discourse, but student bodies were bitterly divided between hawks and doves, and the antiwar movement itself riven between violent and non-violent factions (183). Stan Lee responded to this crisis by ducking the issue. He introduced a new civilian sidekick, Jasper Sitwell, to orient Tony Stark away from Senator Byrd and Congress to the fictional international agency S.H.I.E.L.D. He introduced new antagonists (the Maggia and Whiplash) to reinvent Iron Man as an apolitical hero. And then, just four issues after the hero's fateful encounter with Half-Face, he distanced himself from the title altogether, delegating the tasks of plotting and scripting to Archie Goodwin, who took over starting with the final issue of *Tales of Suspense* and continuing in *The Invincible Iron Man* #1–28.[6]

But even as Lee and Goodwin were wrenching Iron Man from the Cold War to float for a time in apolitical limbo free from contemporary controversy, they signaled an openness to discussion of controversy in the letters column. Having run reader William Martin's negative assessment of the Vietnam Half-Face story in *Tales of Suspense* #96, they inaugurated Iron Man's solo series with a letters column whose title practically invited criticism—"Sock It to Shell-Head"—pressing the point home by printing Chris Barth's attack on Tony Stark as a "sadistic hatemonger" as the column's very first letter. The column in issue 2 opened with a similarly strident declaration, penned by Patricia Huguet of Philadelphia, objecting to the paucity of female super-heroes as "plain discrimination." Noting the appearance of a host of new titles ("Iron Man, Sub-Mariner, Captain America and the Hulk"), Huguet pointed out that Marvel had no "mags" celebrating the exploits of a female superhero: "Women have been doing work considered for men only for years and we have the right to have a super-heroine to admire. I know there are a lot of your female readers who will agree with me." She might have addressed this critique to any of the four new titles she mentioned; the fact that it was run in *The Invincible Iron Man* rather than one of the others suggests the editors' interest in presenting the comic, if not the character, as politically "with it." The editors' appetite for political discussion proved limited, however; later issues carried letters critical of stories and artwork, but after issue 2 politics disappeared from the letters column for several years, reappearing only after the comic itself returned to politics.

Perhaps in deference to a directive from Lee or his assistant Roy Thomas, that return to political relevance was both tentative and gradual under the stewardship of Archie Goodwin. A two-issue story that ran in *The Invincible Iron Man* #10–11 (Feb-Mar 1969) brought Senator Byrd back to respond to photographic evidence, fabricated by the Mandarin, that made it look as if Stark had met with high-ranking Communist officials. Yet the narrative was oddly disjointed from contemporary politics: the photos didn't show Stark in the presence of anyone recognizable, while the situation recollected the Red Scare of the early 1950s rather than, say, late–60s Black Panther Maoism. In a fill-in issue that ran in *The Invincible Iron Man* #14 (Jun 1969), Archie Goodwin experimented with reframing Iron Man's politics by reference to the postcolonial third world. Set in a newly independent Caribbean nation, the story pitted Stark as an agent of technocratic modernization against the mysterious Night Phantom, a masked villain dressed all in black whose appearances were presaged by "voodoo drums." In a denouement worthy of the contemporaneous *Scooby-Doo* (1969–70), this supposedly terrifying embodiment of the island's primitive traditions turned out to be a wealthy white landowner who had hoped to keep the island's culture "pure"—and his grip on power secure—by scaring off Stark and other international investors. Designed as "a reserve piece … out of sequence" to hedge against deadline pressures (letters column, *The Invincible Iron Man* #18), the story was notable for its effort to reengage with the contemporary political scene, the only such story in the period stretching from *Tales of Suspense* #95 (Nov 1967) to *The Invincible Iron Man* #24 (Apr 1970). Of course, international development was not nearly as controversial as the war in Vietnam, but that was precisely the point: the story managed to identify common ground on which Iron Man and his readers might stand in defense of a shared ideal. What's more, Goodwin did so by reconceptualizing the significance of Tony Stark's role as a leading industrialist: no longer a "sadistic hatemonger … turn[ing] out disintegration rays" (as per Chris Barth's letter in *The Invincible Iron Man* #1), but rather a liberal investor and force for progress.

A year later, Goodwin followed up with two stories in quick succession, both of which explicitly addressed controversial issues. In *The Invincible Iron Man* #25 (May 1970), Stark visited another remote outpost of Stark Industries only to discover that his Meridian Island Project had run out of control, exhausting the island's resources and polluting the ocean around it. The Sub-Mariner showed up to offer a neat didactic lesson by turning the pollution back upon the polluters, poisoning the air instead of the water. Although Iron Man traded punches with him, the story's real villain wasn't "Subby" but the project's head, Blane Ordway, an engineer so fixated on technological progress as to be blind to nature's suffering and even that of his workers. The experience converted Stark to environmentalism, but he returned to the mainland only to discover that his fellow industrialists were deaf to his pleas about the need to rein in pollution. Bolder than *The Invincible Iron Man* #14, this new story contained an implicit critique of Stark the industrialist, even as it left room for him to plead ignorance and begin repairing the hurt his company had done by setting a new initiative in motion.

Two issues later, in his penultimate story as a steady writer on *Iron Man*, Goodwin displayed a different side to Stark's newfound political conscience. Set in a blighted black neighborhood of Bay City known as North Side (a reference to Chicago's troubled neighborhoods, the West Side and the South Side), the narrative pitted radical activist Firebrand against a project sponsored by the Iron Man Foundation. Both the costumed villain and the charitable organization were created by Goodwin for the occasion, suggesting the wholesale revision involved in his effort to reposition Iron Man against a domestic political backdrop. Firebrand's fervent opposition to the Foundation's project must have appeared ill-founded to many readers: how could anyone object to building a community center on a vacant lot in the middle of a run-down ghetto neighborhood? But Goodwin channeled real-world radical discourse to give Firebrand some of the best lines in the issue: "Anything the Man puts up, I'm ready to tear down! …. The only way to get anything from the Man is to take it!" (2). And artist Don Heck drew into the story a whole crowd of neighborhood activists that shared this perspective, joining Firebrand in questioning whether any project backed by the establishment could be trusted to benefit the oppressed. What's more, the story's outcome proved Firebrand's distrust to be well-founded: the project's political sponsor, Councilman Bradshaw, was discovered to be on the take, enriching himself through a network of dummy corporations. And Goodwin and Heck were careful to explain how Firebrand, in parallel to many real-world militants in the late 60s and early 70s, was radicalized by the bitter experience of trying to address social wrongs through non-violent protest: "I sat-in for Civil Rights, marched for peace, and demonstrated on campus—and got chased by vicious dogs, spat on by bigots, beat on by 'patriots,' choked by tear gas, and blinded by mace, until I finally caught on: this country doesn't want to be changed! The only way to build anything decent is to tear down what's here and start over!" (11). These separate elements combined to give a certain legitimacy to the story's putative villain: whereas five years earlier Communism could be defeated through a proxy battle with the Titanium Man, the paranoid distrust of Firebrand and his followers could not be simply punched into submission. As Iron Man mused to a riot policeman in the final panels, "It's not Firebrand's escaping that bothers me. It's wondering where the rest of us went wrong—that someone like him should have to come into being at all!" (20).

Haunted by late–60s racial politics, the story addressed an anxiety, then common in white liberal circles, that the middle ground had disappeared from national politics, leaving no viable alternative between violent uprising and stodgy conservatism. In an effort to reference the riots that had engulfed Chicago's black neighborhoods two years earlier in the wake of the 1968 King assassination, the story's action took place in a ghetto, pitting disaffected black activists against an almost wholly white power structure. In this polarized climate, efforts at reasoned dialogue broke down in distrust and *ad hominem* attacks: Tony Stark's friend, the boxer Eddie Marsh, was scornfully dismissed by Firebrand as an Uncle Tom (7), while Iron Man was attacked by the mob as an armored flunky for white hegemony (8). Don Heck's costume design for Firebrand precisely inverted Iron Man's red-on-gold color scheme, reinforcing the impression that this radical stood for the interests of an oppressed minority against Tony Stark's bodyguard, the champion of monied interests. Moreover, Firebrand's chest logo referenced the "black power salute" made famous by track stars Tommie Smith and John Carlos at the 1968 Olympics and later associated with the Black Panther movement. Goodwin and Heck managed to conclude the issue in a way that restored civic peace, carving out a middle ground by discrediting both Firebrand and the corrupt Councilman Bradshaw. But any comic depicting a race riot in 1970 was taking a risk—simply on account of taking a stand on a controversial issue. One measure of that risk is the effort that Marvel's editors went to conceal the issue's real topic from the general public, requesting from Marie Severin a front cover showing Firebrand attacking Iron Man at the head of a mob of angry *white* men.[7]

Thus, while Goodwin's 1968–70 run on Iron Man was characterized for the most part by apolitical stories, the final issues found him groping toward a new articulation of Tony Stark's relationship to contemporary America. The reaction from readers was overwhelming, swamping the letters column for several issues. In a letter printed in *The Invincible Iron Man* #29, Kevin Dawson of Hollis, a neighborhood in Queens, recommended that *The Invincible Iron Man* #25 be mailed to the owners of polluting factories—even though, he acknowledged, these businessmen would likely respond no differently from the fictional ones addressed by Tony Stark at the comic's end. In the same issue, Patrick Rosenkranz of Portland, Oregon, lavished praise on the story's creators: "I have never seen Marvel so violently espouse an issue before, and you could not have chosen a more worthy cause than world ecology." Perhaps in an effort to invoke Stan Lee's words of wisdom in the first issue of *Spider-Man*, "With great power there must also come great responsibility," Rosenkranz made much of the little-recognized "media power" of comics before concluding by praising Marvel for using that power for the greater good: "instead of merely capitalizing on a tested pattern, you have had the courage to use your broadening media power to speak out on controversial issues. You show that winos exist, that students and blacks have legitimate claims, that today is a period of unrest that seriously affects the lives of many people." Three more letters praising *IM*#25 followed in issue 30, along with one noting that *The Invincible Iron Man* had merited mention during a TV news interview with the Florida governor (his daughter had bought him an issue). These letters suggest an audience eager for comics that addressed contemporary ills.[8]

Reaction to Firebrand's debut was far more mixed, suggesting the tricky balance required for crafting a politically relevant comic. Perhaps the most telling response was that of Bruce Long of Montebello, California, who marked his refusal to take the political issue seriously by proposing a silly solution to the mystery of Firebrand's identity, that the villain was really Liz Allen, Flash Thompson's girlfriend from the early issues of *Amazing Spider-Man* (*The Invisible Iron Man* #31). Others responded with political blinders firmly in place. Ralph Hensley of Cincinnati, Ohio, insisted not only that Firebrand was a villain, but that his followers were criminals: "The law was made for all people to obey, but the rioters, regardless of their reasons, were breaking the law. The people were fighting for a cause, but they were going at it the wrong way" (*The Invincible Iron Man* #31). By contrast, Andy Feeny, of Detroit Michigan, pointed the finger of blame squarely at Iron Man, or, rather, at the military-industrial complex that gave him birth:

> In one way, Firebrand is "right on"—and nobody illustrates his point better than Tony Stark. At the end of the issue, you have Iron Man say, "It's not Firebrand's escaping that bothers me! It's wondering where the rest of us went wrong that someone like him should have to come into being at all!" Stop wondering, Tony—your own munitions factory is one place that comes to mind, right away. While Firebrand was marching, trying to bring about a more peaceful world, Stark Industries was probably building weapons for Vietnam, where we "destroyed a city in order to save it" [*The Invincible Iron Man* #31].

The three letters published in response to Firebrand exemplified the very problem enacted in the story's fiction, the total breakdown in civil discourse: Andy Feeny used an *ad hominem* attack to dismiss Tony Stark; Ralph Hensley did the same to the radicals, refusing to listen to their grievance on the grounds of their improper methods; and Bruce Long refused to engage altogether.

Marvel's writers and editors were not dissuaded from reengaging with contemporary politics, however. By my count, in the seven years following Goodwin's last issue (#28), from September 1970 to the July 1977 celebratory issue 100, 58 percent of stories engaged with political issues in some way, almost precisely on par with the 59 percent that engaged with Cold War geopolitics in the *Tales of Suspense* era up through the Half-Face story set in Vietnam. The difference was in the variety of political issues covered: not only the environment, race relations, and radicalized youth (all issues introduced by Goodwin), but also women's rights, the legacy of the war in Vietnam, and the decline of New York City into near-bankruptcy.[9]

It's tempting to attribute this thematic shift to the passing of the generational torch from Stan Lee (who turned 48 in 1970) to the much younger Archie Goodwin (33 in 1970), followed by a series of even younger regulars in the period 1970–77: Gerry Conway, Mike Friedrich, and Bill Mantlo (respectively 18, 21, and 19 in 1970). Notably, this shift only occurred among

Iron Man's writers. The character's regular pencilers, responsible for layouts and story structure, shifted in the opposite direction, from Don Heck (41 in 1970) to Gene Colan (44) to George Tuska (54). What's more, younger writers sometimes brought conservative values into play, as when Mimi Gold (22 in 1970) had Iron Man aiding rebels against a Communist regime on a Caribbean island in *The Invincible Iron Man* #29 (Sep. 1970), a triumphant reimagining of the Bay of Pigs disaster nine years earlier. One can only conclude that the diversity of political themes in the 1970s reflected the diversity of opinion in the title's creative staff.

Yet despite the vibrancy of the title's engagement with the contemporary world, a core problem remained: Iron Man had been designed and built by a manufacturer of weapons systems, and readers would not let Marvel forget it. A steady drumbeat of letters appeared in "Sock It to Shell-Head" in 1971, calling for the comic's creators to address Stark's uncomfortable past. In *The Invincible Iron Man* #33 (Jan. 1971), J.J. Friel of Lansing, Michigan, praised Marvel for taking a big step in the right direction with Firebrand in issue 27, but insisted that the next necessary step would be for Tony Stark "to stop supplying the government with weapons." In *The Invincible Iron Man* #35 Richard Hawkins of Madera, California, concurred, commenting that "the time is right for Tony Stark to quit being a weapons manufacturer ... a merchant of death." In *The Invincible Iron Man* #38, Paul Sanford of Seattle, Washington, posed a tough question to the editors: "when are you going to admit that Tony Stark produces devices to kill people? ... Stark needs to wake up. He needs to invent a way to feed people. He needs to start converting from military to civilian uses. He needs to come to grips with himself and his profits, with human needs and his own luxurious (though responsibly used) existence. Tony Stark is going to have to take a good hard look at himself, or he will soon be very definitely on the baddie side of the ledger." A year later, David Copson of Bucknell University took matters a step further in a letter published in *The Invincible Iron Man* #47 (Jun 1972), arguing that mere reform was not enough: "Stark is a leftover from the days when Marvel heroes all fought the commies. His occupation of weapons inventor was great then, but now turns off the majority of us fans. And you can't change his occupation either, since it is so central to Iron Man's origin and continued existence." The only solution Copson could see was to kill Stark off—along with his solo title—replacing him with a new Iron Man who would appear exclusively in *The Avengers*.

Copson's solution may strike us today as an extreme one, but it's difficult to appreciate the wholesale revaluation that the armaments industry had undergone in the late 1960s. A convenient measure of the magnitude of this shift can be made through a newspaper database search of the phrase "military-industrial complex," for the meaning of this phrase changed significantly and its prevalence increased overwhelmingly over the course of the 1960s. Of course, the phrase was pejorative from the moment it was coined by President Eisenhower, in his January 1961 Farewell Address to the nation. Eisenhower had been frustrated in his efforts to cut the military's budget by generals and congressmen with connections to the munitions industry. So he responded with a critique of cozy relationships that had grown up between industry and government: "In the councils of government, we must guard against the acquisition of unwarranted influence, whether sought or unsought, by the military-industrial complex. The potential for the disastrous rise of misplaced power exists and will persist." But though carrying a negative valence, in this initial formulation the phrase offered a fairly limited critique of the weapons industry, as having the potential to improperly influence the procurement process. Vigilance would be needed to guard against corruption, a sentiment echoed by mainstream journalists for several years.[10]

Almost immediately, though, radical writers began taking up the phrase, eager to cite Eisenhower as a proponent for their vision of an America gone badly wrong. One early instance was Fred J. Cook, whose 1962 book *The Warfare State* presented the military-industrial complex as "the frightening alliance between the Military and Industry ... leading us inexorably toward global war." Cook was a clear instance of a tendency noted by historian James Ledbetter, for the "military-industrial complex" to become entangled with preexisting critiques of the munitions industry, both with "Merchants of Death" (a rhetorical attack directed against arms manufacturers whose "patriotic leagues" lobbied for America's entry to World War I—Ledbetter 21) and with the War Economy thesis of the 1930s (the claim that a dependence on heavy industry had collapsed the distinction between the needs of the military and those of private individuals—27). In this form the phrase appeared in 1962 in the Port Huron Statement, the founding document of the SDS (Students for a Democratic Society, easily the most influential campus protest group in the sixties):

> The most spectacular and important creation of the authoritarian and oligopolistic structure of economic decision-making in America is the institution called "the military-industrial complex" by former President Eisenhower, the powerful congruence of interest and structure among military and business elites which affects so much of our development and destiny. Not only is ours the first generation to live with the possibility of world-wide cataclysm—it is the first to experience the actual social preparation for cataclysm, the general militarization of American society. In 1948 Congress established Universal

Military Training, the first peacetime conscription. The military became a permanent institution [24].

The SDS leadership was no less excited than Cook by the chance to co-opt the former General and President as an exponent of its radical vision. Two years later, on a 1964 tour of east coast college campuses, Berkeley activist Mario Savio re-focused the critique to spotlight the role of military funding at universities, suggesting that scholarship was now "secondary to service to the military-industrial complex" (Buckley 22).

Nonetheless, several more years would pass before the notion of a military-industrial complex began to have a major impact on mainstream thought. Even as Eisenhower's phrase was taking on a new meaning for the radical fringe, its grip on public consciousness had never been strong—and was weakening. A survey of five national newspapers shows a steady decline in the number of references to the "military-industrial complex" through the mid-sixties, from 32 in 1961, to 28 in 1963, to 19 in 1964, to 20 in 1965, to just 15 in 1966.[11] Through this period, the phrase, with its pejorative valence, was competing unsuccessfully with formulations like "weapons system" and "aerospace" that emphasized technological prowess rather than backroom deals. This period saw Iron Man in his Cold War heyday, repeatedly battling the Titanium Man to prove the superiority of American technology and the entrepreneurial spirit over the products of a planned economy based on compulsory labor.

The turnabout, when it came, was sudden: fully one-third of the references to "military-industrial complex" in 1966 fall in December, the first sign of an enormous blow-up that would take place over the rest of the decade: 71 references in 1967, followed by 114 in 1968 and no fewer than 505 in 1969. This change in the phrase's fortunes can be attributed to Michigan Governor George Romney's presidential bid in the 1968 election cycle. As early as March 1966, Romney began employing the "military-industrial complex" rhetorically as a justification for his shift from supporting to opposing the war in Vietnam (Associated Press). The phrase allowed Romney, a Republican, to present his newfound opposition as grounded in the thinking of a centrist Republican president. But the phrase really exploded on the public scene only in the wake of Romney's offhand claim during a television interview on September 4, 1967, that he had been "brainwashed" by the military and diplomatic corps during a 1965 visit to Vietnam (*New York Times* Staff). While Romney didn't mention the "military-industrial complex" in that remark, the phrase featured prominently in the hurly-burly that followed his gaffe, quadrupling the number of references from August to September of 1967. A typical instance from the front page of *The Boston Globe*: "Sen Thruston B. Morton (R-Ky.) said Wednesday that President Johnson has been 'brainwashed' on Vietnam since 1961 by the military-industrial complex and confessed that he himself had been wrong in supporting the war" (Averill). Forged in the heat of an ugly campaign season, Morton's defense of Romney owed more to the radical fringe than to Eisenhower. In suggesting that a sitting President was a puppet of dark forces, Morton brought the phrase from the political wilderness, altered from a critique of military procurement into a paranoid vision of the body politic.

The power in Romney's usage lay in conjuring a scapegoat to take the blame for Vietnam, a conflict that in retrospect seemed not only foolhardy but lacking in noble purpose. And student radicals agreed. They spoke of the war as a vast conspiracy fomented by the military-industrial complex to cement its grip on power and to provide a ready outlet for its products. This explains the manifold targets of student protest, from university research funded by Defense Department grants to campus recruitment by the likes of the CIA and Dow Chemical, the manufacturer of napalm. For links such as these implicated higher learning in the insidious web.

This brief review suggests the weight of public opprobrium that settled on Tony Stark's shoulders in the late 60s and early 70s. The Half-Face story was an early casualty, as we saw earlier. What now becomes clear is just how bad its timing really was: running in the August through October 1967 issues of *Tales of Suspense,* it hit newsstands just as Romney's gaffe focused public discourse on the role of the "military-industrial complex" in promoting war in Indochina. A few months later, in March 1968, Tony Stark's occupation became an explicit target for the first time when Chris Barth called him a "hatemonger" in a letter published in *Iron Man* #1. Shortly after that, as we've seen, the letters column went into a period of political hibernation, during which fans either didn't write controversial letters, or (more likely) editors refused to publish them. But once Goodwin fully reengaged with politics in the environmental fable of *The Invincible Iron Man* #25, the letters column followed suit. And, in the first half of 1971, the editors began to print a steady stream of letters expressing reader outrage about Iron Man's origin.

This apparent change in editorial policy may well reflect an effort to test the waters in advance of launching a major revision of the comic's central character. Letters often ran in the same issue or in the issue just before major changes in thematic focus or visual style, allowing the editors to present that change as undertaken in response to reader demand.[12] But if so, the lead time in this instance was unusually long, with multiple letters run over a period of six months before the issue was finally tackled in *The Invincible Iron Man* #39 (July 1971). A better explanation for this deluge of published criticism might be that an editorial staffer was using the letters column to indirectly lobby one or both of Marvel's senior decision makers, editor-in-chief Stan Lee and publisher Martin Goodman. Such an effort would not be without precedent: in Sean Howe's insider history of Marvel, Frank Brunner tells how he and Steve Englehart used a fabricated fan letter from one Reverend Billingsley of Texas to calm Stan Lee after a particularly dodgy bit of theological speculation in the pages of *Dr. Strange* (143–44). While Iron Man's creative team seems not to have been at a loss for letters to print, they were sufficiently hungry for criticism in this period that they ran in *The Invincible Iron Man* #37 a letter from Richard Hawkins rehearsing the same points Hawkins had made in a letter published just two issues earlier. In any event, the creative team finally felt ready to take action an issue later, leading off the letters column of *The Invincible Iron Man* #38 (Jun 1971) with a long missive from Paul Sanford summing up the case against Iron Man, and then responding with a terse promise of changes to come: "Good points, well taken, Paul. We'll try to explore those problems in the place where they should be explored—in the pages of our mag. Stick with us. We're trying, pal, we're trying."

Over the next four-and-a-half years, from July 1971 through January 1976, a series of writers on *Iron Man* engaged with the problem of Iron Man's origin. The first was Gerry Conway, who in *IM#39* had a villain capture and brainwash (!) Stark, thereby dramatizing the difference between Stark's real self (someone who was planning to turn over a new leaf by speaking before a UN committee on "The Scientist's Responsibility Towards Man") and the sort of sadistic warmonger that critics kept invoking in the letters column, a fiend who expressed excitement about "blueprints ... for a new weapon ... like none we've ever seen before: sonically pressurized pellets—bullets which implode upon impact" (9).

Some time later, Gary Friedrich and Steve Englehart[13] collaborated in *The Invincible Iron Man* #45 (Mar. 1972) on a story that placed Stark at odds with his own company's board of directors. Led by the ruthless Simon Gilbert, the board was trying to put Stark out to pasture out of concern for the financial consequences of Stark's decision to refuse all further military contracts. In a plot that reworked the dynamic from Goodwin's Firebrand story, Iron Man found himself standing once more between a raucous crowd of protesters (chanting "Stark Industries is a Death Factory"—p. 11) and a hierarchic power structure, a corporation more interested in private profit than in the public good. Except this time the tinderbox got sparked not by a left-wing radical but by Tony's erstwhile friend and confidante, Kevin O'Brien, now a reactionary spokesman for the established order. Wearing a suit of green-and-blue power armor and going by the fateful name "Guardsman," O'Brien lashed out at a stone-throwing mob with a repulsor-ray blast that left one protester dead. An angry bystander shouted, "It's another Kent State" (13), referring to the massacre of May 4, 1970, in which Ohio National Guardsmen fired into a crowd, killing four and wounding nine. As Goodwin had done, Friedrich and Englehart used mob protest to dramatize the powerlessness of reasoned dialogue in a society riven by political dissent, as well as the quandary presented by a foe who could not be defeated through violence. Yet the new story differed in one crucial respect: by making Iron Man's doppelgänger an advocate of the established order, Friedrich and Englehart enabled the series' hero to differentiate himself more convincingly from that order: according to the story's logic, Simon Gilbert, not Tony Stark, was the true embodiment of the military-industrial complex, and Guardsman, not Iron Man, its stooge.

For the story's continuation in the following issue, artist George Tuska surreptitiously added a further element, drawing an ingenious, never-before-seen logo for Stark Industries:

$$\$$$

By overlapping the company's initials to form the sign of the almighty dollar, Tuska gave expression to the problem faced by Tony Stark in his effort to disentangle his company from the likes of Simon Gilbert. The symbolism was a potent bit of satire, suggesting that combining "Stark" with "Industries" had always been about making a quick buck. Besides appearing in close proximity to Gilbert's head in issue 46, the logo appeared twice in 47 (penciled by Barry Windsor-Smith), and once each in issues 48 and 50 (both George Tuska), then disappeared forever. The logo was never the subject of comment in the stories or in the letters column, suggesting that it may have been an inside joke among a group of Marvel's artists that got nixed once it came to the attention of upper management.

But the longest sustained effort to address reader objections to Tony Stark's past came from the pen of Mike Friedrich (no relation to Gary). For one thing, Friedrich made corporate reinvention into a running subplot for the whole length of his long stint as writer on Iron Man. Stark spoke to a reporter about his company's "re-ordered priorities" in Friedrich's second issue, IM#50 (Sep. 1972), gave an initial sales report to the board in *The Invincible Iron Man* #55 (Feb. 1973), and toured several of his company's reengineered manufacturing plants on an extended business trip with Pepper in *The Invincible Iron Man* #59–62 (June–Sep. 1973). Using corporate transformation as a subplot allowed Friedrich to present the project as an ongoing process even in stories otherwise unrelated to the politics of the military-industrial complex.

In addition, Friedrich reintroduced Firebrand in *IM#48* (July 1972), filling in the character's backstory so as to transform him from champion of black nationalism into an anti-corporate anarchist. In his earlier debut, Firebrand never removed his mask, but his cause and his raised fist logo—not to mention his use of the phrase "Uncle Tom"—must have struck most readers as clear signifiers of racial identity. In Friedrich's version, however, Firebrand became the disaffected son of Simon Gilbert, Stark's villainous corporate rival. The new backstory presented a neat allegory for the radicalization of white middle class youth. And an anti-corporate radical was better placed to criticize Stark's effort to "reorder priorities" at Stark Industries as too little, too late. But the backstory was also a first step in discrediting Firebrand as a spokesman for social ills. His earlier activities became, retrospectively, the work of a white *agent provocateur* deliberately stoking racial resentments. What's more, his revised origin story made his quest a personal one: brutalized by his abusive father years before being radicalized by social injustice, his commitment to revolution became the expression of a baser desire, to destroy everything his father valued. Whereas Goodwin had given Firebrand some of the best lines in *IM#27*, Friedrich made him a petulant child, one who screamed things like "You freakin' hypocrite!" at his father (9). Goodwin's character had expressed the betrayed idealism of a whole generation, and in the final panels of that issue Iron Man acknowledged his share in the blame. By contrast, Friedrich's Firebrand refocused attention on the personal failures of his father, faults for which Tony Stark bore no responsibility. Hence the crowning irony of the story's ending, when Simon Gilbert, plotting to dynamite one of Stark's factories in a bid to further his takeover of the corporation, died in the resulting explosion. Firebrand blamed Iron Man, transferring all his years of resentful hatred from his father to the man he wrongly supposed to be his father's killer. Subsequent issues further degraded Firebrand until he was functionally no different from any other power-hungry supervillain. In *The Invincible Iron Man* #59 he proved willing to sacrifice the lives of innocents as "pawns" in his now very personal war against Iron Man (26). And in *The Invincible Iron Man* #81 he helped foment a rebellion in an alternate dimension in the hope of becoming its next dictator. In sum, Friedrich's Firebrand was a straw man, voicing arguments similar to those made by Iron Man's more radical critics in the letters page ("the guy ... practically invented the Viet Nam War!"— *The Invincible Iron Man* #74 p18), but behaving in ways that discredited those ideals. Thus, even as Friedrich worked to reform Tony Stark in response to reader demands, he used Firebrand to satirize the most radical among his readers.

Finally, Friedrich introduced a new love interest for Tony Stark in the form of Roxie Gilbert, Firebrand's sister and the daughter of Simon Gilbert. Roxie represented the liberal ideal from which her brother had fallen: a non-violent activist committed to social justice. Stark's interest in her worked hand-in-glove with his efforts to turn over a new leaf, invoking the romantic trope of the man inspired by love to better himself. Naturally, she at first despised him and everything he stood for, but in time she became increasingly convinced of his fundamentally good nature. Roxie had a crucial influence on Stark during this period, at one point bringing him to North Vietnam in search of Eddie Marsh's POW/MIA brother. In a story written during the period between the signing of the Paris Peace Accords in August 1973 and the fall of Saigon two years later, Stark confronted the consequences of his various interventions in the war, both as Iron Man (*The Invincible Iron Man* #68, 7) and as a manufacturer of napalm (*The Invincible Iron Man* #69, 14). What's more, just as Firebrand served Friedrich as a straw man for undercutting Iron Man's most extreme critics, Roxie could be used to voice the doubtful deliberations of another group of readers: "Tony's everything I'm not—from a different kind of life. And I can never forget the murder his munitions rained on Viet Nam for more than a decade. And yet—perhaps I can forgive him those crimes in the name of good intentions" (*The Invincible Iron Man* #64, 23). Stark's efforts to win Roxie thus paralleled Friedrich's efforts to win over liberal critics among his readers.

Yet ultimately Roxie, like her brother, was discredited and set to one side. Just after Friedrich ended his run on Iron Man, Len Wein declared a triumphant end to Stark's lengthy effort to reinvent Stark Industries as "Stark International" in *The Invincible Iron Man* #82 (Jan. 1976), trumpeting the firm's successes on "projects designed to promote the ecology, to discover energy alternatives to fossil fuels, or projects developed to aid in the exploration of space" (6). Appropriately enough, just pages later he staged Tony's triumphant dismissal of Roxie at a penthouse cocktail party celebrating the firm's self-transformation. When Roxie spoke patronizingly of the company's recent efforts at reform, Stark made a cutting reply: "I hate to disappoint you, Ms. Gilbert, but the Iron Man Foundation was begun a number of years ago, before establishing funds to aid underprivileged ghetto children even came into vogue. I may have been a 'warmongering weapons-maker' for far too long a time, Roxie, but I've always cared about the people! Now if you'll excuse me, I've got to see to the rest of my guests" (14). So much for constructive criticism. Despite the issue's enthusiastic rehearsal of Stark's accomplishments, one senses Len Wein's impatience with the years-long reform effort, an eagerness to consign the past to the past.

Wein was not the first to attempt to find closure through a grand gesture. Years earlier, in *The Invincible Iron Man* #47 (Jun 1972), Roy Thomas had stepped in as writer for a single issue to confront the Cold War hero with the question, "Must there be an Iron Man?" Grieving the death of his friend Kevin O'Brien, Iron Man was led to a stern critique of his self-assigned mission. The issue's middle pages retold the hero's Vietnam origin story in detail, scripted and illustrated in close imitation of the original account in *Tales of Suspense* #39. In the pages following, however, Iron Man questioned that story's patriotic optimism: in the years that followed had he lived up to his heroic pledge? Had his weapons systems always been used for good, not ill? In a particularly resonant panel, flanked above and to the right by Tuska's satirical $ logo, Iron Man mused:

My armor—and dozens of other weapons—for the army, for SHIELD— weapons I've sometimes been sorry I designed—weapons that can be used to kill one people, to save another. Sometimes I'm out in a crowd, and I hear somebody's scornful whisper: 'munitions-maker!' And I find myself pondering every action I ever made. But maybe that's all to the good [19].

Roy Thomas thus devoted an issue, lavishly illustrated by Barry Windsor-Smith, to pondering tough questions that the souring of the Vietnam War had raised in many readers' minds. And then he attempted to shut down all further inquiry by answering those questions with a resounding Yes! In the final pages Iron Man realized that self-questioning was somehow "taking the simple way out": "It'd be easy—too easy—to give in to the Gilberts of the world. Because for every person killed because he encountered Iron Man, a hundred more have lived!" (20). The final splash page invoked one of the patron saints of the antiwar movement to assert the end of self-doubt and the beginning of a new era: "Bob Dylan likes to sing about 'New mornings.' This is one of them" (21).

But doubt could not be banished so easily. Another attempt at grappling with Tony Stark's demons followed toward the end of Mike Friedrich's long run. In *The Invincible Iron Man* #78 (Sep. 1975), written not long after the Fall of Saigon, Bill Mantlo wrote a retrospective story explaining how Tony Stark came to rethink both the war and his own work designing weapons systems. The issue opened with Stark pacing the rooms of his 1970s office, ruminating about a traumatic experience he'd had about ten years earlier (judging from Iron Man's armor in the flashback, of a design not seen since *ToS#53* from May 1964). Iron Man had been helping an army platoon field test a high-tech laser-guided cannon when an enemy counterattack destroyed the American position and left his armor badly damaged. In the face of the soldiers' deaths, Stark's fancy weapon now seemed a hollow "promise of a faster kill, a well-oiled war." And when Iron Man turned to confront a Vietnamese soldier who was shooting at him, any thought of vengeance was extinguished by the discovery that his attacker was no cunning communist, but a scared, blind child—a child whose village turned out to have been destroyed by Stark's own weapon. Mantlo's Vietnam story was far darker than anything that had been attempted before with Iron Man, and the issue ended with the hero offering a new pledge of heroism: "I swear, as the man, Tony Stark—as the Avenger fate chose to cast in the role of Iron Man—that I will live to avenge those whose lives have been lost through the ignorance of men like the man I once was—or I will die trying!" (31). This attempt at resolution was the least convincing of all: vengeance is hardly an appropriate response to ignorance. But the pledge's instability made it far more interesting than the others. Far from an end to critique, the pledge seemed to promise a never-ending sequence of searing self-examinations.

In the event, while Wein managed to bring an end to the doubts and self-recriminations of the Vietnam era, Mantlo's vision of Iron Man won out in the long run. Years of responding to reader critique had left their mark on Marvel's gleaming Cold Warrior. Mantlo's genius was in realizing that the burden of the past wasn't a drawback but a central asset, a character flaw on par with Spider-Man's guilt over the death of Uncle Ben. In the celebratory issue 100, editor Archie Goodwin saw fit to publish an excoriating letter from Roger Klorese of Tamarac, Florida, asking why Iron Man had remained "an atavistic throwback to the days of 'Commie Smasher': "The 'old' Iron Man … cold warrior … seems out of place in this age of *detente,* and to a readership many of whom feel that the 'other' side isn't as far from their hearts as is the beaten, synthetic one of millionaire industrialists like Stark…. Is Iron Man a dinosaur?" To which Bill Mantlo answered:

> Roger Klorese's point is one I've given a lot of thought to, and essentially agree with. I don't feel Tony Stark is a dinosaur, a creature unable to change before the weight of time crushes him aside. Yeah, it is hard in 1977 to praise a millionaire industrialist, playboy and former munitions-manufacturer—but it isn't impossible to change that image. Which is what I plan to do. In upcoming issues you'll be seeing what *made* Tony Stark the way he is. While Iron Man gets stronger, more invincible than ever, you'll see the man *within* the metal shell begin to question convictions settled so deep in his subconscious as to have become character traits—and you'll see his struggle to come to grips with himself through his origins and through the loss of that which he's based his life on.

Great stories lay ahead, of Iron Man's public persecution and Tony Stark's descent into alcoholism.

NOTES

1. Lee first gave this account of events in his 2002 autobiography, *Excelsior!* (co-written with George Mair), but he has since repeated it many times in video interviews. Among other instances, on a panel discussing Marvel's history for Very Very Live!, and in a featurette included with the 2-disc edition of the 2008 *Iron Man* movie.

2. As of this writing, Life's full run is available in a searchable archive on Google Books (books.google.com).

3. Here and elsewhere in this article I have used a dash in place of any ellipses that appear in the original comic book, reserving ellipses for places where I have shortened quotations by removing words. I have also judiciously replaced the less fervent exclamation points with periods.

4. The Merry Marvel Marching Society, a fan club started by Stan Lee in 1964 (Howe 4).

5. College and graduate students contributed a substantial fraction of the letters published in *Tales of Suspense, Iron Man,* and presumably other Marvel titles in the 1960s and early 70s. These letters suggest both the vibrancy of this readership and Marvel's pride in being able to claim as readers young intellectuals fond of quoting George Bernard Shaw (*IM*#15) or Ayn Rand (*IM*#24 & 28). Howe argues that the Merry Marvel Marching Society specifically targeted college-age students, and that it was founded after Stan Lee started receiving invitations to speak from campus student organizations in the mid-sixties (54).

6. Lee eventually gave up writing altogether, but he left off scripting Iron Man with the Feb 1968 issue of *Tales of Suspense*, years before other he left other major Marvel titles, continuing to write *Captain America, Thor, The Fantastic Four* and *The Amazing Spider-Man* all through the September 1971 issue.

7. Cover attribution courtesy of the online Grand Comics Database.

8. A year later Marvel defied the Comics Code Authority to run a story in *Amazing Spider-Man* 96–98 (May-Jul 1971) focusing on the problem of drug addiction.

9. I discuss the comic's treatment of the Vietnam War in detail below. Women's right to work outside the house was dramatized when Pepper Hogan (née Potts) came back as Tony Stark's personal secretary, resulting in marital discord with her jealous husband Happy Hogan. A running subplot in *IM*#59–63, 65, and 70 (June 1973 to September 1974), scripted by Mike Friedrich and drawn for the most part by George Tuska, the theme was given special emphasis in issue 62 (penciled by John Romita, Sr., and Craig Russell) when Tony Stark and the estranged Pepper, traveling together on business, met with Stark's first female plant manager, Vicki Snow. Snow turned out to be engaged to a chauvinist boor, Mark Scott, who insisted that once they were married she would be "minding the kitchen for me." New York City's brush with bankruptcy in October 1975 received explicit reference in a narration box scripted by Roger Silfer in *IM*#84 (Mar 1976, p 26) over a scene showing the garbage-strewn bank of the East River, described on an earlier page as "pollution-infested" (18). Later the same year a sequence of issues penciled by George Tuska followed up on this lead, employing the homeless population of gritty New York as the zombified minions of the Controller (*IM*#88–91, Jul-Oct 1976).

10. Tony Stark's recurring trouble with generals and congressmen exercising oversight on his contracts can be seen as an effort to keep Stark Industries free from the taint of Eisenhower's accusation. The theme appeared as early as *ToS*#47 (Nov 1963) and crystalized in the character of Senator Byrd in *ToS*#68 (Aug 1965).

11. These numbers are drawn from a Proquest database search of *The New York Times, The Chicago Tribune, The Washington Post, The Boston Globe,* and *The Los Angeles Times.* These publications provide a rough yardstick of public opinion across the nation, though certainly one with a bias toward the mainstream elite.

12. For example, in *IM*#16 the editors printed Maggie Stebbins' criticism of George Tuska's angular panel layouts, responding with a promise that Tuska would shift back to rectilinear layouts starting with the next issue.

13. The comic lists only Gary Friedrich as "writer," but the online Grand Comics Database adds Englehart as an "uncredited" contributor.

Works Cited

Associated Press. "Flow of News Being Dammed, Romney Says." *The Chicago Tribune.* Mar. 27, 1966. Page E43. ProQuest Historical Newspapers: *The Chicago Tribune* (1849–1990).

Averill, John. "Morton Says Johnson 'Brainwashed' on War." *The Boston Globe.* Sept. 28, 1967. Page 1. ProQuest Historical Newspapers: *The Boston Globe* (1872–1981).

"Bailey Says Romney Owes Apology to 2." *The New York Times.* Sept. 6, 1967. Page 3. ProQuest Historical Newspapers: *The New York Times* (1851–2010).

Buckley, Thomas. "Berkeley Youth Leader Warns of Protests at Other Campuses." *The New York Times.* Dec. 12, 1964. Page 22.

Grand Comics Database (www.comics.org). Accessed 5/1/14. Web.

Heineman, Kenneth J. *Campus Wars: The Peace Movement at American State Universities in the Vietnam Era.* New York: New York University Press, 1994.

Hodgson, Geoffrey. *America In Our Time: From World War II to Nixon—What Happened and Why.* Garden City, NY: Doubleday, 1976. Rpt. Princeton, NJ: Princeton University Press, 2005.

Howe, Sean. *Marvel Comics: The Untold Story.* New York: Harper Perennial, Kindle Edition, 2013.

Kennedy, John Fitzgerald. "1962–09–12 Rice University." jfklibrary.org. John F. Kennedy Presidential Library and Museum. n.d. Web. 15 May 2014.

Lee, Stan, and George Mair. *Excelsior! The Amazing Life of Stan Lee.* New York: Simon & Schuster, 2002.

"Riddle of an Embattled Phantom." *Life* 53.10 (Sept. 7, 1962). 20–29.

Students for a Democratic Society. *The Port Huron Statement (1962).* Chicago: C.H. Kerr, 1990.

Very, Very Live: Marvel Then and Now: A Night with Stan Lee and Joe Quesada. [Los Angeles, Calif.]: Hero Initiative: Maverick Interactive [distributor], 2007. DVD.

Countdown to #100

Escapist Heroism and the Challenges of Modernity in the Late 1970s

John M. Vohlidka

Born in the middle of the Vietnam conflict, Marvel's Iron Man resonated well with readers of the time. He represented by his very nature one of the strengths of the United States: industrial technology. The optimistic days of the early 1960s faded into the turbulence of the later part of that decade. This downturn continued into the 1970s. By the Bicentennial in 1976, society became jaded, self-reflective and critical. In such an environment, the concept of the 'hero' needed careful handling to ensure continued sales. Stories concerning heroes are designed to reassure society of its concerns, as heroes represent the aspirations of a society (Hogan 200). In 1977, *The Invincible Iron Man* issues 95–100, written by Gerry Conway and Bill Mantlo with art by George Tuska, were a microcosm of the concerns of the readership concerning the society in which they lived. Tony Stark is one of Marvel's few lead heroes who specifically uses technology to fulfill his role as a superhero making him uniquely situated to represent a solution to the tensions in American society created by lack of faith in government, globalization and technology.

Marvel reflected society's concerns while rising to the challenge of showing how a hero could still be relevant to readers. Wealthy, flawed, and jaded himself, Tony Stark embodies the fractures in society while at the same time, demonstrating the meaning of heroism. Specifically, in *The Invincible Iron Man* issues 95–100, Stark faces a number of challenges representing issues faced by the country: technology out of control (Ultimo, the Guardsman);

government corruption (Senate hearings); communism, globalization (Sun-fire) and traditionalism (the Mandarin). The Mandarin, who is at the core of much of Stark's troubles during this storyline, is defeated by Iron Man's courage, intelligence, a well-timed judo toss, and his willingness to face certain death and defeat. While Stark needs technology to be super, it is his humanity and his willingness to sacrifice himself in these stories that defines his heroism.

Culture and Comics in the 1970s

Comic books, like any other popular medium, reflect the values and troubles of society, and the troubles of the 1970s were many and deep. The prolonged Vietnamese conflict and the assassinations of prominent figures, such as, Martin Luther King, Jr., and Robert Kennedy seeded a growing pessimism. The civil rights movement along with the coming of age of the baby boomer generation increased racial and generational tensions. All this, combined with a growing distrust of government and elected officials that was sparked by the Watergate scandal caused a series of seemingly overwhelming setbacks for the nation. Nixon's resignation, his failure to admit guilt and his quick pardon by President Ford troubled the country (Olson 179). Confusion, anger and a general sense of malaise gripped the country.

This decade was not the best of times for comic books. The age of the classic hero, who was always on the side of right, seemed to be over as it no longer connected with the readers of that decade. This led to both financial and creative challenges for the comics industry. The two big companies, DC and Marvel, spent much of the 1970s competing with each other over a shrinking market. They tried to increase readership and sales through market saturation along with experimenting with new titles (Gabilliet 74). Both companies attempted to make comics more relevant (Spider-Man and Green Arrow both taking on the topic of drug addiction for example). They also experimented with the genres of fantasy (*Conan the Barbarian*), horror (*Swamp Thing*; *Tomb of Dracula*) and martial arts (*Shang-Chi, The Master of Kung Fu*; *Richard Dragon, Kung-Fu Fighter*). Marvel had some success with these genres (Gabilliet 78). By the end of the decade, the company saw success with movie adaptations (*Star Wars*) and comics based on toys (*Micronauts*; *Rom*) (Gabilliet 80). As Marvel was constantly looking for new hits by widening their field beyond just their classic line up of superheroes, it should be noted that a number of these successful new titles were not heroes in the classic mold, but rather outsiders.

Where did this leave Iron Man? As noted by Jon Hogan, Iron Man is one of the few characters who can change his appearance on a semi-regular basis without creating a fan outcry (Hogan 201). In the 1970s, however, it was not his armor that changed (the look underwent very few revisions), but his actual character. Iron Man did an abrupt turnaround in 1971, going from an anti-communist, war manufacturing cold war warrior to becoming considerably more liberal as Stark Industries went out of the weapon making business (Gabilliet 74). As a character designed as a technological weapon of war, this put Iron Man's identity as a hero in a precarious position. Writers attempted to make Iron Man relevant to readers to ensure continued sales. To keep the book, *Iron Man,* afloat, the character, Iron Man, had to appeal to readers.

Iron Man #95–100—The Conway, Mantlo and Tuska Approach

The storylines in *Iron Man* issues 95–100 were produced by Gerry Conway, Bill Mantlo and George Tuska. Conway is credited with plotting the first three issues. Mantlo is credited with scripting those issues and then noted as writer for the remaining three. It is not clear if Mantlo wrote issues 98–100 based on an idea by Conway or if he decided to wrap up the storyline on his own. In either case, the segmented story flows naturally. George Tuska, who had been the regular artist for most of the 1970s, penciled the issues.

In today's comic world, story arcs, limited series and special anniversary issues are common. In the seventies it was considerably less so. It is clear that *Iron Man* issues 95–100 were meant to be a story leading to a final confrontation between the hero and the villain in #100, but it was not designed as a self-contained story as many story arcs tend to be today. Much of the story seems determined to keep with the dictates of the time by having Iron Man battle someone new in almost every issue. This was done to increase sales and interest. Also, there were subplots (What is Chrissy Longfellow's secret? Who is stealing Iron Man's old armors?) that would not be dealt with until later in the series. The primary purpose of the issues was to keep readers buying, not necessarily to tell a deeper story or to comment on the times. Such comments were inevitable, however, as Conway and Mantlo needed to write stories reflecting the issues of the day if they were to keep readers interested.

Society and Technology: The Political Context

Technology's relationship with humanity has always been a dominant theme in *Iron Man* (Hogan 201). This is certainly the case in issues 95–97.

These issues use Ultimo and the Guardsman to symbolize technology out of control and the fears people have about mechanization and technology in the wrong hands. Ultimo represents the unnatural, inhuman, lifeless side of technology. The monster running rampant near the heart of American government symbolizes the helplessness felt by society not just towards technology, but towards the government as well. In the middle of the cold war with the threat of nuclear annihilation always looming, this was a concern for many.

Issue 95 begins when Tony Stark is in the process of testing his newest armor. He receives a telephone call from Senator Hawk who orders him to attend an inquest in Washington, D.C. to answer allegations that Stark Industries was bribing officials (in the U.S. and other countries) and selling substandard equipment to the U.S.'s defense system. Meanwhile, a Russian submarine penetrates that defense system and fires a torpedo at the coast. The mysterious monster Ultimo, emerges from the torpedo and marches toward the Capitol. Iron Man arrives in Washington with a briefcase, but before he can change into Stark's clothes, he flies off to battle the blue behemoth.

Released from the torpedo, Ultimo marches towards the Capitol with Washington, D.C. representing the center of American society. Ultimo's attack towards the White House is a reflection of what was wrong with society and government. Ultimo is, in essence, a grotesque figure. His large, muscular frame combined with his dead eyes and mechanical looking mouth mark him as unnatural in both shape and appearance. Arthur Asa Berger, who has written about the meaning of the grotesque in comics, refers to it as "an affront to society and suggests that something is wrong with the social order" (Berger 200). Ultimo, then, is symbolic of the problems of 1977 America.

Author Ernest Dichter, writing about horror, states that monsters are "really ourselves" and "a force out of control" (Dichter 192). This is fitting for Ultimo. In this story, Ultimo represents impotent anger over a turbulent decade, focused toward the Capitol and the government, which many blamed for the controversial politics and sense of distrust that permeated society. Ultimo also represents technology out of control. He is clearly a construct, not a human being. That he is powerfully destructive, combined with the fact that he emerges from a Russian torpedo, suggests that he is also symbolic of that most deadly of technological advances: a nuclear weapon. In this sense he represents the helplessness felt by society towards mechanization, mass production and, of course, the nuclear arms race with the Soviet Union, all of which seemed beyond the average person's ability to direct.

At the time, little was known about Ultimo except that he was a silent, hulking android of incredible power. He exudes a sense of menace as he marches slowly, steadily and silently towards the White House. Ultimo can be seen to represent the creeping threat of technology that was pervading everyday life. Iron Man's battle with Ultimo represents a continued American sense of confidence, in that Stark uses technology (the Iron Man armor) along with his human intelligence to defeat the monster.

It is both fitting and telling that this is a foe for Iron Man, a hero who uses and represents technology, mechanization and mass production. Iron Man, the technological hero is pitted against Ultimo, runaway technology. This battle is an attempt to put the genie back in the bottle as it were. Defeating Ultimo would be a symbolic attempt of man using technology to solve the problems technology created. Interestingly, and not surprising, considering the pessimism of the late seventies, both machine and man are found wanting. Issue 95 begins with Stark testing a new armor with a machine that can "punch its way through mountains" (Conway and Mantlo "Ultimo!" 1). Later in the same issue, the armor literally cracks under the pressure of Ultimo's grip. Iron Man depletes his power fighting Ultimo, and the Golden Avenger suffers a heart attack and falls to the ground. His armor was capable of resisting technology in control (the hole punching machine), but not technology out of control (Ultimo).

Iron Man's eventual solution to defeating Ultimo is lacking in finality. Remembering that he had defeated Ultimo in the past by luring him into a volcano, Iron Man uses his repulsor rays to dig a tunnel into the Earth, prompting Ultimo to follow him. When they reach the edge of the outer crust, Iron Man triggers a volcanic reaction. Ultimo is consumed and Iron Man just barely makes it out. Could Ultimo be said to be defeated if Iron Man was simply repeating something he previously tried? Obviously, it had not worked as Ultimo had returned. Incapable of defeating technology out of control, Iron Man simply buried the problem and moved on.

It is significant that the action in these issues takes place in Washington, D.C. Iron Man's troubles during this storyline suggest a national importance, the failure of Stark defense systems to defend the country; and Washington, D.C., was the center of most Americans' disappointment. The Watergate scandal had exposed corruption in the nation's highest office. President Ford attempted to argue that the exposure of the scandal along with Nixon's resignation was an example that the system worked. But cynicism over politics and government had set in (Schulman 48). Ford's pardon of Nixon so soon after the resignation further exacerbated the problem. Ford became seen as an inept bumbler (Berkowitz 74). His approval rating dropped from 71 to 49 percent (Olson 179). Iron Man's solution mirrored the confusion and apathy of the time felt by many Americans (Madrick 12). By simply burying Ultimo, Iron Man was acting neither creatively nor decisively. He was following Ford's controversial decision regarding Nixon. Bury the problem and hope for better times ahead. It was an attitude all too common for the times.

Society and Technology: The Human Context

The conflict with technology out of control is heightened even more in the confrontation with the Guardsman. This battle addresses the concerns over what technology can do to people. Again, the issue is who is in control of the technology, only with this story it is a more personal question. Are we the masters of technology or will technology be the master over us?

In issue 97, Iron Man returns to the Stark plant to find the Guardsman holed up there. Police detective Michael O'Brien (brother of deceased Kevin O'Brien, the previous Guardsman) snuck past the security in Stark's plant and donned the Guardsman armor, vowing vengeance on both Stark and Iron Man. By facing off against this new Guardsman, whose armor also was created by Stark, Iron Man is essentially battling a demented version of himself. Although he is at first defeated and suffers another heart attack, Stark is able to eventually recharge his armor. Doing so allows his heart to beat better. Technology in this case helps him. O'Brien is a different case. In the end, it is the Guardsman who defeats himself as the faulty circuits in the armor make O'Brien go mad. It is revealed in the story that faulty circuitry was also responsible for Kevin O'Brien's erratic and disloyal behavior. Those circuits are also affecting Michael O'Brien's mind so much so that he eventually collapses at the end of the issue. It is clearly stated that his mind was unbalanced to begin with. Iron Man vows to help him saying, "Michael O'Brien's sick— not evil..." (Conway and Mantlo "Showdown with the Guardsman!" 31). Iron Man did not physically defeat the Guardsman, but he did master his own armor (technology), while O'Brien did not. This demonstrates that technology in the hands of a good, or sane man, is used for beneficial purposes: i.e. saving everyone at the plant. Technology in the hands of a sick individual is destructive, dangerous and eventually self-defeating.

Fear of technology running amok is always tempered by the statement that it is how humans use technology, not the technology itself that is dangerous. The story is a parallel of the positive and detrimental aspects of technology; it helps Stark, but hinders O'Brien. Right after Michael O'Brien defeats himself, Stark uses the same Guardsman armor to battle Sunfire. The Avenger is not worried that the armor will affect his mind, as his mind is not unbalanced to begin with. Using the armor to help indicates that his mind is balanced and so the technology is beneficial rather than harmful.

These issues of *Iron Man* offer two very different solutions to the two sides of rampant technology. Ultimo's fate is more of a political, stop gap measure to find a temporary, but immediate fix. The solution with the Guardsman is more human and involves healing. Just as Michael O'Brien needed to heal after losing his brother, so did the country. The remaining issues of the storyline address other concerns of the time, mainly concerns over globalization and traditionalism versus modernity.

Globalization and the West

In issue 98, while Stark is finishing the new armor, his plant is attacked by the Japanese superhero Sunfire, who is enraged over reports Stark Industries was bribing the Japanese government. Without his new armor, Stark dons the Guardsman armor before a restrained and startled Michael O'Brien. Stark, as the Guardsman, rushes off to protect the plant from Sunfire. He fights Sunfire, but his heart begins to give out. The new armor is ready and O'Brien puts it on to save Stark. While fighting Sunfire, O'Brien is mysteriously teleported away.

The attack on Stark Industries by Sunfire makes little sense from a rationalist perspective. Sunfire is enraged that Stark Industries is, reportedly, bribing the Japanese government and bringing shame on his nation. He does not take his anger out on his own corrupt government, instead he travels to the United States to attack an industrial plant. In this issue, two faces of Japan are seen, and seen, of course, through western eyes. Professor Watanabe and his daughter, Fujiko, are clearly the modern Japan, in the sense that they are willing to deal with Stark despite the allegations of corruption against him and their rational (and hence "western") belief that such allegations need to be proven. Sunfire, in contrast, comes across as hot-headed, and babbles on about the honor of his country. In this sense, Sunfire is traditional and backward. Rationalism and legal proceedings mean nothing to him. His costume, patterned after the rising sun flag of Second World War Japan, reinforces this identity of traditionalism. His irrationalism comes into focus with a realization of his aim: to punish Stark and not the officials of his own country.

From a symbolic sense, Sunfire makes a good foil. Iron Man is Marvel's premiere industrialist hero and Japan by the late 1970s was becoming a serious competitor to American produced goods. In the late 1940s and early fifties, Japan's economy struggled to recover from the Second World War. By 1955,

Japan entered the period known as the "Economic Miracle" with the economy expanding at more than ten percent a year (McClain 572). This sudden economic surge meant cheap Japanese goods were being imported into the United States and were becoming a threat to some American industries. The "rust belt" in particular was hard hit with jobs being exported to Japan (Reischauer 376).

This situation continued through the 1970s. Trade imbalances between the two countries led to a series of clashes. President Nixon imposed a tariff on Japanese goods and became more interested in China, as many Americans grew tired of protecting Japan (LeFeber 357). The imbalance grew worse during the decade as Japan's export industries went from a $1.7 billion favorable trade balance in 1974 to $10.4 billion by 1980 (LeFeber 363).

Sunfire, like the Guardsman before him, attacks the Stark plant. The industrial plant became a focal point in a society suffering from a steep recession and then stagflation (Perlstein 33). Plant closings increased throughout the seventies with the blame going to international competition (Berkowitz 69). Sunfire's attack on the plant was symbolic of Japan's economic success which damaged American jobs. He destroys the plant in reflection of the way the Japanese economy was seen to be destroying the livelihood of American workers. His characterization of being traditional, irrational and backward was part of an overall perception that Japan was anti-western. This perception existed as early as 1971, when *Time* magazine blatantly referred to Japan as non-western (LeFeber 358). Sunfire encapsulated American feelings that Japan was arrogant, non-western and destructive to the American labor force.

Stark's battle with Sunfire was, therefore, symbolic of the battle between American enterprise against an encroaching Japanese market. Sunfire himself marks the division between the two forces as he is defending the "sacred honor" of Japan against the "corruption" of the west. Stark, in contrast, demonstrates the ingenuity and enterprise of the west. With his new armor unavailable and his spare armor missing, Stark improvises first with the Guardsman armor and later with an old version of the Iron Man armor. The fact that he wins the battle demonstrates that his perseverance, intelligence and ingenuity mark him as the hero of western capitalism.

Stark's integrity, honor, morals and perseverance all come into play in his conflict with this opponent. With his latest armor undone, Stark must wear the Guardsman armor to battle the Solar Samurai. He is, therefore, not recognized by Sunfire, who presumes Stark to be an armored mercenary. By being anonymous, Stark demonstrates his heroism not by his fame, but by his actions. This is shown by Sunfire's reaction to Stark. At first, he figures Stark a mercenary because he "struck without honor—from behind" (Conway

"Sunfire Strikes Again!" 16). As the fight progresses and Stark continues to fight even though it looks like the odds are against him, Sunfire's respect for his opponent grows with phrases, such as, "so … you find the courage to fight back?! Excellent!" to "you have fought nobly my enemy," until finally, "you were an honorable foe, armored one" (Conway "Sunfire Strikes Again!" 17, 26, 27). This growing respect from Sunfire, who although misguided, is still a superhero, demonstrates to the reader that a hero is made by his actions. So, again, despite the odds against him, it is Stark's human strengths of fortitude and courage which make him the hero.

Traditionalism and the West

Stark, in one of his older armors, defeats Sunfire in issue 99. Then using a complex network of satellite hook-ups, he is able to find O'Brien in Red China. He watches as O'Brien (still dressed as Iron Man) is defeated by the Mandarin and chained to a nuclear missile aimed at the United States. Realizing the Mandarin is behind all his recent troubles, and that the missile will start a nuclear war, Iron Man heads to China. He arrives in China just as the missile launches. He diverts its course, renders it harmless and frees O'Brien. They then switch armors. O'Brien returns to America in Stark's old armor, admitting he was wrong about Stark's involvement in his brother's death. Meanwhile, Iron Man heads off towards his confrontation with the Mandarin in issue 100.

Iron Man defeats the Mandarin's lifeless soldiers and penetrates the villain's fortress and engages in a physical confrontation with his longtime foe. Using one of his alien power rings, the Mandarin freezes Iron Man and proceeds to gloat over how he was responsible for the manipulations against Stark. He explains that he was behind the "Russian" submarine (which was actually manned by his mercenaries) which released Ultimo and it was his agent who was spreading lies in Washington, D.C. which caused Sunfire to fly to the U.S. to battle Stark. His goal was to create distrust in Stark's defense systems so that America would be vulnerable to a missile attack. With the tensions of the cold war amid American fears of international communism, it would spark a world war, allowing him to take over. Iron Man thaws himself and takes the rings. He destroys the Mandarin's view screen, the missiles and even the castle and leaves him there, among the smoking ruins.

Here, the Mandarin represents two aspects of traditionalism: a pride in Asian tradition and hostility to western, i.e. modern, culture. He takes pride in his Asian ancestry, and claims descent from Genghis Khan and considers this claim to rule the world as his birthright. He takes pride in his mastery of karate and refers to himself as his "sublime personage" (Mantlo "Ten Rings to Rule the World!" 11). Of course, the Mandarin in this sense fits the mold of the Yellow Peril. A mold created in various pulp stories, films and dime novels from the beginning of the twentieth century. He is clearly modeled after such villains as Fu Manchu and the Shadow's adversary, Shiwan Khan, who also claimed descent from Genghis Khan.

The Mandarin is also a model for what Ian Buruma and Avishai Margalit have termed an occidentalist, someone who is opposed to western civilization (Buruma and Margalit 6). His entire appearance suggests a traditional and even romantic non-western attitude. Although he appears on a view screen in *Iron Man* #99, the two adversaries do not come face-to-face until issue 100 in the final panel of page seven. Artist George Tuska portrays the Mandarin as a gothic figure, standing in a wood paneled room, his cape flowing about him with one cape laden arm before his face in a pose invoking that classic gothic vampire of Eastern Europe: Dracula. While there are two missiles behind him, the eye of the reader is drawn to the foreground and an axe sticking in the tabletop. It is a wonderful image that evokes romantic traditionalism in a character willing to use modern methods, but who prefers a classic method of dealing out death. While willing to use missiles and his alien power rings, he prefers to defeat Iron Man using karate; otherwise the victory would be "meaningless" (Mantlo "Ten Rings to Rule the World!" 10).

The Mandarin's manner of speaking suggests a link with traditional non-western attitudes. When Iron Man turns the tables on him with a Judo-toss, the Mandarin exclaims "By my ancestors! What—?!?" (Mantlo "Ten Rings to Rule the World!" 11). He describes his destiny to rule the world as a "holy purpose" "decreed by the gods" suggesting a belief in paganism, long since supplanted by the Judeo-Christian tradition (Mantlo "Ten Rings to Rule the World!" 16). This same speech also serves to paint the Mandarin as being hostile to the west. One of the occidentalist critiques of the west is that it is the home of the infidel which must be crushed to form a world of pure faith (Buruma 8). Phrases such as "holy purpose" and "decreed by the gods" place the Mandarin as a character who considers himself more spiritual, while his references to Iron Man repeatedly as "dog" and "fool" suggest that the Mandarin considers the Avenger to be a lackey or tool of the west and all its evils (Mantlo "Ten Rings to Rule the World!" 10, 15). The Mandarin's plan to ignite a global holocaust wherein he will then step in and take over connects to the idea of creating a new world order, one untainted by western ideals.

This portrayal of the Mandarin as an occidentalist is reinforced further by the location of his stronghold: "Red" China, an eastern country hostile to the west. Although the Mandarin's connection with China is dubious (after all, his plan is to start a war between the U.S., Russia and China, wiping them all out), it is telling that his hidden castle is not in say, westernized Japan, or even upstate New York. He is clearly situated in a non-western locale to emphasize his antagonism to the west.

The conflict then is between the west in the form of Iron Man, who utilizes and masters modern technology and the east in the form of the Mandarin who, while willing to use technology, prefers traditional methods and harbors a deep dislike for the west and all it stands for. Iron Man demonstrates the superiority of western values by defeating the Mandarin and not killing him. Moments after the Mandarin destroys his Washington agent, Iron Man destroys the Mandarin's plans, rings, missiles and castle, but refrains from killing the Mandarin himself. "Remember that, Mandarin!," says Iron Man at the conclusion of the story, "there was a time Iron Man could have killed you—and didn't! And that he refrained out of strength—not weakness!" (Mantlo "Ten Rings to Rule the World!" 31). By refusing to sink to the Mandarin's level, Iron Man emerges the true victor.

Faith in Government

Some themes are not confined to just a single issue of the series and carry throughout the six issues. These include government corruption, heroism in a Christian context, and Stark's humanity. While they began with both Conway and Mantlo sharing the writing chores, these themes were continued under Mantlo alone.

Throughout the storyline, there is a sub-plot of Stark facing allegations of corruption with the U.S. Senate. As previously mentioned, in issue 95, Senator Hawk ordered him to Washington, D.C., but when Stark arrived there he flew off to battle Ultimo, leaving his briefcase behind. While Iron Man and Ultimo duke it out a second time in issue 96, a mysterious someone picks up the briefcase. In issue 97, Hawk, realizing that it was Stark Industries' defense systems that failed, issues a subpoena for Tony Stark and we see Hawk's assistant carrying the stolen briefcase. In issue 99, Hawk's assistant declares he has proof against Stark and prepares to open the briefcase. It takes him until the following issue to do just that, but instead of evidence the case releases a smoke bomb and rather un-climactically, we learn Senator Hawk had helped set a trap for his assistant, who, it turned out, was working for the Mandarin.

This subplot appears mainly to provide Stark with as much trouble as possible. Problems impossible to overcome reflected the malaise of the time (Pustz 138). With Watergate and then the controversial resignation and pardon of Nixon, faith in the federal government was plunging downward. A storyline where Stark is in trouble with the U.S. Senate and the cause of it might be a conspiracy was quite timely. It is interesting to note that the whole conspiracy was a red herring. At the very climax of the story, it is suddenly revealed that Senator Hawk and Stark were working together to smoke out the traitor.

At least on the surface, the storyline argues that we can trust in the innate honesty, or goodness, of elected officials. This contradicts the more subtle criticism of government in the issues dealing with Ultimo. This could be because by the end of the story, Mantlo was sole writer, but more likely it reflects an overall trend in comics not to overtly criticize elected officials, which might alienate readers.

The Hero in the Judeo-Christian Tradition

There is also a strong case to be made that Iron Man is a hero in a Christian mold. This may seem odd for the 1970s, which is mostly remembered for disco, hedonism and narcissism. There was, in fact, a religious revival during the decade (Schulman 121). Also, the plotter of three of the issues in the storyline, Gerry Conway, acknowledged the impact his religious upbringing had on his writing (Buttery 9). "...I think the Christian mythology also speaks to our need to understand life and to find a purpose in death," said Conway (qtd. in Buttery 9).

This is not to argue that Iron Man, as written by Conway and Mantlo, is overtly a Christian hero. Iron Man never sports a cross on his chest. Rather, his heroism is based on a pattern that is Christian in nature. This is shown in four ways: one, a willingness to sacrifice oneself for others; two, refusing to take vengeance on enemies; three, the fight against injustice; and four, redeeming a lost soul.

One pattern that is consistent is Stark's willingness to sacrifice himself to save others. He uses up most of his power to prevent the Washington Monument from toppling on the crowd during his battle with Ultimo. To save Washington, D.C., he lures Ultimo down to the Earth's crust and is almost fried himself. To prevent the Guardsman from hurting the workers at his plant, he confronts the madman, even though he recently experienced a heart attack and is well aware that he is in no shape to fight. Likewise, he battles Sunfire in the Guardsman armor, an armor that cannot keep his heart beating.

This concern for others is an integral part of the character. It is highlighted by dialogue from various characters from "Are you trying to tell me that a man with a history of heart trouble is sacrificing himself to save us all?!!" to "Stark's finished! He's throwin' his life away while his employees get t'safety!" (Mantlo "Sunfire Strikes Again!" 22, 23).

Another pattern is the fight against injustice. In most of these battles, Iron Man is fighting to protect others. Yet, in the battle with the Mandarin there is a deeper conflict. The Mandarin despises the west and the modern world. His plan to start a world war, one that would wipe out millions of innocent lives, is unjust. This makes Iron Man's fight against the Mandarin a fight against injustice. At the same time, he was also fighting secretly alongside Senator Hawk, trying to save the name of Stark Industries which had been unjustly placed under suspicion as part of the Mandarin's plan.

Refusing to take revenge on an enemy, demonstrating forgiveness rather than punishment, is very Christian in nature. One of the major aspects of Christianity is the willingness to forgive one's enemies. He displays this tendency in the sequence with Michael O'Brien. O'Brien dons the Guardsman armor because he believes his brother Kevin was betrayed and killed by both Stark and Iron Man (not realizing until later in the story that they are one and the same). After he becomes confused and collapses, Iron Man does not take vengeance on him, but rather vows to do whatever is in his power to help him.

A slightly similar pattern occurs at the end of the story when Iron Man defeats the Mandarin. He destroys everything around the Mandarin, but steadfastly refuses to kill him. He leaves the Mandarin alone, contemplating this, although it is by no means certain that any of it has sunk in (and considering later appearances by the Mandarin it is certain that it was a lesson not learned).

The lesson was learned by O'Brien, who was redeemed by Stark's willingness to forgive. Stark does not act as a stern judge and simply condemn O'Brien for his acts. He places O'Brien under Avengers' custody (not letting the police take him), and works to help him, showing an interest in O'Brien's redemption. By donning the Guardsman armor before O'Brien to battle Sunfire, O'Brien was surprised by Stark's bravery. Then, O'Brien remembers that Stark has a weak heart, meaning that Stark could die at any minute during the battle. That is when O'Brien realizes he might be wrong.

O'Brien comes to the realization that he was on the wrong path. He frees himself, but rather than escaping or trying to kill Stark, he dons the newly finished Iron Man armor to save Stark and continues the battle with Sunfire, imitating the heroism he just witnessed. After Iron Man saves him from the Mandarin, they switch armors and O'Brien discovers that both Stark and Iron Man are one and the same. This marks this as a story about transcendence, where a major character becomes a better person by being in contact with the hero. With this revelation, O'Brien realizes just how wrong he was and is truly saved, not just from the Mandarin and his missile, but saved from going down the wrong path. His acknowledgement that Stark is a hero is part of his redemption. Iron Man is, thus, a hero in a Christian sense wherein he saves O'Brien's physical person, but more importantly his soul as well.

Humanity

Another factor defining Stark's heroism during those troubling times is his humanity. Unlike many of the Marvel superheroes of the time, Stark lacked any superpowers. His abilities came solely from the armor he wore. His armor is his creation, conceived by a human mind and built by human hands. Therefore, his armor is an extension of his humanity and not a mutant power, alien technology or something from mythology. His heroism comes from the fact that he is a human being. This humanity, as well as, its relationship with technology is emphasized throughout the story.

At points in the storyline, Stark once again needs his armor to stay alive. His synthetic heart, which had freed him from his dependence on his armored chest plate, cannot stand up to the challenges. While oncoming heart attacks force Stark to abandon some fights to recharge his armor and lessen the strain on his heart, his compassion, sense of justice and right, his true 'heart,' never falters. It keeps bringing him back into the fight to protect innocent lives. Further, even though he needs the chest plate to stay alive, he is still the master of his armor. As he says in issue 98, "Tony Stark may be a prisoner of his life-saving chest-device, —but at least I'll be the master of my armor, unlike the O'Brien brothers…" (Mantlo "Sunfire Strikes Again!" 2). When his artificial heart is functioning properly, he does not need the armor to stay alive, and hence, could give up being a superhero at any time. He chooses to continue to be Iron Man. That choice puts him in control of the armor.

His concern for others even affects his personal life. "…next time whoever wants to strike at me through my friends, and employees might not stop at taking them hostage! Unless I can make it seem that Tony Stark is as cold and unfeeling as the armor he wears," he says, reaffirming his decision not to get involved with anyone romantically for fear they could come in harm's way (Conway and Mantlo "Ultimo!" 3). Stark is willing to separate himself from his friends to protect them, another sacrifice. Willing to be seen as selfish and self-absorbed to protect his friends from his enemies, shows his first concern is for others which is part of what makes him a hero.

Issues 95–100 reinforce Tony Stark's humanity by pitting him against non-human foes. Ultimo clearly is not human. He is a manufactured creation with no direction of his own. His only motivation is to destroy. O'Brien's desire for revenge overtook his soul and he lost his humanity in the armor. Again, destruction is the goal of this enemy. The Mandarin returned from the dead by transferring his "mind-force" into his power rings. Is he truly human? He certainly has no regard for humanity since he plans to destroy it. This is in sharp contrast to Iron Man, whose armor is a triumph of human strength and used for good. By contrasting Iron Man with these disparate foes, Stark's humanity comes into focus. His sense of justice keeps him wearing the armor. His sense of compassion keeps him fighting. Unlike his adversaries who are defeated, he keeps fighting even as he struggles against impossible odds.

Finally, it is his struggles that showcase his humanity. Iron Man struggles with a myriad of problems that seem impossible to overcome. This reflects the feelings of the country in the 1970s. Time and again, he is beaten down, only to get up again and keep fighting. At one point he says he feels "like a wrung-out dishrag..." (Conway and Mantlo "Only a Friend Can Save Him" 11). It would be easy to stop, but he continues the fight. It is this constant struggle and not his superpowers that readers identify with. As the readers struggle in their everyday lives, and with comics having an older readership more aware of the troubles in society, Stark's struggles made him human and a more relatable hero.

Conclusion

The 1970s was a difficult time for comic books. The apathy and general malaise which gripped the country made the traditional superhero seem out of touch. Decreasing sales and an overall uncertainty in the industry led the big companies to experiment with other genres, such as fantasy and horror which placed the more traditional hero Iron Man in a precarious position. In a time when sorcerers or anti-heroic barbarians were more popular, it was up to the writers, artists and editors to find ways to make heroes more relevant and important to the audience.

This is seen in *The Invincible Iron Man* in a countdown of sorts leading to his one hundredth issue. Conway, Mantlo and Tuska needed to keep finding ways to make Iron Man relatable to a readership that was growing older and had lost a great deal of faith in American institutions and government. In the related stories, Iron Man was pitted against a number of challenges reflecting the concerns of the society of the time: from government corruption and modern technology in the form of Ultimo, to technology out of control with the Guardsman, to globalization with Sunfire and finally to the Mandarin who represented a non-western and traditionalistic threat to modern western society. These stories reflected an attempt to define heroism in the malaise of the late seventies.

For Conway and Mantlo, Iron Man was made to be the hero by having him become a champion of technology in control and of western ideals. His battles with both Ultimo and the Guardsman were attempts to keep control of technology in an age where technology advanced all the time, a fact which made many people feel helpless. Although he was more successful with the Guardsman than with Ultimo, this conflict made him a relevant hero. His battles with Sunfire and the Mandarin both made him a champion of the West and its ideals of rationalism, industrialization, and ingenuity. With both victories, Iron Man proved the worth of western society.

Iron Man was also the hero, not because he defeated his enemies or because he was invincible, but because of his continued willingness to sacrifice himself in the cause of the innocent. Stark continually fought to save others even at the possible expense of his own life. He did not always win the fight, but he was winning the war by saving the lives of others, reinforcing faith in our elected officials and even redeeming the soul of a sick man. This last was the greatest triumph of the storyline. Michael O'Brien went from being sick, violent and anti-social to becoming an individual who acknowledged his failing and understanding true heroism and therefore becoming a complete human being. This was Iron Man's true victory and made him truly invincible.

WORKS CITED

Berger, Arthur Asa. *The Comic-Stripped American: What Dick Tracy, Blondie, Daddy Warbucks, and Charlie Brown Tell Us About Ourselves.* New York: Walker, 1973.

Berkowitz, Edward D. *Something Happened: A Political and Cultural Overview of the Seventies.* New York: Columbia University Press, 2006.

Buruma, Ian and Avishai Margalit. *Occidentalism: The West in the Eyes of its Enemies.* New York: The Penguin Press, 2004.

Buttery, Jarrod. "Hulk Smash! The Incredible Hulk in the 1970s." *Back Issue* 70 (February 2014): 3–18.

Conway, George (w), Bill Mantlo (w) and George Tuska (a). "Only a Friend can Save Him" *The Invincible Iron Man* # 96 (March 1977). New York: Marvel Comics.

_____. "Showdown with the Guardsman!" *The Invincible Iron Man* #97 (April 1977). New York: Marvel Comics.

_____. "Ultimo!" *The Invincible Iron Man* #95 (February 1977). New York: Marvel Comics.

Dichter, Ernest. *The Strategy of Desire.* New Brunswick: Transaction, 2004.

Gabilliet, Jean-Paul. *Of Comics and Men: A Cultural History of American Comic Books.* Translated by Bart Beaty and Nick Nguyen. Jackson, MS: University Press of Mississippi, 2010.

Hogan, Jon. "The Comic Book as Symbolic Environment: The Case of Iron Man." *ETC* (April 2009): 199–214.

LaFeber, Walter. *The Clash: U.S.-Japanese Relations Throughout History.* New York: W.W. Norton, 1998.

Madrick, Jeff. "Can We Trust Government Again?" *The Nation* (April 9, 2012): 11–13.

Mantlo, Bill (w), and George Tuska (a). "At the Mercy of the Mandarin!" *The Invincible Iron Man* # 99 (June 1977). New York: Marvel Comics.

_____. "Sunfire Strikes Again!" *The Invincible Iron Man* #98 (May 1977). New York: Marvel Comics.

_____. "Ten Rings to Rule the World!" *The Invincible Iron Man* #100 (July 1977). New York: Marvel Comics.

McClain, James L. *Japan: A Modern History.* New York: W.W. Norton, 2002.

Olson, Keith W. *Watergate: The Presidential Scandal That Shook America.* Lawrence: University Press of Kansas, 2003.

Perlstein, Rick. "Books & the Arts. That Seventies Show." *The Nation* (November 8, 2010): 25–34.

Pustz, Matthew. "'Paralysis and Stagnation and Drift': America's Malaise as Demonstrated in Comic Books of the 1970s." In *Comic Books and American Cultural History: An Anthology,* edited by Matthew Pustz. New York: Continuum, 2012. 136–51.

Reischauer, Edwin O. and Marius B. Jansen. *The Japanese Today: Change and Continuity.* Cambridge, MA: The Belknap Press of Harvard University Press, 1996.

Schulman, Bruce J. *The Seventies: The Great Shift in American Culture, Society, and Politics.* New York: The Free Press, 2001.

Demon in a Bottle and Feet of Clay

David Michelinie and Bob Layton on Iron Man

Jason Sacks

From the first moment that viewers of *Iron Man* see Robert Downey, Jr., playing billionaire industrialist Tony Stark, riding through Afghanistan in his military Humvee, "Back in Black" streaming from the speakers and with a glass of fine, expensive scotch whiskey in his hand, it is immediately obvious that Stark is an alcoholic. The handsome, dashing and charismatic munitions manufacturer is shown in the first few minutes of this wildly successful film with a crystal tumbler of good alcohol in his hand, and it's obvious it's not an unusual experience for him. In fact, Stark's alcoholism one of the aspects of the first *Iron Man* film that is best-known by casual fans. It's also one of the aspects of *Iron Man* that fans really latched onto, since Downey himself has had well-documented struggles during his life with drugs and alcohol.

Part of the power of Tony Stark's story arc in *Iron Man* lies in how he triumphs over the demon alcohol, at the same time that he battles a takeover of his corporation by the nefarious Obadiah Stane. In the film, viewers could watch both a heroic costumed superhero and a heroic human being—a perfect multileveled crossover hit that laid the groundwork for the wildly successful Marvel cinematic universe. Downey was praised by both critics and fans for the way that he portrayed Stark, while giving viewers a fun post-modern thrill that allowed them to see Downey's own struggles filtered through. It could be argued that the entire explosive success of the Marvel film franchise rested on Downey's beloved performance in this film.

Stark's alcoholism seemed a natural fit for both Downey's performance and for the character of a multibillionaire industrialist. However, it may have surprised some readers to learn that the problem of alcoholism was not always part of the character. It had been introduced to Stark's life only in 1979, some sixteen years after Iron Man was initially introduced in *Tales of Suspense* #39 (Mar. 1963). But from the moment that writer David Michelinie and inker and co-plotter Bob Layton introduced Stark's struggles with alcoholism to *Iron Man* beginning when they took over the title, it seemed the perfect problem for a spoiled billionaire to have. As with many important innovations in comics, the idea of an alcoholic super-hero emerged organically, without any consideration by the creators that it would be innovative. It also emerged as an extension of a classic Marvel formula: flawed heroes who have resonance with readers, and represent a key feature of the Marvel brand that made the line stand out against DC's heroes.

Heroes with Flaws

One of the major attributes of Marvel's super-heroes that differentiated them from their counterparts at DC was that Marvel's heroes had flaws that came from within themselves rather than from outside themselves. Daredevil was blind, Spider-Man was filled with angst, and Iron Man had a heart condition that prevented him from getting too excited and often caused him tremendous weakness in major battles. This contrasted with Superman's famous weakness when confronted with kryptonite, an external element over which he had no control. It's been asserted that one of the reasons why Marvel passed DC in linewide sales in the early 1970s was precisely because of this difference.[1] Marvel's characters had problems with which young readers could empathize, while DC's heroes seemed to have adult complications that were outside the concerns of most readers. Marvel's characters also lived complicated, messy lives that contrasted to the much simpler and more homogenized lives of DC's heroes.

As comic book historian Sean Howe explains:

> To Marvel readers, the personalities of the DC characters were interchangeable, their lives static and flat…. Although they were, in truth, charming and inventive in their own right, they couldn't hold a candle to the blend of humor and pathos and grandeur that Lee, Kirby and Ditko had concocted [68–9].

But while many Marvel heroes such as Spider-Man and the Fantastic Four were thriving in the 1970s, some other heroes were not as popular and experienced periods of drift. The Sub-Mariner, once a front-line Marvel character, saw his series canceled in 1974 after an ill-fated shift to a slick black and yellow costume from his green swim trunks, and other heroes fell into periods of decline during that era. Iron Man was one of those characters who seemed to have lost his momentum by the late 1970s. The glory days of Stan Lee's writing and Gene Colan's art were long past for the Golden Avenger by that time, replaced by an ever-changing series of writers. Indeed, within a seven-issue span in 1976, *Iron Man* had five writers working on it, finally landing on journeyman Bill Mantlo with *Iron Man* #95 (Feb. 1977). Mantlo was joined on art by long-time comics veteran George Tuska, who had drawn crime comics in the 1950s, with inks by senior talents Don Perlin and Mike Esposito (and later, with artwork by veterans like George Kida and Carmine Infantino), the series felt somewhat old-fashioned and out-of-date to many readers. Letter-writer Roger Klorese summed up that feeling in a letter in *Iron Man* #100 (July 1977), stating:

> Why is it that some super-heroes grow up, while others seem to go on in perpetual emotional childhood? Iron Man seems to be one of the latter; despite his romantic problems and health hassles he seems, now as ever before, an anachronism, an atavistic throwback to the days of "Commie Smasher" and blacklists.... Bill Mantlo has taken the character on at a point when all seems almost hopeless. The "old" Iron Man ... cold warrior ... seems out of place in this age of *détente* (sic), and to a readership many of whom feel that the "other" side isn't as far from their hearts as is the beaten, synthetic one of billionaire industrialists like Stark. And all attempts at a more human, more humane Iron Man have run into the ground ... they just don't wash [Klorese].

Sales tracked aesthetics, and *Iron Man* seemed in trouble in an apathetic and ever-shrinking comic book market by 1977 and 1978.[2]

Change would be needed to keep the Golden Avenger's comic book from falling prey to the executioner's ax. But like a classic super-hero adventure, the elements of Iron Man's salvation lay in the despair of his near-defeat. Writer Mantlo had introduced a number of plot-threads that would soon be reprised by a more modern and polished team of creators and would bring a new renaissance to Iron Man. In one extended Mantlo-scripted storyline, the corpulent arch-villain Midas engineers a take-over of Stark International, a scheme that the hero defeats heroically with the help of his friends—including an ally whom Stark places in an iron suit of his own. That ally is just one of a number of supporting characters that Mantlo brings in, including a girlfriend with a dark secret and several employees of Stark International. After his victory over Midas, Stark rebuilds his corporate campus as a high-tech hub, anticipating changes that would happen soon. All of these concepts would be reprised to greater effect by Michelinie and Layton. And, perhaps both innocently and fatefully, readers witness Iron Man ordering a brandy on a cross–Atlantic airline flight. Though nobody suspected it at that time, the drink would prove to be a damning choice for Stark to make and a precursor to a move that would make Iron Man more iconic, giving him a fateful weakness.

Buffing the Armor

David Michelinie and Bob Layton became friends when they worked together at DC on *Claw the Unconquered* and *Star Hunters*, ongoing series that were canceled by DC in 1978. DC was in one of its boom-and-bust periods that year, as it often was in the 1970s. Marvel editor-in-chief Jim Shooter wooed the team over to his company when their comics were canceled; as Layton recalls:

> David had never been a Marvel guy. He had always been a DC guy. So he wasn't sure about the characters and all that kind of stuff. I said "Trust me." They offered us our choice of three books that were in danger of cancellation. That's the only way you got work back then, and when we were offered *Iron Man*, I told David, "Take it, take it, take it", because I'd loved that character my whole life [Sacks].

As Michelinie recalls, Marvel's editorial staff gave the team freedom to do what they wanted with the formerly moribund series as long as events were created in smart ways:

> We were only given one criterion to follow. We were told to do it well. Marvel gave us a lot of trust. It was a good story and they let us go. I don't remember … any time when we were doing that story arc that Marvel said, "Don't do this," or "pull back on that" [Johnson].

John Romita, Jr., then new to the industry, arrived to pencil *Iron Man* in issue #115 (Oct. 1978) with Michelinie and Layton arriving one month later as Mantlo went on to script *Micronauts,* a licensed comic that Mantlo had persuaded Marvel's management to arrange for publication.

Iron Man #116 (Nov. 1978) was an auspicious arrival, and the team immediately had plans for the series:

> Dave had never really worked with an artist who had so many ideas for his concepts. So we just fed off each other. By the time we got to Marvel we set up this 50/50 partnership with the story. It was a fun time, but we decided we had to do a lot of changes. That's why we set with Bob at page five with the very first issue we got rid of a lot of stupid characters. Then it was the matter of

recreating the whole Iron Man universe. It was pretty stupid. If you go back and read *Iron Man,* it was a pretty dumb book for most of his history. One of the things that we needed to do was that by that time technology had gotten to the point where heart transplants were regular visits. People were getting them all the time. So see, him having a heart problem is ridiculous. Even now in the movies they're finally had to get rid of it because just … you know. Just give him a transplant of a new heart, and give him any rejection drugs and boom. We're off to the races, right? [Sacks].

Indeed, *Iron Man* #116 and #117 were a classic "clearing of the decks" for the creative team. They jettisoned Stark's love interest, the tragic Whitney Frost, a.k.a Madame Masque, who betrayed Tony to try to save her father the evil Count Nefaria, with issue #116. With issue #117 Michelinie and Layton brought in a new paradigm by disposing of some of the dead weight that had accumulated around the series: Life Model Decoys, robots that looked like Tony Stark but allowed him to appear as both Stark and Iron Man at public events (and therefore both echoed the dull Superman and provided an endlessly convenient *deus ex machina),* were destroyed. Tony was kicked out of his Long Island condo by his irate fellow tenants and moved into an apartment on the Stark International campus. As well, a group of rogue employees decide that "Stark International is too important to leave in the hands of a do-gooder like Stark" and thus engineer a corporate takeover of the company by S.H.I.E.L.D. (Michelinie, "The Spy…"). Immediately upon the arrival of Michelinie and Layton, the entire status quo all changed for the new Iron Man creative team.

Maybe most fatefully, in *Iron Man* #117 (Dec. 1978), Tony attends a white-tie reception for an Ambassador at a swanky mansion (at which a Senator Mountebank reminds Stark that he hasn't attended one of those shindigs for months). While there, Stark takes another drink—ominously, a tray of champagne is framed in a cut-out panel that shows Stark's hand snatching the drink eagerly—and meets a beautiful redhead named Bethany Cabe.

The framing of the alcohol and the reassertion of the playboy image brought alcoholism to center stage in the comic; as Layton recalls, that decision was made with deliberate thought:

We really thought about how we needed to give him a weakness. It wasn't hip to have him running out of energy and looking for a light socket every few pages, or having a heart attack every time Ultimo was fighting him. So we discussed it and we thought that we would give him the corporate man's disease. Something that would always haunt him. Something that would struggle with regardless if he was Iron Man or Tony Stark. It was just the villain of the month. It was what we wanted to set up. So we never thought of a time that we were doing it where we thought we would make comic book history. If you set out to make history, you probably won't. Unless it's something infamous, but in that particular case we were just doing our job. We were reshaping that universe for another generation, and it just made sense [Sacks].

During 1979, S.H.I.E.L.D. were actively working to take over Stark International in order to get it to produce more munitions and military grade material. Thus Tony was forced to deal with a coup organized by his longtime friend Nick Fury. As mentioned, Stark was evicted from his upscale apartment because his neighbors were constantly afraid of attacks. Maybe most significantly, Iron Man was framed for a murder that he didn't commit, which led to tense confrontations with police and other authority figures. Ultimately acquitted of the killing, the hero nevertheless had to deal with scandal attached to his name. To cope with his manifold problems, Stark began to drink heavily.

This was a new and different side of a superhero, and a plotline that Michelinie and Layton developed slowly, showing the power of monthly periodical comics. In fact, Tony Stark became one of the few truly heroic lead characters of any entertainment franchise to that time to fall victim to substance abuse. The first hint of the hero's passion for alcohol is in *Iron Man* #117 (Dec. 1978), in which he ponders at a black-tie party, "the only way I'm getting through this is with a little bubbly" – the same party in which he begins a tempestuous affair with the lovely Bethany Cabe (Michelinie, "The Spy..."). By *Iron Man* #120 (March 1979), Stark has begun to hit the bottle hard, downing at least four martinis on board an airplane, thinking to himself "after all, I'm drinking for two men," a clever allusion to his second life as Iron Man (Michelinie, "The Old Man..."). In *Iron Man* #123 (June 1979), Cabe professes worry that her boyfriend is hitting the bottle too hard, telling him, "Don't you think you've had enough? I know you need to unwind, but couldn't we find some ... other way?"—a not-so-subtle indicator of the healthy sex life that Cabe and Stark share (Michelinie, "Casino..."). But billionaire playboys are given a long leash, and Stark was seen just as a hedonist engaging in drinking, an active sex life, and borderline dangerous behavior. Until, that is, he hit bottom.

Feet of Clay

In *Iron Man* #128 (Nov. 1978), Stark confronts his "demon in a bottle" and finds that his personal problems are far more difficult to overcome than the threats of villains like Whiplash and the Melter. On the cover of that fateful issue, readers were presented an image the likes of which hadn't been seen since Green Arrow's ward Speedy dealt with his heroin use in *Green Lantern/Green Arrow #85* in 1971. Readers were granted the unusual image of a sweating and unshaven Tony Stark confronting himself in the mirror with a bottle of Canadian Club whiskey to his right and his Iron Man mask to his left. Clearly our hero was going through some real pain in his life.

As the issue begins, Stark soliloquizes to his helmet in much the same way that Hamlet soliloquizes to Yorick's skull, listing all of his recent flaws as he sips courage from a crystal glass. After three pages of moping, Stark flies out his office window—forgetting to open it—and proceeds to the site of a train derailment—where he makes a stupid mistake and accidentally exposes the area to toxic gas. Finally, Bethany Cabe steps in. Bethany tells Tony the terrible story of her ex-husband, a man who seemed to be completely successful but who had an addiction to pills—a problem that eventually killed him, as he drove himself off a bridge one tragic night. In a fury, Bethany demands that Tony take steps to handle his alcoholism and after a tense moment in which he's tempted by a bottle of whiskey, the hero finally agrees to kick his habit. For days, Bethany helps Tony with his abuse until, finally, he begins to triumph over his addiction. In the story's dramatic denouement, our hero stands at the bar in his office, bottle of Jack Daniels in his hand. Stark wants nothing more than to toss back a drink, but Bethany pleads with him to stop himself. If Tony drinks, he won't just lose his business, he'll lose everything that makes him a good person, including her love. In the end, he puts the bottle back on the shelf, and as Bethany drives her sports car into the sunset, Stark says, "I'm going to win" (Michelinie, "Demon…").

This was the first time that the title character of a comic book was shown as a substance abuser. And though the plotline was unusual, Michelinie and Layton were given the freedom to do what they wanted on the series. For one thing, *Iron Man* wasn't a strong seller so there was little that the creative team could do to affect sales. For another, the creators were trusted to produce a storyline that grew organically out of the machinations that Tony Stark was going through. As Layton recalls:

> I think we presented it in such a way that it made sense. As long as we didn't have Tony vomiting on camera or taking a piss on a flower pot in the lobby of Stark International, we were going to be fine [Johnson].

For the first time in mainstream comics, a lead character in a comic series had become involved with substance abuse, though supporting characters had similar struggles previously. This was a new and significant change to the core Marvel concept of heroes with flaws. Where previously Tony Stark had suffered from a condition—heart disease—that was outside of his control, the new paradigm of alcoholism came from inside the billionaire industrialist. His problems came from his own weakness; in fact, Stark's problems ironically came from his own strengths.

The emergence of alcoholism as Stark's struggle was also significant in that it was reflective of the new audience reading comic books. In the early part of the 1970s, the popular media noted with amused novelty that college-age people were reading Marvels and identifying with the problems that Spider-Man and the Hulk were experiencing. However, older comic book fans were a distinct minority. Comics were cheap, disposable entertainment mainly intended for elementary and middle school aged kids; it was a cliché of the era that boys would start to outgrow comic books at about the time that they discovered their attraction to girls. By the late 1970s, however, that paradigm had begun to shift in a major way. The direct sales market, strongly skewed towards older readers and collectors, grossed $6 million in sales by 1979 (Thompson). To spur that market, a new generation of *auteur*-driven comics series were emerging that became extremely popular, due in major part to the power of the direct market. Frank Miller's *Daredevil* and Chris Claremont and John Byrne's *X-Men* became popular, because of their slick storytelling, and because they took on mature themes that had resonance in the lives of the older cohort. Alcoholism was a relatable problem for those older readers and had a resonance stronger than heart disease. Alcoholism seemed adult, real, and important in a way that mere heart disease could not.

As a tragic hero, Stark is shown to have feet of clay. And like a true hero, Stark is able to become a better man because he has transcended his own faults. Older readers, who had grown emotionally attached to Tony Stark and who had followed his deepening problems with booze since the beginning, found pleasure in the way that he worked through his problems—something that found resonance three decades later, when Downey was cast in the lead for the *Iron Man* film.

Alcoholism in the Media

Many heroes in popular film and TV have drunk alcohol over the years, but few ever struggled with alcoholism in anything approaching a realistic way. Film and television had a bit of a two-sided approach to the issue, sometimes glorifying and sometimes condemning drinking. Cowboy heroes in film and TV would wander to the tavern for a drink, but their drinking seldom affected their ability to fire a gun or battle the week's bad guys. Alcohol was frequently portrayed as a regular aspect of adulthood, and even as heroism in heroes; a man who was able to toss back a drink was also one who was able to fight for justice and gain a night of passion with a beautiful woman. Indeed, James Bond's famous martini, "shaken not stirred," has been an iconic aspect of that globally popular character since his first film, *Dr. No*, in 1962. The 1965 comedy *Cat Ballou* portrayed Lee Marvin as a former gunfighter who had become so much of an alcoholic that he even got his horse drunk. That approach continued into the early 1980s. A rough contemporary film of the Michelinie/Layton *Iron Man* was the Dudley Moore film *Arthur*, in which the character's constant drunkenness was portrayed for laughs. *Arthur* was the fourth-highest grossing film of the year 1981.

But alcoholism was also portrayed at times as a tragic consequence of weak characters. The 1945 Ray Milland film *The Lost Weekend*, directed by Billy Wilder, portrayed the tragic consequences of a writer's drunken life and the way that drinking shattered his existence; as one of film's most famous "preachies," it advocated for temperance among film-goers lest they suffer Milland's character's fate. That film won the Best Picture Oscar in 1946. Similarly, *The Days of Wine and Roses* from 1962 starred Jack Lemmon and Lee Remick as a husband and wife who fight a terrible drinking problem that causes them to nearly burn down their house and for Lemmon to nearly lose his job before shaping up his life. Ultimately, the pair join Alcoholics Anonymous and set their lives straight, but not before nearly destroying everything that they built up.

In comics, alcohol was almost never mentioned except as a throwaway line in westerns. Nearly all the attention around substance abuse was devoted to hard drugs, and that attention followed a rough parallel to its treatment in the media. R. Crumb drew a number of comic strips around the effects of getting stoned, and other underground cartoonists—both prominent and obscure—showed the profound influence that drug use had on them. S. Clay Wilson, Rick Griffin and Victor Moscoso were just three of Crumb's cohort who dove deep into psychedelia.

Mainstream comics only briefly discussed drug abuse, and invariably from a negative viewpoint. In a notorious pair of issues of *Green Lantern*, the ward of Green Arrow, who is ironically nicknamed Speedy, is discovered to be a heroin abuser. In a roughly contemporary trio of issues of *Amazing Spider-Man*, supporting character Harry Osborn is shown as a user of psychedelics and an African-American student throws tries to throw himself off a building. In one memorable scene in that storyline, Peter Parker confronts drug pushers in the campus of the fictional Empire State University with an upright, heroic statement: "Before you go sleepy-bye, remember one thing—

and remember it good—if I ever see you pushing that stuff—anywhere again—you'll think that this was just a playful picnic" (Lee).

Stark, under Michelinie and Layton, walked a third ground: he was a high-performing drunk before completely tumbling into an alcoholic stupor. Indeed, a completely drunk hero could never have defeated the attempted S.H.I.E.L.D. takeover or successfully defend himself against criminal charges. But ironically those same triumphs also helped to foster Stark's disease. Things that might drive a sober man to feel arrogant pride instead drove Stark to drink more, only deepening his problems.

Tony Stark and Robert Downey, Jr.

It's been noted many times that the role of Tony Stark was perfectly cast in the persona of Robert Downey, Jr. Downey, once a member of the Hollywood "bad boys" Brat Pack in the 1980s, had his own well-documented history of drug and alcohol abuse including publicly acknowledged arrests for drug-related charges involving cocaine, marijuana and heroin, and eventually nearly a year spent at California Substance Abuse Treatment Facility and State Prison in Corcoran, California. As Downey recalled on *Oprah*, he hit bottom and decided to try to bounce back:

> I said, "You know what? I don't think I can continue doing this." And I reached out for help, and I ran with it. You can reach out for help in kind of a half-assed way and you'll get it and you won't take advantage of it. It's not that difficult to overcome these seemingly ghastly problems ... what's hard is to decide to do it [Winfrey].

The rehab worked, and the actor started moving back into the Hollywood mainstream; first, starring in smaller movies such as *A Guide to Recognizing Your Saints* and the drug-fueled *A Scanner Darkly*. Because of his problems—not to mention his outstanding acting skills and his magnetic personality—Downey brought a verisimilitude to Stark's struggles, combined with an approach to his character that seemed in some ways to be a more adult version of the Brat Pack characters with which he was well identified. Downey had his own feet of clay, so who would be better to portray a lead character who was both emotionally strong and deeply flawed? His portrayal of Stark and Iron Man combined a brash and cocky attitude with a humbleness around his flaws—a combination that viewers found irresistible.

Perhaps a deeply flawed Robert Downey, Jr., cast as the deeply flawed Tony Stark, hits a certain powerful point in a world economy that in 2008 was in the midst of its worst financial crisis in a generation. The world could see hope in a billionaire industrialist who discovered new technology that would help him transform his life and lift up the world. In the very roots of his own weakness, Downey-as-Stark found hope, aspiration, and ultimately, triumph. If you can defeat an alcohol addiction, you can defeat many things. The Golden Avenger, embodied by perhaps the most deeply flawed (and deeply talented) actor of his generation, represented hope to a world that felt it was on its knees.

It's perhaps appropriate that the 2008 triumph of *Iron Man* had its roots in one of the deepest recessions of the 20th century. The late 1970s were a tumultuous time for America, with sky-high interest rates, the Iran hostage crisis and a sense of malaise. Heroes were hard to find, but heroes with feet of clay were uniquely resonant in that era.

There had been nothing done in comics up to the late 1970s that was similar to the work that Michelinie and Layton did with Tony Stark's alcoholism. No lead character had ever succumbed to the Demon in a Bottle before, much less risen from his addiction to become a hero again. In their depiction of Stark's struggles, Michelinie and Layton didn't just bring glory back to a moribund title and earn their paychecks. They brought Tony Stark to a whole new level of heroism that would reverberate decades later and resonate with millions of film fans. Their reformulation of the classic Marvel trope of the "hero with feet of clay" would become iconic.

Notes

1. There were, to be sure, other reasons for Marvel's success, including less formal story structures, more popular artists and writers and a feeling that reading Marvel Comics was a bit of a rebellion against authority. Stan Lee's hipster Soapbox column didn't hurt either.

2. Estimates in 1978 were that DC lost millions of dollars per year in sales of monthly titles; declining sales forced DC executives to cancel a planned expansion of their line called "The DC Explosion." In fact, rumors of the cancellation, which resulted in a cutback of 40 percent of their comics, was a major reason that Michelinie and Layton came to Marvel.

Works Cited

Howe, Sean. *Marvel Comics: The Untold Story.* New York: Harper Collins, 2012.

Johnson, Dan. "Marvel's Metal Men: Bob Layton and David Michelinie" *Back Issue #25* (Dec. 2007). Raleigh, NC: TwoMorrows.

Klorese, Roger. Letter of Comment in *Printed Circuits*. Iron Man #100 (Jul. 1977). New York: Marvel Comics.

Lee, Stan (w), Kane, Gil (p) and Giacoia, Frank. "The Goblin's Last Gasp!" Amazing Spider-Man #98 (July 1971). New York: Marvel Comics.

Michelinie, David (w), Romita Jr., John (p) and Layton, Bob (i). "Casino Fatale!" Iron Man #123 (June 1979). New York: Marvel Comics.

_____. "Demon in a Bottle" Iron Man #128 (Nov. 1979). New York: Marvel Comics.
_____. "The Old Man and the Sea Prince!" Iron Man #120 (Mar. 1979). New York: Marvel Comics.
_____. "The Spy Who Killed Me!" Iron Man #117 (Dec. 1978). New York: Marvel Comics.
Sacks, Jason. "Bob Layton: The "Corporate Man's Disease" Hits Tony Stark." Accessed 14 May 2014. http://comicsbulletin.com/interviews/6740/bob-layton-the-corporate-mans-disease-hits-tony-stark/
Thompson, Kim. "Marvel Hires Direct Sales Manager." The Comics Journal #54 (March 1980)
Winfrey, Oprah. "RDJ on O3" Accessed 14 May 2014, at https://www.youtube.com/watch?v=0_K_3h1KBS8.

War Machine

Blackness, Power and Identity in Iron Man

Julian C. Chambliss

In the last decade scholarly interest in superheroes has skyrocketed. The adaptation of superhero characters for film and television project opens the door to broader questions. As Marc DiPaolo suggests, these characters help us understand the "hopes and fears of the average American" within a broader social and political context (DiPaolo 3). These fantastic stories communicate cultural ideas that inform and reflect societal expectations (Inge 140–143). In the case of Tony Stark/Iron Man, this seminal character has long offered commentary on the United States concerns with security, nationalism, technology, and masculinity during the Cold War (Chambliss; Genter). In recent years, with the importance of anti-terrorism to U.S. policy, Iron Man's fictive narrative has evolved to engaged with those concerns. In doing so, key elements of Iron Man's universe have been re-imagined. In particular, James "Jim" Rupert Rhodes, also known as the hero War Machine, has risen to public awareness and become a visible space of intersection around questions of community and identity. Since his introduction in *Iron Man* #118 (1979) Rhodes has served as employee, confidant, protégé, and successor to Tony Stark/Iron Man. This essay examines Rhodes' evolution and argues that his progression serves as a window on broader questions of race and identity in the U.S. experience. One of the few African American superhero characters, Rhodes both challenged *and* affirmed expectations about community, identity, and responsibility linked to the African American experience.

Superhero stories stress values, ideas, and concerns central to U.S. experience in a manner that allows the audience to contextualize changing contemporary circumstances with established societal expectations. Yet, as Kenneth Ghee suggests, "there is a dearth of serious cultural bound hero archetypes available to the youth in black culture…" that affirm their culture and worldview (Ghee 227). This point has become more crucial as the superhero genre has been positioned as a metaphorical landscape in popular culture that allows Americans to at once affirm and question U.S. society (Rosenberg and Coogan xvii–xviii). Arguably, the net effect of this imagined backdrop on the question of race is to present a white identity as the normative baseline and all other individualities as markers of difference. As scholar Marc Singer explains, superhero comics embrace "every fantastic race possible," but ignore the struggles that define the reality of actual minorities (Singer 111).

The limited number of minorities suggests little concern about diversity in comic books, but as Nickie D. Philips and Staci Strobi point out, racial presentation are not static, instead "…there is a plethora of constructions that sometime privilege certain racial identities over others" (Phillips and Strobl 169). Bradford Wright's *Comic Book Nation: The Transformation of Youth Culture in American* supports this view and his work addresses the appearance of black superheroes as a significant marker of social transformations in the United States. Yet, Jeffery A. Brown's *Black Superheroes: Milestone Comics, and Their Fans* highlights how black superheroes struggle to overcome the challenge of the comic community's **expectations** linked to identity. Recently Adilifu Nama's *Super Black: American Pop Culture and Black Superheroes* provided a post-structural analysis of black superheroes to spotlight the aspirational symbolism inherent to these characters is worthy of consideration even if their numbers are limited.

Marvel Comics' emergence in 1961 marked the beginning of the Silver Age and was connected to the changing social landscape of the 1960s. Both *Sgt. Fury and His Howling Commandos* and the *Amazing Spider-Man* had black supporting characters. Moreover, Marvel debuted the first black superhero, the Black Panther in 1966 and the first African American hero, The Falcon in 1969. Despite the presence of black characters, initial representations of black superheroes in Marvel Comics tended to present these characters in circumstances without overt racial themes informing their origins or actions. Marvel was aware and embraced youth culture challenging the racial status quo, but it was not a counter-culture media voice. As Stan Lee explained in 1967, "We [Marvel] stand for the good virtues" (Sloane). The presence of an African American hero then, was calculated and reflected a belief that a black (or other minority) character would not challenge white expectations.

Instead, these characters affirm 1960s public sentiments that minorities share the values and outlook that justify their inclusion into the mainstream (Wright 219).

While the inclusion of characters such as Black Panther in the *Fantastic Four* or Falcon in *Captain America* broke new ground by presenting people of color as heroes, in many ways *The Invincible Iron Man* lagged behind other Marvel titles in the 1960s. Debuting in 1963, Tony Stark/Iron Man served as a counterpoint to adolescent and outsider heroes such as Spider-Man or the X-Men. Instead, a founding member of the Avengers and a corporate symbol, Stark/Iron Man offered a powerful commentary on Cold War fears and anxieties (Chambliss 164). Because of this, Iron Man lagged behind in the area of diversity. Indeed, with an origin tied to Vietnam and an emphasis on anticommunism and defense, creators utilized super villains linked to Cold war threats such as China. Thus, the Mandarin, a classic Iron Man foe continued a legacy of anti–Asian caricatures begun in pulp adventure magazines of the 1920s and 1930s (Chambliss and Svitavsky). Nonetheless, Iron Man began to break from this pattern in the 1970s. Surprisingly, the inclusion of African American perspective did not start with Jim Rhodes.

Tony Stark/Iron Man first hand picked successor was actually a man named Eddie March. A former boxer and friend to early Stark bodyguard/chauffeur Happy Hogan, March was trained to be Stark's replacement after he became concerned his heart would fail (a recurring theme in the series). March dons the armor for one solo adventure fighting the Crimson Dynamo in *The Invincible Iron Man #21* (Jan 1970). Seriously injured, Stark reclaimed the mantle of Iron Man and vows never to shirk his responsibility again. March's tenure as replacement was more a story device than an effort at diversity. Nonetheless, James Rhodes' first appearance in *The Invincible Iron Man* #118 (Jan 1979) was a *lesser* debut. Created by David Michelinie, John Byrne, and Bob Layton, he appears in *one* panel. His full back-story is not revealed until *Invincible Iron Man* # 144 (March 1981). It is in this story that readers learn Rhodes' connection to Iron Man goes back to Vietnam. Rhodes was the first person Stark encountered after escaping from the communist base where he was held prisoner and built the Iron Man armor. Together, the two overcome Vietcong threats, steal a helicopter, and make their way to the U.S. embassy. This adventure establishes Rhodes' importance in the Iron Man universe, but more importantly it sets Rhodes apart from African American characters that had appeared in Marvel Comics after the 1960s.

The early 1970s saw Marvel's few African American heroes shift to reflect the Black Power politics that challenged mainstream white expectation. While Black Power's opposition to structural racism and advocacy for cultural uplift offered a complex critique of mainstream white society, its portrayal in popular entertainment did not reflect its thoughtful substance. The entertainment industry mimicked black militancy in film, television, and print by reveling in the violent resistance associated with radical groups such as the Black Panther Party (Lendrum 361). It inspired Marvel's *Luke Cage: Hero for Hire*. Created in 1972, Cage was the first major African American superhero with his own monthly title (Wright 247). Born and raised in Harlem, Cage's backstory included a time in a street gang, wrongful incarceration, and experimentation in prison that gifted him with superhuman strength and durability. Thus, Marvel's most prominent African American character mirrors the pattern of hyper-masculinity and infantilized personality that reinforced popular racial stereotypes (Mastro and Robinson).

As the decade progressed, portrays of African American reflected competing ideology about agency and power. By the late 1970s a conservative ascendency shifted public dialogue toward a "law and order" philosophy that rebuked collectivism and embraced individual agency as a vehicle for community betterment. African Americans, conservatives argued, needed to embrace personal responsibility as the ultimate tool for self-improvement (Schulman). Rhodes' biography, born and raised in South Philadelphia with military service getting him out of the ghetto, mirrored conservative commentary. The U.S. military was lauded as the single U.S. institution that effectively implemented racial integration in the postwar period and thus was a space of legitimate African American achievement (Moskos; Phillips).

These elements combined to position Rhodes in a manner that resonated with a renewed emphasis on military power and patriotic entertainment during the presidency of Ronald Reagan (1981–1989). Reagan's career as a movie actor seemed to shape his approach to the presidency and public perception at home and abroad. Reagan leveraged the pop culture landscape in service of communicating political ideas (Ashby 443). Reagan's perspective rejected the post Vietnam retrenchment and championed an aggressive stance against communism around the globe. These sentiments were echoed by positive portrays of Vietnam veterans on television and film, a contrast to the damaged soldiers that dominated popular culture in the 1970s. Rhodes illustrated these points, proving himself to be a steadfast and willing ally facing Justin Hammer's super villain army (*Invincible Iron Man* #122 (May 1979)–#127 (October 1979) and almost losing his life while aiding Stark against the machination of Obadiah Stane (*Invincible Iron Man* #163 (October 1982)–#169 (April 1983).

Created by Dennis O'Neil and Luke McDonnell, Obadiah Stane was a former chess prodigy that employed psychological tactics to undermine Tony

Stark's emotional stability, leading to alcoholism. Collected and reprinted as "Demon in a Bottle," Stark's battle with alcohol abuse is generally lauded as an example of a socially relevant storytelling in superhero comics (Karczekski). David Michelinie and Bob Layton established Stark's drinking problem, but writer Denny O'Neil crafted the relapse storyline that featured Stark's collapses, Stane's takeover of Stark International, and James Rhodes taking on the mantle of Iron Man. Coming after John Stewart debuted as "replacement" Green Lantern in DC Comics, Rhodes' stint as Iron Man began in *Invincible Iron Man* #170 (May 1983) and was a rare example of an African American replacing a white hero in comic books. Far from a triumphant moment, the story opens with a caption that reads, "His name is James Rhodes. He is by profession, a pilot and by occupation, an employee of Stark International. He is probably Anthony Stark's best friend. He has no desire whatsoever to be a hero … but sometimes one has no choice." Forced to protect an inebriated Stark, Rhodes battles Magna, a villain with a grudge against Iron Man. Ultimately, Rhodes defeats Magna with the assistance of The Knight, a henchman dispatched by Stane to insure Stark's manufacturing facilities are not destroyed. Rhodes' tenure as Iron Man is plagued by uncertainty.

From the beginning Rhodes, as loyal confidant and friend, wanted Stark to *take back* his armor and responsibilities. He is shocked when Stark prefers to continue abusing alcohol rather than fulfill his duty. Reflecting on Stark's actions he thinks, "Okay, I can't keep him from destroying himself, but maybe I can keep others from destroying everything he's built, everything he's accomplished" (*Invincible Iron Man* #170). Thus, a pattern that will define Rhodes' tenure begins. He is caretaker to Tony Stark's legacy. His actions in his early adventures merely serve to consolidate his role as protector of the Stark legacy. Rhodes quits the Avengers (*Invincible Iron Man* #170), he disposes of Stark's extra armors to keep them away from enemies, and he resigns from Stane International (formerly Stark International) as Iron Man and himself. All the while, he acknowledges that he does not possess the knowledge to operate the Iron Man armor. Despite the fact he is a trained combat pilot and has years of military experience, he needs help to be Iron Man. It is only the instructions given to him by Morley Erwin, a Stark employee, which allow him to act. Rhodes' own thoughts confirm this assessment. "Without you [Erwin] to figure out how the various gadgets work, the tin suit would be no more to me than a set of chrome long johns" (*Invincible Iron Man* #171, June 1983). Unable to mirror Stark's scientific understanding; Rhodes often solves his problems by relying on physical force. Not surprisingly, fans share Rhodes uncertainty, as one letter in Printed Circuits, the *Invincible Iron Man* letter page explains,

"Make Tony better soon or make a super hero out of Rhodey *real* fast" (*Invincible Iron Man* # 175 (Oct 1983).

As Stark hits rock bottom and begins recovery, Rhodes becomes more enamored with being Iron Man. Stark's quest to recover prompts him to join Rhodes, Morley Erwin and Clytemestra Erwin (Morley's sister) to start a new electronic firm. Under Stark's scrutiny Rhodes begins experiencing headaches, having emotional outbursts, and acting defensive about his role as Iron Man. Rhodes and Stark act as Iron Man in a series of adventures before Stark take back the role full time in new high tech armor. Moreover, Rhodes' headaches and erratic behavior are explained by the armor's cybernetic controls not being calibrated for him. Yet, these experiences merely serve to highlight the illegitimacy associated with Rhodes' tenure as Iron Man. Indeed, as Adilifu Nama explains a significant portion of Rhodes' "agency and self-definition" was robbed by his mimicry of Stark during his tenure (Nama 79). Conversely, Rhodes' time as Iron Man can be understood as a deeper commentary on identity politics in the 1980s. Responsible, but overwhelmed, Rhodes' tenure as Iron Man paralleled conservative arguments that emphasized minorities elevated into position of power were ultimately hurt by the experience (Brown et al. 1–3).

While Rhodes' term as Iron Man in the 1980s was mixed, in many ways it enhanced his position as confidant and ally to Tony Stark. Rhodes shares an understanding of being Iron Man, yet happily returns to his role as pilot and bodyguard for the rest of the decade. While he would take up the armor to assist when necessary, his time as a hero was over. However, with Stark's health in jeopardy, Rhodes became Iron Man again in the 1990s. *Iron Man* #284 (Sept 1992) features the demise of Tony Stark. In a story entitled "Legacy of Iron," extraordinary circumstances once again put Rhodes in the role of Iron Man. Suffering from massive neurological deterioration and facing death, Stark gives his armor to Rhodes. The Variable Threat Response Battle Suit, dubbed "War Machine Armor" by Stark, is a weapons laden black and silver armor created for all out war. Unlike the previous stint as Iron Man, Rhodes inherits Stark's empire becoming CEO and Iron Man (Mangels 144). While recent research suggests racial diversity in superhero comics lagged behind other media in the 1980s, by the 1990s African American presence in popular culture experienced a new level of saturation and Rhodes' second outing as Iron Man reflected that shifting experience (Peterson and Gerstein).

Serving as CEO in his second outing as Iron Man seemingly placed Rhodes on equal footing with Tony Stark. Balancing the role of hero and CEO, Rhodes exhibits little of the uncertainty associated with his first tenure as

Iron Man. Instead, he asserts a moralism that challenges the technocrat realism associated with Tony Stark. Like Stark he faces corporate/industrial threats such as Spymaster, Whiplash, and Beetle who attempt to steal company secrets (*Iron Man # 285*, Oct 1992). However, after confronting Atom Smasher, a villain seeking to draw attention to environmental abuses in Stark Enterprises owned power facilities, CEO Rhodes makes the decision to divest the company of its nuclear holdings, overruling objections from the board of directors (*Iron Man #287*, Dec 1992). Rhodes' second tour as Iron Man again falls apart when he discovers Stark faked his death. He resigns his dual roles, but Stark gives him the War Machine armor saying, "You want to leave here hating me, all right. Maybe I deserve it. But that armor on the floor is yours. It always was. Don't leave without it" (*Iron Man #289*, Feb 1993). Rhodes takes the armor, giving birth to a new hero called War Machine.

Determined to create a heroic legacy distinct from Tony Stark, he joins the West Coast Avengers (*Avengers: West Coast #94*, May 1993). Rhodes' tenure as an Avenger is short lived; the group is disbanded shortly thereafter. Nonetheless, War Machine allows Rhodes to create a heroic identity with a worldview and identity distinct from Stark. In doing so, his adventures mirror African Americans' experience in the broader culture. The era's identity politics influence Rhodes' War Machine adventures. This period saw stereotypical markers of blackness embraced in white mainstream consumer culture even as African Americans faced marginalization based on that imagery (Tate 5–8). Despite or perhaps because of this, African American creative endeavors in the comic industry in the 1990s placed visible emphasis on markers of identity and culture.

Projects such as *Brotherman Comics* or Milestone Media presented culturally diverse and socially complex narratives that attempted to merge traditional superhero comic narratives with "unfettered sense of escapism and exploration" for black people (Lackaff and Sales 68). In creating a monthly title based on Rhodes' adventure as War Machine, Marvel Comics reflected this dynamic within its fictive universe. *War Machine* ran for twenty-five issues between April 1994 and April 1996.

Shaped by his African American identity, Rhodes' solo adventures as War Machine saw him use military technology and question national security in a manner that differed from Tony Stark/Iron Man. However, rather than engage with problems in the United States, *War Machine*'s initial adventures focus on an African context. Written by Scott Benson and Len Kaminski with art by Gabriel Gecko, *War Machine* touched on post Cold War geopolitical shifts, spotlighting assumptions of free market capitalism's legitimacy (Brown 17–18). Yet, it also fetishized contemporary social and political discourse linked to the African continent in the West. These views marked Africa as a space of famine, war, and injustice (Falola and Agwuele 4).

The initial storyline in *War Machine* provided readers with tangible analogs to real African events. Bolstered by U.S. media that reported on African humanitarian incidents caused by civil conflicts, refugee emergencies, and intervention debates in Somalia (1990–1995), Rwanda (1994), and Liberia (1989–1996), the popular discourse opened the door to a role at once new and familiar for Rhodes. This role, which utilized military technology within an individualistic moral framework, mirrored the actions of Tony Stark as Iron Man, but drew on his African American identity to inform his actions (Chambliss 172).

War Machine's first story arc starts with Vincent Cetewayo, a noted African human rights activist, approaching Rhodes to lead Worldwatch Incorporated. Cetewayo founded the organization to pursue human rights on the African continent (highlighting the region's deficit in the area). Although Rhodes declined the offer, he is drawn in after Imaya's (Cetewayo's home country) military dictator kidnaps the activist. Interacting with Cable (of X-Force), but ultimately teaming up with Deathlok (Michael Collins), War Machine leads a revolution that overthrows the brutal regime. War Machine acts outside the bounds of law, ignoring warnings from S.H.I.E.L.D. (Strategic Hazard Intervention Espionage Logistics Directorate) and the Avengers. However, his action mirrors those undertaken when he served as CEO of Stark Industries, pursuing morally correct actions regardless of established policy.

Beyond furthering the moralism attached to Rhodes' character, this storyline offers a unique pairing of two African American heroes in a story that centered on a corrupt government in Africa. As such, this story represented both stereotypes and possibilities within the Marvel Universe. As Lysa Rivera writes, Deathlok's presentation in the 1990s, established by writer Dwayne McDuffie, took the trope of dehumanization often assigned to cyborgs and used it to reimagine blackness as a "complex, diasporic cultural production" that explored the meaning of black identity (Rivera 107–108). Rhodes' actions as War Machine hinted at the possibility that he too could engage in a more complex narrative linked to the African diaspora. However, this story did not establish this path for the *War Machine* series. Despite the strong start, writers never again explored African diaspora themes in the title. Indeed, as was the case in his previous adventures, Rhodes' link to Stark and reliance on his technology leads to a confrontation with Iron Man. Stark disagrees with Rhodes' intervention actions. Stark asks, "What do you think you're doing with the suit I gave you? Have you lost your mind?" Going further, Stark criticizes Rhodes' morality, saying, " I thought I gave the suit to a highly moral man, Jim ... a man of principle. But you've used it like a bully, a common vigilante—with no regard for international law or the sanctity of human life" (*War Machine* #8, Nov 1994). In confronting each other a subtext of race and power in the Rhodes/Stark relationship is made clear:

> STARK: "I don't know what happened to you, Jim. The James Rhodes I knew was a sensible man.
> RHODES: "Sensible" meaning he did what you told him to, right? #%&@ that noise! It must really burn your butt that I'm through steppin' and fetchin' on your say so.
> STARK: You are wrong about that. But you are right about one thing: You're through.

With those words, Stark hacks into Rhodes' armor and deactivates it, telling him, "Your days as War Machine are over (Benson, Kaminski, and Gecko). As is the way of superhero adventure, a new threat from the Mandarin forces the two men to put aside their problems and confront his latest evil plot. While Adilifu Nama writes that the Stark/Rhodes relationship "symbolized very little" about U.S. race relations, the confrontation captures the contested landscape around identity in the 1990s (Nama 81). The Stark/Rhodes confrontation resonated with wider debates about how African American culture was visible, but that visibility did not equate to full societal acceptance or success. As Henry Louis Gates, Jr., explained the "the cultural centrality" of blackness "coexisted with economic and political marginality" that rendered African Americans, especially males, more likely to end up uneducated, underemployed, or imprisoned (Gates, Jr. xvi–xv). Such debates clearly inform the evolution of Rhodes' persona. Yet, as it did in the 1980s, Rhodes' adventures moved away from racial allegory in favor of fantastic adventure that assured readers whatever his views, Rhodes embraced common heroic values.

The series moves onto fantastic ground as a time traveling adventure leads to the War Machine armor being destroyed (*War Machine* #15, June 1995–*War Machine* #17, August 1995). In its place, Rhodes is given Eidolon Warwear, bio-organic armor of alien origin. Using the warwear Rhodes plays a pivotal role opposing a plot conceived by Kang the Conquer that led to the corruption and death of the adult Tony Stark and his replacement by a time travelling younger self! Marvel's cancellation of the *War Machine* series coincided with a period of broader industry adjustment. Fan backlash against crossovers and collector oriented marketing cut deeply into sales at both Marvel and DC. Yet, arguably Marvel suffered more from the aggressive expansion by owner Ronald Perelman. Under Perelman's guidance, Marvel acquired Skybox and Fleer, trading card manufacturers, Hero World Distribution, a comic distributor company, and a minority stake in ToyBiz, a toy maker that manufactured Marvel action figures ("Remembering Two Titans' Marvel Duel"). These efforts did not translate into greater readership. Indeed, critics and fans charged that the quality of comic books declined. In response, Marvel reduced the number of comics it published and stabilized prices (Wright 283). The reduced publication line sacrificed lesser titles and concentrated on core characters. As a result James Rhodes' place in the Marvel Universe shifted.

As with the previous decadal transition, James Rhodes' representation in the 2000s reflected new national concerns. As Bradford Wright explained, "September 11 forced comic book makers to step back and reevaluate the place of their industry in American culture" (Wright 288). The attack, coming just as the comic industry recouped from the decline in the 1990s, also parallels a creative and business renaissance at Marvel. Under the leadership of Toy Biz executives Avi Arad and Isaac Perlmutter the company consolidated publications, crafted new film deals based on its characters and sought new ways to attract readers. Initially, these changes *marginalize* Rhodes. Officially retired and no longer a regular supporting character in *Iron Man*, Rhodes made sporadic appearances in various publications. In Christopher Priest and Joe Bennett's *The Crew,* we learn that Rhodes has founded and lost a marine salvage business when he comes to New York to investigate his sister's death. An attempt to broaden his backstory and add depths to the perspective introduced in *War Machine*, the series was quickly cancelled (Priest and Bennett). Next Rhodes appeared in *Sentinel Squad ONE*, a five-issue miniseries linked to Marvel's X-Men: Decimation event. Both appearances hark back to Rhodes' link to Tony Stark and his career as War Machine. Indeed, *Sentinel Squad ONE* cast Rhodes as "commanding officer and combat instructor" for raw recruits being trained to pilot next generation Sentinel robots. Rhodes' first action as training officer was to "washout" a recruit that expressed anti-mutant prejudice. Rhodes explains, "If you wanna make it to the sentinel squad, every last member of the team is your brother. That understood?" (Layman and Lopresti). Continuing the pattern of racial awareness associated with the character, Rhodes' identity is leveraged for greater utility in this post 9–11 world. Rhodes' expertise as a combat pilot and experience using armor technology add value to his identity and bolster his stature. Writer John Layman stresses these facts with idle chatter in the first issue: "used to be a big shot at Stark International—heard a rumor he used to be Iron Man—oh yeah? I heard he used to War Machine" (Layman and Lopresti). This series orients Rhodes' identity to Iron Man, reestablishing that his utility and ability are linked to Iron Man and his world. This point is crucial to understand Rhodes in the post September 11 comic world. In the context of the United States' "War on Terror," *Iron Man*'s traditional emphasis on national defense and military technology was given renewed emphasis and visibility across the Marvel Universe.

In January 2005, writer Warren Ellis and artist Adi Granov reimagined *The Invincible Iron Man*. Offering an updated origin firmly rooted in Middle Eastern military experience (displacing the original Vietnam context), the new Iron Man narrative mirrored concerns growing from U.S. involvement in Afghanistan and Iraq (Ellis and Granov). In a series of storylines that reverberated across the Marvel Universe, Tony Stark/ Iron Man became a central player emphasizing the need for security. In *Civil War*, writer Mark Millar and artist Steve McNiven pitted pro-registration forces led by Iron Man against anti-registration forces led by Captain America (Millar and McNiven). Drawing creative inspiration from contemporary debates around preventative war and terrorist surveillance programs, the comic narrative placed emphasis on moral and ethical uncertainty. While Matthew J. Costello writes the debate over registration fails to privilege the moral position of either side, it does elevate Iron Man and *his* technology to a central place in the Marvel Universe (Costello 237). Tony Stark/Iron Man emerges as director of S.H.I.E.L.D. and the fifty state initiative designed to train and garrison licensed superheroes across the United States (Slott and Caselli).

In the security centric narrative universe, Rhodes' military background and armor expertise combine with his relationship to Tony Stark to make him a useful protagonist. Echoing the legitimation associated with military service that characterized his initial introduction to the Marvel Universe, the United States' contemporary focus on fighting terrorism heightens Rhodes' utility. His expertise valued, Rhodes' agency remains constrained by his relationship with Tony Stark. In the first issue of the *Avengers: The Initiative*, it is revealed that Rhodes was severely injured in a terrorist attack and Tony Stark has rebuilt him as a cyborg, melding Rhodes' damaged body to his armor. With cybernetic elements visible, Rhodes' "enhanced" status means he is now figuratively and literally built by Stark. Adding to the contrast, Stark too has undergone a biotechnological transformation thanks to the Extremis, a biosynthetic virus that allowed Stark to integrate elements of his Iron Man armor *within* his body (Ellis and Granov).

The difference in the outcome of these technological interventions on each man's body—Stark looks human, Rhodes does not—serves to make Rhodes' body a space of contested negotiation around the war on terrorism. Rhodes' body indicates the danger posed by continual conflict even as his expertise as soldier and fighter is lauded in the new status quo. His body manipulated by the military industrial complex, Rhodes' fate easily elicits criticism rooted in the Vietnam era that disproportionate numbers of African American men (and women) have fought and died in service to a morally questionable policy (Lucks 6–7; Lutz 170–173).

In the aftermath of a company wide event entitled *Dark Reign*, Norman Osborn (the villain Green Goblin) emerges as the leader of world security (Bendis et al.). Once again spun off in his own series, *War Machine* (February 2009 to February 2010), Rhodes travels to the Middle East kingdom of Aqiria. There Rhodes confronts Eaglestar International, a military contractor that has committed war crimes such as torture and experimentation on prisoners (Pak, *War Machine—Volume 1*). Mirroring many of the tropes of the 1990s series, Rhodes' identity and moral viewpoint force him to act, and his efforts uncover misdeeds over the objections of established authority. This time as a cyborg, his commitment to justice affirms his humanity even as his body no longer projects it. The conclusion of the second *War Machine* series places Rhodes on trial for war crimes. With the assistance of his allies, he is able to punish, in a limited way, the corporate and government authorities responsible for the morally bankrupt actions in the Middle East (a victory most Americans cannot claim). This final story arc also allows Rhodes to transfer his mind into a cloned body, thus returning the outward signs of his humanity (Pak, *War Machine—Volume 2*).

The focus on terrorism and security has allowed writers to continue to utilize Rhodes' military experience to explore contemporary debates about a decade of conflict. As Americans laud the sacrifice associated with military service, they question the abuse associated with defense subcontractors and the suspicions linked to corporate profiteering. Indeed, as the Marvel security versus liberty narrative unfolded in the pages of *Invincible Iron Man*, the majority of Americans believed the original decision to invade Iraq was wrong and concerns about private military contractors shaped public debates (Street et al.; Mazzetti and Risen). In this landscape, Rhodes' established identity as a soldier and a morally responsible hero perfectly situates him to explore these concerns as the Marvel Universe expands into films.

The centrality of Iron Man in Marvel Comics mirrored the character centrality in the Marvel Studios film. Indeed, *Iron Man* (2008), *Iron Man 2* (2010) and *Iron Man 3* (2013) form a benchmark franchise for the studio and the heart of a shared universe narrative that replicated the comic book format in a live action setting. Tony Stark (played by Robert Downey, Jr.) is the head of Stark Industries much like the one found in the comic book. However, Jim Rhodes (played by Terrance Howard in *Iron Man* and Don Cheadle in subsequent films) is the military liaison to Stark Industries. While *Iron Man* did not feature Rhodes as War Machine, subsequent films featured Rhodes' character acquiring Stark created armor and joining the action. The arc of Rhodes' character in the films highlights the acceptable traits built around the character in the comics. He is a successful military officer and loyal friend to Tony Stark. Synthetic by nature, the cinematic James Rhodes emerges as War Machine and in that role helps Tony Stark navigate the complexities of balancing his moral code and the government's demands for Stark Technology for national defense (Favreau; Favreau and Branagh; Black).

The success of the cinematic version of War Machine is reflected in James Rhodes' continued comic adventures. While Matt Fraction, the writer for *The Invincible Iron Man* from 2008 to 2012, insists he had no direct understanding of Rhodes' cinematic path prior to the release of 2008's *Iron Man,* his development of the character mirrored the film (Siuntres). Fraction took established continuity around Rhodes and shaped a storyline that eventually required Rhodes to rejoin the military and serve as War Machine (Phillips and Strobl 184). As a supporting player in the pages of *Iron Man*, Rhodes evolves further into his role as protector of the Stark legacy (Fraction). Indeed, in the first issue of a new title focused on Rhodes, *Iron Man 2.0*, his status as proxy is given new gravitas:

> STARK: I did want to say—I mean, I am sorry to be putting you in a spot like this. I know it isn't easy.
> RHODES: Tony, Look—It is what it is. If Stark doesn't supply Iron Man to the military, someone else will supply an Iron Man to the military. Better us than them" [Spencer].

A direct and clear proxy for Stark, *Iron Man 2.0* summarizes the reconciliation between agency and race linked to Rhodes. He effectively occupies a heroic space legitimated by loyalty, enhanced by his experience, and inspired by his background. *Iron Man 2.0*'s cancellation did not end Rhodes' responsibilities. Thanks to the success of *Iron Man 3*, which featured the cinematic Rhodes' transformation into the Iron Patriot, Marvel launched a new comic book of the same title in March 2014. Written by Ales Kot with art by Garry Brown, the masthead of *Iron Patriot* affirms the heroic identity constructed for James Rhodes over thirty-five years—"*James Rupert 'Rhodey' Rodes is an American hero. He's served his country in the armed forces, stepped in for an ill Tony Stark as Iron Man and battled bad guys in top secret conflicts as War Machine. Now he wears a new red, white, and blue suit of armor with a promise of protecting the home land as IRON PATRIOT.*"

Succinctly weaving together the responsibility narrative that distinguished Rhodes from Iron Man, *Iron Patriot* also links Rhodes to recent African American social grievances. Set in New Orleans, the comic touches on environmental inequality in its first pages as Iron Patriot sends drones under the city to "assess the damage" and determine if the city will indeed "go offshore before this century ends." In the midst of these actions, Rhodes verbally spars with his father about this duty to mentor his niece (a prodigy) while continuing to serve as Iron Patriot. His response reminds readers of his ethical stance, "I have to stand by my principles. I have to help this country. I protect it. Therefore I protect you. I'm protecting mom. I'm protecting Lila." As Iron Patriot, Rhodes' familial commitment and personal responsibility becomes a framework to address the home front. As always, race is a contextualizing element. Set in a city with social and economic challenges defined by the African American experience, in this new series Rhodes publicly defines his Iron Patriot's role by promising "to help you if you ever need my help regardless of your color, nationality, or belief because our primary foundation is that of freedom and love." To accomplish this goal, Rhodes commits himself to limiting his involvement "in military operations to those occurring on American soil unless they are rescue missions, in which case I intend to always be ready help, regardless of the country involved" (Kot). *Iron Patriot* couples the positive stereotype of African American military service with community-oriented heroism that aligns Rhodes' identity and actions in a pattern of validation central to his placement in the Marvel Universe.

The evolution of James Rhodes highlights the limitation linked to race in superhero comics. As an inheritor of the Iron Man legacy, Rhodes' status has evolved from faithful sidekick to nationalistic hero. Nonetheless, his actions remain defined by the tension between his identity and the expectation of heroic agency. A figure representing the wider social discourse on the African American community, his greater visibility opens the door to questions about values, actions, and motivations defining the African American experience. Never free from this racial dialogue, Rhodes' relationship to Iron Man becomes a marker of valuation and limitation as cultural tensions in the wider racial landscape define the milieu for his action. Ultimately, James Rhodes and War Machine are both cogs in a wider societal apparatus that struggles to define the evolving meaning of race in the United States.

WORKS CITED

Ashby, LeRoy. *With Amusement for All: A History of American Popular Culture since 1830*. Re The University Press of Kentucky, 2012.

Bendis, Brian Michael et al. *Dark Reign: Accept Change*. S.l.: Marvel, 2009.

Benson, Scott, Len Kaminski, and Gabriel Gecko. *War Machine*. One. New York, N.Y.: Marvel Comics, 1994. Web. 14 June 2014. 25 vols. 8.

Brown, Deward Clayton. *Globalization and America Since 1945*. Rowman & Littlefield, 2003.

Brown, Michael K. et al. *Whitewashing Race: The Myth of a Color-Blind Society*. Berkeley: University of California Press, 2003.

Chambliss, Julian C. "Upgrading the Cold War Framework: Iron Man, the Military Industrial Complex, and American Defense." In *Ages of Heroes, Eras of Men*. Newcastle upon Tyne: Cambridge Scholars Publishing, 2013.

_____, and William Svitavsky. "From Pulp Hero to Superhero: Culture, Race, and Identity in American Popular Culture, 1900–1940." *Faculty Publications* (2008): n. pag. Web.

Costello, Matthew J. *Secret Identity Crisis: Comic Books and the Unmasking of Cold War America*. New York: Bloomsbury Publishing, 2009.

DiPaolo, Marc. *War, Politics and Superheroes: Ethics and Propaganda in Comics and Film*. Jefferson, N.C: McFarland, 2011.

Ellis, Warren, and Adi Granov. *Extremis*. New York: Marvel, 2013.

Falola, Toyin, and Augustine Agwuele. *Africans and the Politics of Popular Culture*. Rochester, NY: University of Rochester Press, 2009.

Fraction, Matt. *The Invincible Iron Man, Vol. 5: Stark Resilient, Book 1*. New York: Marvel, 2011.

Gates, Henry Louis, Jr. *Thirteen Ways of Looking at a Black Man*. New York: Vintage, 1998.

Genter, Robert. "'With Great Power Comes Great Responsibility': Cold War Culture and the Birth of Marvel Comics." *The Journal of Popular Culture* 40.6 (2007): 953–978. *Wiley Online Library*. 10 June 2014.

Ghee, Kenneth. "Will the 'Real' Black Superheroes Please Stand Up?!": A Critical Analysis of the Mythological and Cultural Significance of Black Superheroes." In *Black Comics: Politics of Race and Representation*. New York: Bloomsbury Academic, 2013.

Inge, M. Thomas. *Comics as Culture*. Jackson: University Press of Mississippi, 1990.

Karczekski, Kacper. "More than Just Iron Man: A Brief History of Comic Books and Graphic Novels." Journal. *Crossroads*. N.p., 19 Mar. 2014. Web. 14 June 2014.

Kot, Ales. *Iron Patriot*. Vol. 1. New York, N.Y.: Marvel Comics, 2014. Web. 22 June 2014. Iron Patriot 1.

Lackaff, Derek, and Michael Sales. "Black Comics and Social Media Economics: New Media, New Production Models." In *Black Comics: Politics of Race and Representation*. New York: Bloomsbury Academic, 2013.

Layman, John, and Aaron Lopresti. *Sentinel Squad One*. Vol. 1. New York, N.Y.: Marvel Comics, 2006. 5 vols.

Lendrum, Rob. "The Super Black Macho, One Baaad Mutha: Black Superhero Masculinity in 1970s Mainstream Comic Books." *Extrapolation (pre-2012)* 46.3 (2005): 360–372,293.

Lucks, Daniel S. *Selma to Saigon: The Civil Rights Movement and the Vietnam War*. University Press of Kentucky, 2014.

Lutz, Amy. "Who Joins the Military?: A Look at Race, Class, and Immigration Status." (2008): n. pag. *Google Scholar*. Web. 13 Nov. 2014.

Mangels, Andy. *Iron Man: Beneath the Armor*. New York: Del Rey, 2008.

Mastro, Dana E., and Amanda L Robinson. "Cops and Crooks: Images of Minorities on Primetime Television." *Journal of Criminal Justice* 28.5 (2000): 385–396. *ScienceDirect*. Web. 14 June 2014.

Mazzetti, Mark, and James Risen. "Blackwater Said to Pursue Bribes to Iraq After 17 Died." *The New York Times* 11 Nov. 2009. NYTimes.com Web. 18 June 2014.

Millar, Mark, and Steve McNiven. *Civil War*. New York, NY: Marvel Comics, 2007.

Moskos, Charles C. "Success Story: Blacks in the Military." *The Atlantic* May 1986. *The Atlantic*. Web. 14 June 2014.

Nama, Adilifu. *Super Black: American Pop Culture and Black Superheroes.* University of Texas Press, 2011.

Pak, Greg. *War Machine—Volume 1: Iron Heart.* New York: Marvel, 2009.

_____. *War Machine—Volume 2: Dark Reign.* New York; London: Marvel, 2010.

Peterson, Bill E., and Emily D. Gerstein. "Fighting and Flying: Archival Analysis of Threat, Authoritarianism, and the North American Comic Book." *Political Psychology* 26.6 (2005): 887–904.

Phillips, Kimberley L. *War! What Is It Good For?: Black Freedom Struggles and the U.S. Military from World War II to Iraq.* Chapel Hill: The University of North Carolina Press, 2014.

Phillips, Nickie D., and Staci Strobl. *Comic Book Crime: Truth, Justice, and the American Way.* New York: New York University Press, 2013.

Priest, Christopher, and Joe Bennett. *The Crew.* 1st ed. Vol. 1. New York: Marvel, 2003.

"Remembering Two Titans' Marvel Duel." *New York Times,* 31 Aug. 2009.

Rivera, Lysa. "Appropriate(d) Cyborgs: Diasporic Identities in Dwayne McDuffie's Deathlok Comic Book Series." *MELUS* 32.3 (2007): 103–127.

Rosenberg, Robin S., and Peter Coogan. "Introduction." *What Is a Superhero?* New York: Oxford University Press, 2013.

Schulman, Bruce J. *The Seventies: The Great Shift in American Culture, Society, and Politics.* Cambridge, MA.: Da Capo Press, 2002.

Singer, Marc. "'Black Skins' and White Masks: Comic Books and the Secret of Race." *African American Review* 36.1 (2002): 107–119. *JSTOR.* Web. 13 June 2014.

Siuntres, John. "Matt Fraction on Iron Man, The X-Men, Thor and More." Podcast. *Wordballon.* N.p., 9 May 2008. Web. 18 June 2014.

Sloane, Leonard. "Advertising: Comics Go Up, Up and Away." *New York Times* 20 July 1967. *ProQuest.* Web. 7 June 2014.

Slott, Dan, and Stefano Caselli. *Avengers: The Initiative, Vol. 1: Basic Training.* New York; London: Marvel, 2008.

Spencer, Nick. *Iron Man 2.0—Volume 1: Palmer Addley Is Dead.* New York: Marvel, 2011.

Street, 1615 L. et al. "Public Attitudes Toward the War in Iraq: 2003–2008." *Pew Research Center.* N.p., n.d. Web. 18 June 2014.

Tate, Greg. *Everything But the Burden: What White People Are Taking from Black Culture.* New York: Broadway, 2003.

Wright, Bradford W. *Comic Book Nation: The Transformation of Youth Culture in America.* The Johns Hopkins University Press, 2003.

From Armor Wars to Iron Man 2.0

The Superhero Entrepreneur

Jean-Philippe Zanco

The powers of the Fantastic Four appeared after a space expedition went wrong and they were exposed to cosmic rays. Hulk was the result of Dr. Banner's exposure to massive gamma radiation. Spider-Man was born as a consequence of a radioactive spider's bite. The X-Men are defined as the children of the atom. Daredevil was the victim of an accident with radioactive waste. In the 1960s, technology and science played the key role in the origin of most superheroes in the Marvel universe. Superheroes are most often presented as the victims of what could be called—using economic terminology—an *externality* of technical progress. Iron Man, though, is an exception: he is not a victim of technological progress. On the contrary, technology is his salvation. First, the Iron Man armor allows Tony Stark to survive by magnetically blocking the deadly progression of the shrapnel lodged in his chest. But it not only keeps him alive, it also gives meaning to his life: "My ticker would stop beating if the plate were removed or didn't receive its regular booster-shot! Ah! Electrical energy is pouring back! Now I can continue living … to help humanity as Iron Man!" (Lee, "Iron Man Versus…").

Another fundamental difference between Iron Man and other superheroes is that the relentless pursuit of innovation is a key motivation of the character, rather than altruism (Superman), revenge (Batman), or guilt (Spider-Man). In only the second Iron Man story, the armor is reduced to a "collapsible form" through "microscopic transistors" and can be carried in a attaché case (Lee, "Iron Man Versus…"). The drive for new, better, more innovative technology continues throughout the early issues. In "Trapped by the Red Barbarian," Tony Stark works on "a pocket-size disintegrator ray" (Lee and Bernstein); in "The Mad Pharaoah!" he experiments a "fluoroscope" (Lee and Bernstein); in "Iron Man Battles the Melter!" Stark redesigns his armor "making it entirely out of tough extruded aluminum" (Lee); and, of course, in "The Mysterious Mr. Doll!" he builds the first famous red and gold armor, the "Mark III" costume that becomes Iron Man's most iconic look (Lee).

In 1960, shortly before the very first adventures of Iron Man, the American economist Walt Whitman Rostow theorized five stages of the economic growth in a book whose subtitle, *A Non-Communist Manifesto*, clearly showed the author's intentions: demonstrate the superiority of capitalism over all other economic models. According to Rostow, the United States at the dawn of the 60s was about to reach the end of the final stage, while other democratic capitalist countries, imitating the American model, began to enter it:

> We come now to the age of high mass-consumption, [...] a phase from which Americans are beginning to emerge [...]. In the 1950's Western Europe and Japan appear to have fully entered this phase, accounting substantially for a momentum in their economies quite unexpected in the immediate post-war years. (Rostow 9)

By contrast, writes Rostow, "the Soviet Union is technically ready for this stage, and, by every sign, its citizens hunger for it; but Communist leaders face difficult political and social problems of adjustment if this stage is launched" (10). The first adventures of Iron Man echoed the context of the Cold War and the diplomatic, military and also industrial rivalry West and East. And the very anti-communist accents of the early–60s *Tales of Suspense* were in the tone of Rostow's *Manifesto*. Iron Man embodied the American genius of industry, continuous innovation, he proved the superiority of the capitalist economic model and the repeated failures of The Crimson Dynamo and his various avatars illustrated the difficulty of the Soviet economy to move towards "the age of high mass-consumption [...with] which Soviet society is engaged in an uneasy flirtation" (Rostow 11).

Armor Wars

It must be noted that, like Iron Man, Tony Stark's enemies are often technologically powered. The story arc titled "Armor Wars," published in 1987–1988, moves away from the early Iron Man tales that presented the idea of inherently superior American technology and describes the difficulties of the hero battling complex, equal armored supervillain competitors. Tony

Stark was too confident in his technological leadership and failed to protect his inventions against the competition. Moving from the Cold War Soviet threats of the 1960s Tony Stark must now face the backstabbing corporate politics of the 1980s. His lawyer laments, "I'm sorry, sir, but defense attorneys insist that the technology in question was never patented ! They suggest that your inventions are in the public domain!" (Michelinie and Layton, "Stark Wars, Ch. 1"). In the storyline, Stark realizes that some elements of his technology have been stolen and he may have no legal recourse. Iron Man's superheroic battles come to mirror Stark's corporate fights, a struggle for competitiveness in a market increasingly open and increasingly crowded, against competitors more aggressive and more numerous (Shockwave, The Beetle, The Controller, The Mauler, Stilt-Man…).

The economic context of the 80s was no longer the time of the original Iron Man, and the series with an industry titan as the lead character needed to reflect the changes brought on by the Reagan years' deregulation, borders opening, tariffs and trade barriers lowering, and high-tech industry development (the NASDAQ was created in 1971). U.S. companies were competing for leadership on an increasingly globalized market. Stark Industries was like IBM threatened by Dell and young Apple, then overtaken by DEC in the mid–1980s, or like the aeronautics leader Boeing threatened by Airbus.

This is no longer the idea of a linear evolution of economy, as theorized by Rostow. "Armor Wars" is an illustration of Raymond Vernon's theory of product life cycle. In stage 3 ("Maturity") of this economic model of the late 60s, the company is facing fierce competition and can only remain competitive by lowering its production costs. As a purposeful businessman, Tony Stark responds with another strategy: the elimination of all competitors, by fighting or confiscating their technology. Despite this, the most aggressive of all armored villains, Firepower, defeats Iron Man and destroys the armor at the end of product life-cycle stage 5 ("Decline") [Iron Man #230, May 1988]. The Iron Man armor is destroyed because, as a product, it is a victim of its obsolescence. Tony Stark, of course, survives, and as the perfect model of an American entrepreneur, he relaunches the innovation process. As announced on the cover of Iron Man # 231 (Jun. 1988), "The new Iron Man," a more powerful Mark VII version of the armor will finally stop Firepower. At the same time, the Mark VIII revives the product life cycle (stage 1: "Introduction," then Stage 2: "Growth"). In the same way, to refer back to a previous example, the rapid growth of DEC (especially because of the success of the PDP-11, an upgradable computer designed for mass and low-cost production) threatens IBM's position as world's number one computer company. DEC's stock quotation finally overtakes IBM's in the mid–1980s; but IBM rebounds with its

PC microcomputer, and DEC, which still believes in the minicomputer, collapses less than ten years later.

The product life cycle theory rejoins the broader cyclic vision of the economy developed by the economist Joseph Alois Schumpeter in the 30s. While the so-called "classical" economists see the economic system tending towards a natural balance, Schumpeter thinks in terms of evolution and cycles whose dynamics depends on the actions of economic actors. Among them, the entrepreneur is a key figure of capitalism:

> The function of entrepreneurs is to reform or revolutionize the pattern of production by exploiting an invention or, more generally, an untried technological possibility for producing a new commodity or producing an old one in a new way [Schumpeter 132].

Portraying the entrepreneur, Schumpeter probably had in mind a few important figures of twentieth century industry—Thomas Edison or Henry Ford—and the heroic dimension is obvious: supernormal intelligence and energy account for industrial success and in particular for the founding of industrial positions in nine cases out of ten (Schumpeter 16). In the early co-creation of Iron Man Stan Lee has never denied being inspired by another great entrepreneur of American economic history: Howard Hughes. It is said that Tony Stark's father's first name was Howard, and beyond the similarity between the activities of Hughes Aircraft Company and Stark Industries, Tony Stark and Howard Hughes share several traits: arrogance, their playboy reputation, even Stark's face being modeled on Hughes'. There is also a curious parallel between Hughes' morphine addiction and paranoia in his last years and Tony Stark's alcoholism and depression.

Of all the superheroes, Tony Stark is the most notable that is driven by profit. Stark combines the spirit of adventure with economic risk taking, as evidenced, for example, by this dialogue with Spider-Man:

IRON MAN: And that web-goo of yours…. How many hundreds of pounds is it tested against? Have you patented it? You could be making a fortune on this stuff.
SPIDER-MAN: Yeah, no. No, not for me. Thanks but…
IRON MAN: Millions of dollars you're leaving on the table.
SPIDER-MAN: No, I…
IRON MAN: Billions [Fraction, "The Five Nightmares: Epilogue"].

The extraordinary powers of the Iron Man armor are not what make it an innovation in the Schumpeterian sense: as such, it is no more than an expensive prototype. Innovation is not just an invention, it is an invention that turns to an economic success, that is to say, which finds an application in the production process. Utility is what gives value to a good or a service;

a useless invention does not exist economically. Unquestionably, the Iron Man armor has a value, that Tony Stark can accurately assess at least at the cost of investment if needed: "four-point-some billion dollars in R&D. Including some near-priceless repulsor patents I've sat on... (Fraction, "The Five Nightmares: Part 1). Does it have an economic utility? Tony Stark, played by Robert Downey, Jr., in the *Iron Man 2* film, answered cynically: "I've successfully privatized world peace" (Favreau).

Iron Man 2.0

Competition is a recurrence in Iron Man universe: super-enemies are almost always like him, technologically-enhanced characters. In both of Jon Favreau's Iron Man films the narrative pattern remains the same: in *Iron Man,* the superhero faces Obadiah Stane, his former partner who steals part of Tony Stark's invention and develops the Iron Monger armor. In *Iron Man 2,* the threat comes from the son of a former employee of Stark Industries, Ivan Vanko, who retrieves some of his father's patents to build the weapons of Whiplash. The entrepreneur always awakens vocations and inevitably imitators. As Schumpeter argued:

> ... the successful appearance of an entrepreneur is followed by the appearance not simply of some others, but of ever greater numbers, though progressively less qualified. [...] we see first of all the single appearance of an innovation— overwhelmingly in business created ad hoc—and then we see how the existing businesses grasp it with varying rapidity and completeness, first a few, then continually more. We have already come across this phenomenon in connection with the process of eliminating entrepreneurial profit [229].

Schumpeter also concludes that while imitation is less innovative than the initial design, it does increase the supply on the market and thus lowers prices. Twenty years after "Armor Wars" reflected an earlier stage of the economic cycle, this latter stage is the threat that faces Iron Man in the story arc "The Five Nightmares" by Matt Fraction and Salvador Larocca. The expressed fourth nightmare that haunts Stark is that "Iron Man becomes disposable. Cheap and replaceable like a cell phone. [...] And there's the fifth nightmare. The big one. The bad one. That the person who makes the Iron Man cheap, easy to use, and disposable ... wouldn't be me" (Fraction, "The Five Nightmares, Part 1"). Of course, Tony Stark's fears become true: "My biggest nightmare has come true : Iron Man 2.0 is here.... And I'm not the one that made it" (Fraction, "The Five Nightmares, Part 1").

"The Five Nightmares" marks a further step in the parallel between the adventures of Iron Man and American economic reality. Stark Industries is no longer the "young company" it was at the time of "Armor Wars." As expressed in *The Invincible Iron Man* #5 (Nov. 2008):

> Stark Industries has facilities on every continent and in more than thirty countries around the world. [It] began as a defense contractor and aeronautics concern before branching out into nearly every technological aspect of modern life. Factories that once made bombs and the planes to drop them today make everything from toasters to medical equipment and beyond [Fraction, "The Five Nightmares, Part 5"].

Stark Industries has become a world high-tech consortium. So rises a new kind of opponent, not only a competitor, but a real entrepreneur who is able to provide an equally effective but less costly alternative to Iron Man. This is a true innovation, in the Schumpeterian sense, as explained by the bad guy of the story, Ezekiel Stane: "The innovation here—the genius of what I'm offering—is that the hardware costs are negligible. [...] The Iron Man suit cost, what, billions? I can offer the same firepower with an organic power source for a fraction of that cost (Fraction, "The Five Nightmares, Part 2"). This is the real "weapon of the poor" Ezekiel Stane worked out, which he uses for terrorist purposes—a single-use weapon, which involves the sacrifice of its operator and paves the way for a new kind of war: "This isn't the future of warfare—this is the face of asymmetrical warfare. Welcome to the 21st Century" (Fraction, "The Five Nightmares, Part 5"). The comparison with Islamic terrorism, the dominant American collective fear since 2001, is evident, especially as Stane's bombers sacrifice themselves shouting "God is great! God is power!" (Fraction, "The Five Nightmares, Part 5").

Iron Man should have died, killed by Ezekiel Stane just as the "romantic" Schumpeterian entrepreneur was inevitably killed by desk consulting. But in the never ending cycle of superhero narratives, inevitably there is a rebirth. After Stark has taken over and relinquished bureaucratic duties, Stark recovers his freedom and his creative genius. To escape a new foe, Tony Stark engineers and builds a mark 0 armor, in fact a copy of the 1963 grey mark I armor, and the cycle begins again, because "capitalism [...] is by nature a form or method of economic change and not only never is but never can be stationary" (Schumpeter 82).

Works Cited

Fraction, Matt (w) and Salvador Larroca (p). "The Five Nightmares: Epilogue." *The Invincible Iron Man* #7 (Jan. 2009). New York: Marvel Comics.

_____. "The Five Nightmares, Part 1." *The Invincible Iron Man* #1 (Jul. 2008). New York: Marvel Comics.

_____. "The Five Nightmares, Part 2." *The Invincible Iron Man #2* (Aug. 2008). New York: Marvel Comics.

_____. "The Five Nightmares, Part 5." *The Invincible Iron Man #5* (Nov. 2008). New York: Marvel Comics.

Lee, Stan (w) and Steve Ditko (a). "Iron Man Battles the Melter!" *Tales of Suspense #42* (Nov. 1963). New York: Marvel Comics.

_____. "The New Iron Man Battles … 'the Mysterious Mr. Doll!'" *Tales of Suspense #48* (Dec. 1963). New York: Marvel Comics.

Lee, Stan with R. Berns (w) and Jack Kirby (a)."Iron Man versus Gargantus!" *Tales of Suspense #40* (Apr. 1963). New York: Marvel Comics.

_____. "Trapped by the Red Barbarian!" *Tales of Suspense #42* (Jun. 1963). New York: Vista Publications.

Michelinie, David and Bob Layton (w) and Mark Bright (a). "Stark Wars, Part 1." *Iron Man #225* (Dec. 1987). New York: Marvel Comics.

Rostow, W. W. *The Stages of Economic Growth: A Non-Communist Manifesto*. New York: Cambridge University, 1990.

Schumpeter, Joseph Alois. *Capitalism, Socialism and Democracy*. London: George Allen and Unwin, 1976.

_____. *The Theory of Economic Development: An Inquiry into Profits, Capital, Credit, Interest, and the Business Cycle*. New Brunswick: Transaction Publishers, 2004.

Vernon, Raymond. "International Investment and International Trade in the Product Cycle," *Quarterly Journal of Economics* vol. 80, May 1966.

Cold Warrior at the End of the Cold War

John Byrne's "War Games" in an Era of Transition

Joseph J. Darowski

Byrne's Three Stories

In 1990 John Byrne was asked if he would take over writing duties for Marvel's comic book, *Iron Man*. Byrne was a popular creator at the time, a significant force in the industry as both an artist and a writer. He rose to fame collaborating with writer Chris Claremont on an acclaimed run of the X-Men comic books and having worked as both writer and artist on *The Fantastic Four*. Through his years at Marvel, which included stints as co-plotter, artist, writer and creator on several additional titles, he had become "the most popular artist in the industry" (Howe 289). He had also, notably, worked with Marvel's chief rival when he wrote and drew the successful reboot of Superman following DC Comics' *Crisis on Infinite Earths* event in the 1980s. On *Iron Man* he would be dropping his artist duties and acting solely as writer.

There were a few caveats placed on him by Howard Mackie, the editor of the series, and Byrne insisted on a few caveats of his own. The previous writing team, David Michelinie and Bob Layton had left the series unexpectedly. The title of what had been their next planned story arc, "Armor Wars II," had already been announced and solicited to retailers, so Byrne had to tailor his first storyline to that title. Byrne was willing to conform to that requirement, though his tale would depart significantly from the previously planned outline for "Armor Wars II." Byrne informed Mackie that were he to take on the writing duties for Iron Man he had three stories to tell, though it could be possible that while writing those he "might think of more, but that seemed unlikely" (Byrne, "Re: JB..."). True to his word, Byrne would write three interconnected story arcs across twenty issues of *Iron Man*. The first, as solicited, was "Armor Wars II," the second was "The Dragon Seed Saga," and the third was called "War Games." In 2014 Marvel Comics collected the entirety of Byrne's run as writer of *Iron Man* into a single trade paperback with the title "War Games."

With three Iron Man stories he was prepared to tell and the opportunity to collaborate with John Romita, Jr., as artist, Byrne was happy to begin what he called an "adventure," though one that, in retrospect, he would admit was "less than satisfying" (Byrne, "Re: JB..."). First, his collaboration with Romita Jr. was not as long lived as Byrne hoped. Of the twenty issues Byrne wrote, Romita Jr. penciled fewer than half. Romita Jr. genuinely enjoyed working with Byrne. Byrne had begun in the industry as an artist, then become known for writing and penciling his own comic books, but was happy collaborating with an artist as he took on the writer's duties for *Iron Man*. Romita Jr. recalls that Byrne employed more of what is referred to as the "Marvel method" of comic book scripting, in which an artist is given more of a general plot outline than a panel-to-panel script to follow, and the writer adds in the dialogue later based on the artist's images:

> I remember John Byrne's first plot on "Iron Man" back in the '90s. I think it was two pages. He was so open to letting me to do whatever I wanted. I smiled at the compliment of it and because it was so much fun to work on. And then he put my name first in the credits. That's why I'll always be a fan of John Byrne. John Byrne was an artist first and working with him was a true pleasure. He's a great guy, a friend, a brilliant talent, but that was the most fun I'd had. When he sent me that plot and at the end said, "Knock yourself out" [Deuben].

Byrne has said that working with Romita Jr. was "one of THE great pleasures of [his] career" (Byrne, "JR..."). During Byrne's run as writer of *Iron Man* he would also collaborate with Paul Ryan, Mark D. Bright, and Tony DeZuniga as pencilers.

In addition to his disappointment that Romita Jr. would leave the title, Byrne also had to deal with a change in editors. Howard Mackie had asked Byrne to take over the series, but left the title during Byrne's run. Byrne has referred to Mackie and Romita Jr. as "two of the legs of [his] Iron Man tripod," so both of their departures likely detracted from any possible interest that may have begun in telling a fourth Iron Man story (Byrne, "Re: JB…"). Additionally, the new editor, Nel Yomtov, changed the ending of Byrne's final story without consulting Byrne, and Byrne had to argue for its restoration (Byrne, "Re: JB…"). Disappointed and frustrated, Byrne chose to not even pursue the possibility of additional Iron Man stories.

Communists After the Cold War

Whether it was intentional or not, and artist intent is an inherently a tricky point to argue, with hindsight it is plain that Byrne's issues of *Iron Man* are reflective of the transitional period when they were published. Produced in the early 1990s, Byrne's issues carry themes and narrative elements that are indicative of the end of the Cold War and the uncertainty that brought with it.

It is difficult to give an end date for the Cold War with exactness for many reasons. It encompassed so much of the globe that changes marking the end of that era were not simultaneous. Even when those changes were clearly happening, precision in declaring a date can still be difficult. For example, the Berlin Wall stood as a great symbol of the political, ideological, cultural, and economic divides that drove the Cold War. Its fall was a great symbolic moment for the easing of tensions and erosion of the Cold War climate in the world. But when did it happen? In late 1989 East Germany announced that its citizens could visit West Germany, and there were celebrations and for several weeks citizens chipped away at portions of the Berlin Wall, but the Wall by no means literally fell. Official work on the demolition of the Wall did not begin until several months later in the summer of 1990. Of course the removal of the Wall was another symbol of German reunification, but the official date of political reunification of East and West Germany is in the Fall of that year, October 3, 1990. And the demolition was not actually completed until 1992. So at what moment did the Wall fall, providing a clear symbol that the Cold War was ending? The transition period where it was clear the Cold War was moving towards a close begins in the mid-to-late 1980s, and the dissolution of the USSR in 1991 is one of the most frequently cited end dates. Byrnes' issues of *Iron Man* have cover dates from July 1990–February 1992.

Historian Jeffrey K. Johnson succinctly sums up many of the most significant shifts that were occurring in this period:

> How do heroes, and nations, define themselves when their enemies have been vanquished and the never ending battle is over? This is the chief problem that

the government and citizens of the United States faced during the 1990s. The U.S. had won the Cold War and the Soviet threat was ended, but on what should Americans now concentrate? The U.S.S.R. had been a threatening and stable adversary for over four decades that had provided a consistent "them" as a mirror to better clarify the American "us." Now that the Soviet Union no longer existed, how would the U.S. Define itself and what would be its new mission? [150].

Or, as John Darowski put it, "Given the bipolar nature of [the Cold War], American society both justified its course of action and sublimated its concerns and anxieties by projecting any negative values onto an external other" (93). Iron Man comics had successfully mined America's cultural Othering of Soviet Communists for villains since its earliest issues. Bradford W. Wright noted that Tony Stark/Iron Man was important as a piece of Cold War propaganda in both his civilian and superhero guise. Stark was vital to America's war effort as a member of the military-industrial complex, and Iron Man a key figure fighting "Communist agents and [battling] Soviet supervillains in symbolic Cold War contests of power and will" (Wright 222). With that iconic external threat disappearing, how would Stark/Iron Man engage a new global stage?

Byrne's storyline simultaneously addresses, highlights, removes, and avoids the Communist threat that had, for decades, defined not only the United States in the real world but the titular character of the *Iron Man* comic books. *Iron Man* #258 (Jul. 1990), with the ominous and melodramatic title "Lo, A Spectral Enemy Rises," features Iron Man fighting an unseen foe who is destroying one of Tony Stark's factories. Of course, upping the stakes and highlighting a key component of the Cold War, this is not just any factory, but a nuclear factory that is becoming increasingly unstable due to the unknown foe's attack. The final splash-page reveal shows the reader that the foe is none other than Iron Man's old communist enemy, Titanium Man.

While Titanium Man was a recurring villain, for consistent readers of Iron Man's adventures this reveal would have been especially unexpected as Titanium Man had been killed in an earlier battle with Iron Man. Most comic book character's relationship with death is not as permanent as one might expect, so the return of a dead character while surprising, was not unheard of. Titanium Man makes reference to his death at Iron Man's hands, declaring "I have a gift for you my old foe. A very special gift. You might say I am returning a favor, Iron Man. The gift I bring is death. And it is only fair that I should be the one to bring it to you ... since it was you who killed me!" (Byrne, "Lo..."). At first Iron Man believes that he is indeed fighting "the ghost of the Titanium Man," (Byrne, "Like All Secrets...") but it is revealed in subsequent issues that he is truly battling the Living Laser, who was trying to psychologically weaken his enemy by appearing as an old arch-nemesis that was believed dead.

With this opening chapter, seemingly reintroducing one of the most iconic Russian Communist foes Iron Man battled in his career, but then revealing it all to be a shadow play and manipulation, Byrne establishes how Communism will be addressed in much of his run—a constantly shifting force, an indeterminate and unknowable enemy. The Titanium Man, symbolic of the Soviet Communist threat for several decades of Iron Man's comic book adventures, is not really the enemy Stark/Iron Man faces. The specter of Communism is raised and brought front and center, and then revealed to be nothing at all. Similarly, the Black Widow, a former Communist but now ally of America, will play a prominent role in later issues, and Stark's life will be saved by a Chinese scientist after Stark/Iron Man makes an uneasy truce with the Communist government of China. Communism is a constant presence in the stories, but not in the same clearly jingoistic and ideological way it was in the earlier Iron Man stories when "over one-third of the stories between 1963 and 1966 pitted him against Communist adversaries" (Costello 63).

While there are, of course layers, twists, and subplots throughout the story, eventually two primary threats emerge during Byrne's run: the Mandarin, classic arch-nemesis of Iron Man, and rival businessmen, constant foes of Tony Stark. The significance of the Mandarin will be addressed shortly, but it is notable that in the early 1990s the attacks on Stark's factories and on Stark himself are all business related. Much as Byrne reimagined Lex Luthor from being a mad scientist and transformed him into a business leader when he rebooted the Superman mythology in 1986, Stark's enemy is not his classic Communist foe, but American business rivals who will stoop to any means to gain an advantage over Stark. These efforts include hiring supervillains and mad scientists to commit corporate espionage. With the film *Wall Street* being released in 1987 and a general condemnation of what was seen as a culture of excess of the 1980s prominent in the early 1990s, making the villains of the story into unscrupulous corporate raiders was indicative of the mood of a large segment of society. Yes, the ghost of Soviet Communism still haunted America, but perhaps there were enemies closer to home doing more harm.

Byrne not only raised the ghost of Communism only to cast it aside, he removed Communism entirely from the character's iconic origin. In *Iron Man* #267 (Apr. 1991) and #268 (May 1991) a portion of the issues retells, and reimagines, Tony Stark's first adventure as Iron Man. Byrne has made something of a name for himself in updating characters' origins, most famously on DC's Superman. In this updated version, Vietnam and Communism are not mentioned once. When Stark is disembarking from his plane his colleague welcomes him only to "Southeast Asia" where Stark is coming to address a situation with one of his factories (Byrne, "The Persistence..."). There is no ideological battle line being drawn, rather this is a "direct attack on Stark Industries" as someone is stealing shipments out of Stark's new factory in the region (Byrne, "The Persistence"). It is revealed that Wong Chu, the local warlord responsible for disrupting the factory's output, is only acting under the orders of the Mandarin. None of the democracy versus communism or America versus Vietnam rhetoric that existed in the original origin story is present in this updated retelling of the tale.

As America is stepping out of the shadow of the Cold War, Byrne is redefining Stark and his motivations. While the character had been anti–Communist to the point of pure propaganda, he was now being presented as a businessman who happened to also be a superhero in order to protect his capitalistic endeavors. Iron Man can no longer be defined solely by what he is not (not–Communist was enough motivation to be a superhero in the 1960s) and Byrne is now establishing a character who is largely free of anti–Communist inspired motivation. As Matthew J. Costello explains:

> Everything becomes part of the corporate tale of Tony Stark, and thus the story becomes internally driven with no reference to outside context. By the 1990s Marvel's most political of characters has become devoid of politics, a mere cog in the capitalist machinery. Defending democracy, promoting national security, and securing some notion of justice is no longer relevant in these tales. Justice, for Iron Man, is whatever benefits Tony Stark [179].

This new origin becomes the tale of an individual, not of an ideological system. This suits America's new identity emerging form the Cold War, as elements of that earlier era's ideology (individualism, capitalism, personal freedom) took on new and greater meaning independent of the Cold War. Stark's enemies were not America's enemies, per se, but those threats to his personal goals.

However, it should be noted that Byrne does explicitly show that Stark is not willing to sacrifice anything for personal gain. He does retain values that cannot be sold and those values contain a distinct Cold War echo. Despite the removal of a Communist threat in this new origin, Byrne does still bring Communism front and center in his stories. When visiting Communist China in a subsequent issue Stark sees a former American business associate who believes Stark is there to establish business ties with the country. The unnamed businessman congratulates Stark on "...finally getting back into China," noting that it must have cost his company "a bundle" to have pulled out all of his business "after that little fracas in Tiennamen Square." Stark reveals that he is in China for personal reasons, not business, leaving such arrangements to "vultures who fancy they can put a dollar value on freedom" (Byrne, "The Price...").

Additionally, the ideological barbs fly freely between the visiting Americans and their Chinese hosts. Though this is the heightened reality of superhero comic books, real world political issues and events are referenced. When landing in the country Stark's friend and ally Jim Rhodes, who is wearing the Iron Man armor, is impressed with the modernity of the airport, thinking to himself, "You'd think we were landing in L.A.X., not in the middle of a country that still thinks the best way to deal with student unrest is to run over 'em with tanks" (Byrne, "The Price"). Stark and his guide/translator, Mr. Li, also question the validity of their respective political systems:

> STARK: ...I've lived too long in a nation that treasures personal freedom above all else to really believe a billion people could be so content to surrender theirs.
> Li: Perhaps. But, then, the freedom your people embrace with such devotion seems also to include the freedom to be uneducated, unemployed. To be starving in that which calls itself the richest nation on Earth. (Byrne, "The Price")

However, the relationship is not purely antagonistic, as both sides need one another. Stark requires the aid of a Chinese scientist, a beautiful woman who predictably falls for his charm, to restore him to full health. The Chinese government requires the aid of Iron Man, who at this point in Marvel continuity is believed to be Tony Stark's bodyguard. The Mandarin has conquered a third of China, and due to Iron Man's many battles with the Mandarin it is believed he has the best chance of defeating the Mandarin where China's army has failed. Stark and the Chinese government set aside their respective differences in order to aid each other in their moments of need. Even though there are clearly self-serving motivations for each side, in previous eras it is likely the ideological divide would have been too great to overcome.

Iron Man Versus the Mandarin

The common thread that runs through much of Byrne's story is the dual blessing/curse of Iron Man's technology and the looming threat of the Mandarin. Byrne highlighted the technology that powered Iron Man, making it even more integral to Tony Stark's ability to function than had previously been the case for the character. In the course of Byrne's run as writer Tony

Stark comes to rely on technology that is designed to provide his body with both "voluntary and involuntary" functions, from walking to breathing (Byrne, "Dragon Flame"). Byrne has affirmed his belief that technology is what makes Stark an interesting character (Mangels 53). Clearly, Iron Man is defined by his technological superiority. That is how the character gains his powers. The superiority of his technology was a part of the character's pro–American appeal during the Cold War.

As a foil, Byrne brought back the classic Iron Man foe Mandarin. The character of the Mandarin has a long history with many writers changing aspects of the character or ignoring previously aspects while highlighting others. Byrne fully embraced the magical side of the Mandarin, presenting it as a counterpoint to Iron Man's technological powers. Regarding some of the problematic aspects of the Mandarin, particularly the negative stereotypes that are often presented in his appearance, motivations, and plots, Byrne said, "Calling the Mandarin a racial stereotype is like calling Captain America a racial stereotype [...] The Mandarin is representative of a particular part of Chinese culture" (Mangels 54). While the positive and negative aspects of their respective cultures that are prominently espoused in the characters of Captain America and the Mandarin may reveal Byrne's comparison to lack necessary nuance, the Mandarin portrayed in Byrne's run is quite different from the devilish character introduced in the 1960s. The Mandarin had been "a Chinese anticapitalist who in the early stories worked for the communist government although he himself was not a communist (Costello 63). Byrne clearly distinguishes the Mandarin from the communist government of China in his issues, as the two wish nothing more than to see the other destroyed.

The magical aspect of the Mandarin is especially prominent to make the character a more menacing foe for Iron Man. There is a long and problematic tradition in American storytelling that highlights Oriental mysticism, and the Mandarin carries many elements of the Yellow Peril stereotypes. While those issues remain, highlighting Mandarin's magical powers may have served another purpose. In comic books, the supervillains are often nearly mirror figures of the hero (Iron Man versus Titanium Man, two normal humans in powered armor) or they are near total opposites (Superman versus Lex Luthor, a nigh all-powerful godlike figure versus an unpowered human). With Iron Man and the Mandarin we have technological futurism versus ancient mysticism. This is made particularly prominent in *Iron Man #261* (Oct. 1990). In this issue, Tony Stark and the Mandarin are on dual paths of recovery. Stark is battling for his life following attacks by the Living Laser and technology attacking his nervous system, while a weakened Mandarin is attempting to regain his full mystical power. The stories are told in a manner that highlights the narrative strengths unique to the comic book medium.

The art and layouts by John Romita, Jr., reveal the parallel journeys of Iron Man and the Mandarin. The issue opens with a page split vertically, Iron Man lying prone on the left side, Mandarin lying prone on the right. The remainder of the issue shows both characters progressing, Stark through science, the Mandarin through magic, in their quest to strengthen themselves. The pages are each split, generally with the top half telling Iron Man's story, and the bottom half telling the Mandarin's. We see Stark use the best science in the world to steady his condition. In the portion of the comic that is telling Stark's story, we also have an interlude revealing that his corporate enemies have weakened him to his current state through an unknown attack on his nervous system. In the end, Tony decides he needs help, "the best money can buy, the best in the world" (Byrne, "Untitled"). This quest will take him to China, where one of the premiere neuroscientists in the world will help repair his nervous system. Conversely, the Mandarin has been seeking ancient, forgotten mystical aid. The final page of the issue reveals that whereas Stark is seeking the most cutting edge science in the world, the Mandarin has sought the aid of the dragon named Fin Fang Foom (Byrne, "Untitled").

During Stark's trip to China we again, as with the "ghost" of Titanium Man, have a case where the specter of Communism is raised, but not really the enemy. Stark and his Chinese hosts trade clearly dislike each other and trade verbal insults, but the true enemy is the Mandarin. While the Mandarin previously had some ties with Communism, here he is explicitly an enemy of the communist state.

In Byrne's run, there are echoes of the old Iron Man tales, but a new identity and purpose is being presented. This is particularly true of the new origin story for Iron Man, which no longer carries the explicit trappings of the Cold War. As America was transitioning into a new post–Cold War identity, Iron Man is shedding his past as one of Marvel's most iconic Cold Warriors. His enemies are businessmen and mystic conquerors, not inferior Soviet imitations of himself.

WORKS CITED

Byrne, John. "Re: JB, Questions about Iron Man." *Byrne Robotics*. The John Byrne Forum, 26 April 2012. Web. 4 November 2014.

_____. "Re: JR Jr. Recounts Iron Man with JB." *Byrne Robotics*. The John Byrne Forum, 13 March 2014. Web. 4 November 2014.

Byrne, John (w) and John Romita, Jr. (p). "Lo, A Spectral Enemy Rises!" *Iron Man #258* (Sep. 1990). New York: Marvel Comics.

_____. "…Like All Secrets, Easily Revealed." *Iron Man #259* (Aug. 1990). New York: Marvel Comics.

_____. "Untitled." *Iron Man* #261 (Oct. 1990). New York, Marvel Comics.

Byrne, John (w) and Paul Ryan (a). "Dragon Flame." *Iron Man* #271 (Aug. 1991). New York, Marvel Comics.

_____. "First Blood." *Iron Man* #268 (May 1991). New York, Marvel Comics.

_____. "The Persistence of Memory." *Iron Man* #267 (Apr. 1991). New York, Marvel Comics.

_____. "The Price." *Iron Man* #270 (Jul. 1991). New York, Marvel Comics.

Costello, Matthew. *Secret Identity Crisis: Comic Books and the Unmasking of Cold War America*. New York: Continuum, 2009.

Darowski, John. "The Earth's Mightiest Heroes and America's Post-Cold War Identity Crisis." In *The Ages of the Avengers: Essays on Earth's Mightiest Heroes in Changing Times*. Jefferson, NC: McFarland. 2014. 92–102.

Deuben, Alex. "The Lightbox: John Romita, Jr. on Collaboration, Character Creation & Design." CBR.com. *Comic Book Resources*, 12 March 2014. Web. 7 Oct. 2014.

Howe, Sean. *Marvel Comics: The Untold Story*. New York: Harper Collins, 2012.

Johnson, Jeffrey K. *Super-History: Comic Book Superheroes and American Society, 1938 to the Present*. Jefferson: McFarland, 2012.

Mangels, Andy. *Iron Man: Beneath the Armor*. New York: Del Rey, 2013.

Wright, Bradford W. *Comic Book Nation: The Transformation of Youth Culture in America*. Baltimore: Johns Hopkins University Press, 2001.

"I would be the bad guy"

Tony Stark as the Villain
of Marvel's Civil War

JOHN DAROWSKI

Written by Mark Millar with art by Steve McNiven, Marvel Comics' mini-series event *Civil War* (published May 2006-February 2007) dramatically pitted Avengers stalwarts Iron Man and Captain America against each other over the Superhero Registration Act, which required heroes to register their secret identities and become government employees. The story mirrored society as a thinly-veiled allegory of the debate surrounding the fears and positions around the issues of security versus freedom in post–9/11 America. Throughout the series, Marvel claimed to give equal representation to both the pro- and anti-registration camps. Editor Tom Breevort stated: "What makes this interesting is, too, the fact that nobody is being painted as wrong or being the bad guy [...] This is legitimately characters who are men of principle and ideal having a difference of opinion that plays out in a very major way and they all believe ardently in their position" (Millar Podcast).

However, the tagline "Whose side are you on?" invited readers to choose which side was right and which was wrong. Given the inherent dichotomy of conflict in superhero comic books, this invariably led readers to view one side as the heroes and the other as the villains. A search of internet polls reveals that fans overwhelmingly supported Captain America's anti-registration side by as wide a margin as eighty percent to twenty percent (ComicBookResources).[1] This implies that Iron Man, as the figurehead of the pro-registration movement, was the villain of the piece. Why was Tony Stark, a hero for over forty years, suddenly the bad guy? While some of Iron

Man's deeds during the mini-series can be interpreted as villainous, the shift is more a response to the challenge of the traditional ideal of the superhero in a post–9/11 world. To understand this, it is necessary to examine Iron Man's actions and motivations, as well as the intentions of the creators and the response of the fans.

The terrorist attacks on September 11, 2001, created a paradigm shift in society that resulted in a culture of fear that dominated the rest of the decade. Numerous laws, such as the USA Patriot Act, endeavored to further the War on Terror and help citizens feel safe, although at the expense of some personal freedoms. This fear was reflected in the Marvel Universe as superheroes came to be viewed less as saviors and more as persons of mass destruction. Tony Stark saw two possible outcomes of this situation: registration or a complete ban on superheroes (Millar, #5, 40).

The spark that started the Civil War came when the New Warriors, teenage superheroes filming a reality show, confronted a group of villains in Stamford, Connecticut. Nitro, a villain with the ability to explode, did so in front of an elementary school, killing six hundred civilians, including children. In the wake of this tragedy, the Superhuman Registration Act (SHRA) was passed, requiring superheroes to register their identities with the government and receive similar training and accountability as law enforcement officers undergo prior to service. When Captain America is asked to lead the ironically named Capekiller Squad to hunt down unregistered heroes, he declines, as he views the law as a violation of personal freedoms. Cap instead goes underground while Iron Man becomes the leader of the pro-registration camp, seeing the SHRA as a way to make the world safer (Millar, #1, 8, 31, 43).

Stark attempts to build support for the SHRA by having popular heroes, such as Spider-Man and himself, unmask to the public (Millar, #2, 35, Jenkins #1, 18). He also lays various traps to capture unregistered heroes. One such encounter results in the death of Goliath by a clone of Thor, which was created by Iron Man, Mr. Fantastic, and Yellowjacket (Millar, #4, 12). The mini-series culminates when a prison break from Number 42, Stark's secret prison in the Negative Zone, spills onto the streets of New York City. When Captain America realizes they aren't fighting for their principles anymore but just fighting, he surrenders. "We were winning back there," says Spider-Man (who had switched sides to join Cap), to which Cap responds, "Everything except the argument" (#7, 27). As Mark Millar states, *Civil War* became "a story where a guy wrapped in the American flag is in chains as the people swap freedom for security" (qtd. in Johnson, *Super-History* 183). Tony Stark becomes the head of the peace-keeping organization SHIELD, in charge of all the registered heroes. On the way to his arraignment, Captain America is assassinated in a plot by his archenemy, the Red Skull.

Iron Man fought for registration as a "twenty-first century overhaul" that preserved as much as possible of superhero system that saved more live and more property than it had ever destroyed (Millar, #3, 18, White 67). However, in doing so Tony Stark increasingly compromised his moral compass, as evidenced by various acts that are typically associated with supervillains.

This all actually began on the road to Civil War. First came the revelation to readers that Stark had years ago established a secret group, the Illuminati, to try and prevent major superhuman conflicts. Consisting of Iron Man, Mr. Fantastic, Professor X, Doctor Strange, and Namor, the Illuminati acted without oversight or transparency in deciding what was best for the planet. This included the decision that the Hulk was too dangerous to remain on Earth and to exile him into space (Mangels 116). Additionally, when Stark initially argued against the SHRA in Congress, before the events in Stamford, he secretly hired Titanium Man to start a fight with Spider-Man in the hopes of proving a point about the value of superheroes, which naturally backfired (White, "Did Iron Man..." 67).

Stark's actions during *Civil War* continue the slippery slope towards villainy. There are the traditional tropes, such as using subterfuge to lay a trap for the heroes, creating an evil clone, and teaming up with other supervillains. As part of the SHRA, villains who register could also work for the government. The newest incarnation of a Marvel superhero team called the Thunderbolts, now comprised of murderers and psychopaths, had chips implanted in their heads to prevent them from becoming too violent (Millar, #4, 31). Captain America briefly considered an alliance with villains, but was stopped by the Punisher (who is generally considered an anti-hero) (Millar, #6, 16).

Tony's and the pro-registration side's questionable actions extended to the denial of civil liberties. Unregistered heroes are treated as enemy combatants, despite war not actually being declared. Those arrested are sent to Number 42, a secret prison in the Negative Zone away from the prying eyes of the media, without due process. A clear parallel to oversea detention camps such as Guantanamo Bay, Number 42 can be considered cruel and unusual punishment; not only are unregistered heroes taken off planet, but the way the Negative Zone interacts with some superpowers results in adverse physical or mental effects (Jenkins, #5, 18). Additionally, Speedball, the only New Warrior to survive Stamford, is denied legal counsel and tortured during his interrogation (Jenkins, #2, 16–19).

One of the more shocking turns of events in the series was when Spider-Man unmasked himself on national television. Secret identities have been a trope of the superhero since their inception and few have guarded theirs as closely as Peter Parker. Villains have often tried to discover the identity behind the mask in order to threaten a hero's loved ones or personal life. While Spider-Man's, as well as Iron Man's, unmasking adds a level of transparency to the SHRA, there is a disturbing undercurrent to the proceedings. Matthew J. Costello, noting that the United States has lacked a national consensus after the Cold War, states: "Without a common language of progress and virtue, only individualism remained as an American value to be asserted" (228). Individualism leads to the cult of celebrity, which, with its inherent narcissism, now ties America together rather than the pursuit of virtue or progress. By pushing for Spider-Man to unmask, Tony is guilty of the same hubris as the New Warriors in filming a reality show.

Even though Stark imitates the tropes of the supervillain, that does not necessarily make him villainous. Peter Coogan, in *Superheroes: The Secret Origin of a Genre*, defines the supervillain as having "a selfish, anti-social mission. The supervillain seeks something—typically wealth or power, but often fame or infamy in addition—that will serve his interests and not those of others or the larger culture. He works at cross purposes to contemporary society" (77). Also, while a hero embodies the values and morals of a culture, a villain represents an inversion of those values (61). In *Superheroes: A Modern Mythology*, Richard Reynolds sees the villain as particularly inverting a hero's devotion to justice and moral loyalty to the state, even though he is above the letter of the law (16).

Tony Stark is not on a selfish, anti-social mission. He is acting for the greater good by enforcing the law at great personal sacrifice. This is only at cross purposes with the will of society to the extent that society itself is divided on the best course of action. As such, Iron Man continues to embody the values and morals of at least part of the culture. Miriam Sharpe, the mother of one of the children killed at Stamford who led the push for the SHRA, thanks Stark for his efforts saying, "I hate how much it's cost you personally. I never would have asked if I'd known your lives would get torn apart like this." To which Tony responds, "We knew what we were taking on, Miriam. There's no shame in making enemies if it means making people safer" (Millar, #6, 21).

Tony was clearly not motivated by evil. Then why did so many of his actions seem so? Because, as philosopher Mark D. White points out, Stark is a utilitarian, which means that the action that creates the most good compared to bad is the most ethical; in other words, the ends justify the means (White, "Superhuman Ethics..." 7, 9). Principles can then be sacrificed to achieve the best solution. "It was the right thing to do!" Tony declares to Captain America's corpse, "And— and—and I was willing to get in bed with people I despise to get this done" (Bendis 17).

Some fans felt that this portrayal of Iron Man was out of character. Tom Breevort responded: "Tony Stark has fairly consistently been portrayed as a guy who will do whatever he thinks is necessary when he believes himself to be right. This goes back at least as far as the "Armor War" story in the '80s..." (Mangels 116). In fact, when the mini-series was first being planned, it was thought that Captain America would be the one to support registration and the government and that Iron Man would be the maverick rebel, but it was decided this ultimately didn't fit their characters (Mangels 118).

Tony was willing to compromise his values because he was in a unique position to understand all sides of the issue. As one of the few heroes who does not possess innate superpowers, he is able to see both the human and the super perspectives. He also personally understands that superheroes make mistakes (White, "Did Iron Man..." 29). Referencing the "Demon in a Bottle" storyline when he became an alcoholic, Tony explains, "You know how dangerous a drunk is behind the wheel of a car? Imagine one piloting the world's most sophisticated battle armor" (Gage 20). Being more realistic, Iron Man must choose to prepare for the worst (White, "Did Iron Man..." 69).

"But I knew that I would be put in the position of taking charge of this side of things. Because if not me, who? Who else was there? No one. So I sucked it up. I did what you [Captain America] do. I committed" (Bendis 16). Despite his good intentions, there is a credibility gap between Iron Man's motivations and actions during *Civil War* because he violated the implicit social contract of the superhero with society.

In *The Myth of the American Superhero*, John Shelton Lawrence and Robert Jewett establish a type of this social contract in the form of the American monomyth:

> A community in a harmonious paradise is threatened by evil; normal institutions fail to contend with this threat; a selfless superhero emerges to renounce temptations and carry out the redemptive task; aided by fate, his decisive victory restores the community to its paradisiacal condition; the superhero then recedes into obscurity [6].

In this case, the hero exists to protect American utopianism (Reynolds 83). However, this ideal always exists in a mythic past and society is striving to recreate something that never actually existed.

Richard Reynolds puts forth slightly different idea of the social contract:

> A key ideological myth of the superhero comic is that the normal and everyday enshrines positive values that must be defended through heroic action—

and defended over and over again almost without respite [...] The normal is valuable and constantly under attack, which means almost by definition the superhero is battling on behalf of the status quo [77].

There is a tension between these two concepts—in one the superhero seeks to recreate the past and in the other he protects the present. However, in both the hero is reacting to a threat. "Something has to happen—the status quo needs to be threatened—before a superhero can jump into action" (Bogaerts 163).

If the hero is responsible for maintaining the status quo, then it is the villain who is concerned with change (Reynolds 51). In *Civil War*, Iron Man is an active agent of change. He is no longer there just to protect, but to reform (Fingeroth 161). And when a superhero becomes proactive, it can set him on a trajectory towards villainy. Peter Coogan observed: "The problem for the creator is that the proactive superhero runs into the trap of most [science fiction] supermen: he risks becoming a ruler, savior, or destroyer, essentially a villain in the first and last role" (114).

It may seem like Stark is being proactive, but he is actually still reacting. While most heroes react to the present, Iron Man reacts to future circumstances (Spanakos 139). "I've told you—this is what I do. I'm an inventor. I can envision the future [...] I knew there would be a war of heroes. I knew it" (Bendis 10). Because of this insight, Tony saw that the best solution, the one that would cost the least number of lives, was registration.

One aspect of this type of social contract is that the superhero only acts when the status quo is threatened or the paradisiacal condition is fallen. This can only occur when traditional institutions fail to protect society. Superhero stories tend to rise in popularity during times uncertainty or mistrust of governing bodies. By the time *Civil War* was published, U.S. citizens' trust in their government was plummeting. While the majority of Americans had initially supported the war in Iraq, by 2007 it was opposed by sixty-seven percent. And the lack of evidence for weapons of mass destruction led fifty-four percent to believe that the war was not morally justified (Costello 229). Additionally, the government itself was split by increasing partisanship.

During such crises, the superhero emerges as a selfless savior, embodying a refined form of societal values. Even though they do not act within the letter of the law, these heroes are often guided by a moral code more stringent than that of the legal system. (Costello 221). A culture allows the hero to function outside the law because the hero's ethics are agreed upon as correct by and beneficial to society. However, when there is no consensus on a set of values, then any assertion of a higher moral duty is looked on with suspicion (Costello 238). Heroes must then either move "up" into formal participation with the governance of society or "down" and out of superheroics (Coogan 216).

But, as Captain America asserts, "Super heroes need to stay above that stuff [politics] or Washington starts telling us who the super-villains are" (Millar, #1, 30). By registering and becoming super powered police officers, Iron Man and others sacrifice their moral autonomy, rendering heroism impossible (Costello 236–7). Captain America and the anti-registration side act heroically by maintaining their moral compass, especially as it alienates them and puts them in conflict with society (Donovan and Richardson 198). As Cap tells Iron Man between his arrest and assassination, "We maintained the principles we swore to defend and protect. You sold your principles. You lost before it started" (Bendis 30).

Tom Breevort notes: "It's always easier to write a story where your guy is pushing against the omnipresent evil oppressive government than it is to push for your guy out there following what amounts to the rule of law in an unpopular situation" (Mangels 118). But, by violating the superhero's social contract, Tony Stark becomes an increasingly ambiguous and morally uncertain character. He has compromised his own principles and can no longer be guided by them, but by the dictates of the government. He also becomes the director of SHIELD, making him the moral compass for the licensed superhuman community. Instead of being a hero or a villain, he can be read as neither.

On writing the series, Mark Millar stated: "I am hesitant to make anyone the underdog because that immediately makes the reader sympathize with them more than the other guy" (Richards). However, as the pro-registration camp has the financial and military backing of the U.S. government, it automatically casts the anti-registration side as an underdog. Tony admits, "I knew the world favors the underdog and that I would be the bad guy" (Bendis 17). At the very least, that appears to be how readers interpreted events.

This is key; it was the readers, the fans, who interpreted Tony Stark as the villain of *Civil War*. In the Marvel universe, Iron Man was primarily viewed as a hero and being granted a position of power as director of SHIELD was a reward. But the social contract is also a contract with the reader which establishes expectations of how a superhero should act. In order to understand why Stark deviated from this norm, it is necessary to examine the creator's intentions.

On creating the mini-series, Mark Millar stated: "I think the reason the story came about is, obviously, you know, any writer writes about what influences them. And for some guys that might be old comics or it might be old movies or whatever. But for me, generally, it's the world I live in" (Millar Podcast).

In 2006, the world that Millar and readers lived in was one dominated by a culture of fear. After 9/11 and a subsequent anthrax scare, some viewed terrorism as an external threat against which national consensus could be defined. But terrorist groups also lack a consensus ideology and unified identity. Without that stable external Other, instead of bringing the U.S. together as a nation, society became more divided and fractured. In addition to an unpopular war in Iraq and Afghanistan, which had no clear goal, controversial programs such as the Guantanamo Bay prison, a domestic surveillance program, and the Patriot Act fostered a mistrust of the government.

This was the world Millar and McNiven reflected in *Civil War*. Unregistered heroes, like Captain America, become terrorists and Iron Man and the registered heroes represent an untrustworthy government with the SHRA as controversial legislation. However, the SHRA is only controversial for the reader; in the Marvel Universe, it was popularly accepted and Tony Stark was a hero. A friction exists between fiction and reality.

Superhero stories are a powerful fantasy of wish-fulfillment (Fingeroth 60). They are a form of escapism which allows the reader the vicarious experience of empowerment. While such stories may be read as a reflection of the contemporary society (as the other essays in this volume attest), this is often accomplished through metaphor requiring a close reading.

Editor Tom Breevort stated:

> It's the difference between, sort of, the fantasy world of the Marvel Universe and the real world approach that, you know, I live with just living in the world. So it's really a case where, in *Civil War*, you know, we examine that dichotomy and play with it without, sort of, knocking the pins out from under it, the fantasy element of the guy and his secret self putting on a mask [Millar podcast].

By emphasizing the tension between fantasy and reality, *Civil War* moves away from being a closed narrative towards becoming a cultural commentary (Costello 229). This confrontation with reality can challenge preconceived notions of what a superhero story should be and creates a discomfort in the reader.

Tony Stark receives the lion share of the blame for this discomfort because, as evidenced above, he is changing the traditional idea of what a superhero is. Two of the superhero's most important traits are the ability to change over time and to always serve as a symbol of American values. A failure to transform risks the character becoming irrelevant and forgotten (Johnson, "This Isn't..." 199, 205). *Civil War* put these two traits into conflict: Cap as a symbol of traditional American values and Iron Man as the ability to change. Because he is creating change, Iron Man comes to represent an unknown future and uncertainty, while Captain America presents a comforting image of stability. It's no wonder that readers tended to side with Cap.

However, this challenge to the idea of the superhero was necessary. Heroes often function as a metaphor for reality. But when a paradigm shift occurs, such as 9/11, society and culture become uncertain and the previous metaphors lose their meaning. Robert Wilonsky perceptively noted: "In a post–Sept. 11 world, even the phrase, 'Look, up in the sky! It's a bird! It's a plane!' sounds different; its awe has been replaced by shock and revulsion. The sense of escapism comic books provided no longer exists; the fantasy world must give way to the real one" (qtd. in Wright 288–9).

Fantasy does not necessarily have to give way to the real world; it just takes time to create new metaphors. Breevort explained the new reality:

> …if there were guys running around Manhattan who could knock down buildings with a beam from their hands, and then on top of that they were masked—nobody knew who they were or what they represented, nobody had any oversight or control over them … I would be petrified if I lived in a Manhattan like that, and you'd bet I'd want to know that there was some oversight on them. (Mangels 118)

Civil War was an attempt to find a new role for the superhero in the twenty-first century as represented by Tony Stark.

Given the support for Captain America's side, as well as the boom of superhero movies that occurred following 2008's *Iron Man*, there appears to have been a backlash against this new metaphor and a turn to nostalgia for the traditional role of the superhero. More likely, rather than the paradigm shift that Iron Man was promoting, there has been a process of synthesis between the two poles of tradition and change. This may be evidenced by Bucky Barnes, a more complicated and tragic character who took up the mantle of Captain America after the assassination of Steve Rogers.

Wars tend to be viewed in monolithic terms of good versus evil. It is easy to interpret Captain America as the hero and Iron Man as the villain in *Civil War*. However, the mini-series shows that the issues are more complicated. Millar admitted: "Because, even now, the series is almost concluded for me and I still don't know who's right because they are both right and they are both wrong" (Millar podcast).

"It wasn't worth it," Tony Stark admits to the body of his friend, Captain America, after *Civil War* is over (Bendis 18–9). While his motivations may have been heroic, his actions were not. Iron Man sacrificed his moral principles in order to create a secure America, rather than a free one. In doing so, he challenged the traditional idea of the superhero and confronted the reader with the friction between fantasy and reality. All this made Tony Stark the villain of *Civil War*. But this was necessary in order to initiate a re-evaluation of the role of the superhero in society in the twenty-first century. Besides, characters often become more heroic by redeeming themselves after a fall from grace.

NOTES

1. The number for this specific poll was 82.46 percent to 17.54 percent. Though hardly scientific, an internet search for "Marvel Civil War Poll" immediately brings up a half-dozen different website polls, all siding with Captain America by a majority. Such a search is now complicated by the recent announcement of Marvel Studios' *Captain America: Civil War* film.

WORKS CITED

Bendis, Brian Michael (w) and Alex Maleev (a). *Civil War: The Confession* #1 (May 2007). New York: Marvel Comics.

Bogaerts, Arno. "The Avengers and S.H.I.E.L.D.: The Problem with Proactive Super-heroics." In *Avengers and Philosophy: Earth's Mightiest Thinkers*, edited by Mark D. White. Hoboken: John Wiley & Sons, Inc., 2012.

Coogan, Peter. *Superheroes: The Secret Origin of a Genre*. Austin: Monkeybrain Books, 2006.

Costello, Matthew J. *Secret Identity Crisis: Comic Books and the Unmasking of Cold War America*. New York: Continuum, 2009.

Donovan, Sarah K. and Nicholas P. Richardson. "Does Tony Stark Use a Moral Compass?" In*Iron Man and Philosophy: Facing the Stark Reality*, edited by Mark D. White. Hoboken: John Wiley & Sons, Inc., 2010.

Fingeroth, Danny. *Superman on the Couch: What Superheroes Really Tell Us about Ourselves and Our Society*. New York: Continuum, 2006.

Gage, Christos (w) and Jeremy Haun (p). "Rubicon." *Iron Man/Captain America: Casualties of War* #1 (Feb. 2007). New York: Marvel Comics.

Jenkins, Paul (w) and Ramon Bachs (p). "Embedded Part One." In *Civil War: Frontline* #1(Aug. 2006). New York: Marvel Comics.

Jenkins, Paul (w) and Ramon Bachs (p) and Steve Lieber. "The Accused Part Two." in *Civil War: Frontline* #2 (Aug. 2006). New York: Marvel Comics.

_____. "The Accused Part Five." In *Civil War: Frontline* #5 (Oct. 2006). New York: Marvel Comics.

Johnson, Jeffrey K. *Super-History: Comic Book Superheroes and American Society, 1938 to the Present*. Jefferson: McFarland, 2012.

_____. "This Isn't Your Grandfather's Comic Book Universe: The Return of the Golden Age Superman." In *The Ages of Superman: Essays on the Man of Steel in Changing Times*, edited by Joseph J. Darowski. Jefferson: McFarland,2012.

Lawrence, John Shelton and Robert Jewett. *The Myth of the American Superhero*. GrandRapids: William B. Eerdmans Publishing Company, 2002.

Mangels, Andy. *Iron Man: Beneath the Armor*. New York: Del Rey, 2013.

Millar, Mark (w) and Steve McNiven (p). *Civil War* # 1 (July 2006). New York: Marvel Comics.

_____. *Civil War* #2 (Aug. 2006). New York: Marvel Comics.

_____. *Civil War* #3 (Sept. 2006). New York: Marvel Comics.

_____. *Civil War* #4 (Oct. 2006). New York: Marvel Comics.

_____. *Civil War* #6 (Dec. 2006). New York: Marvel Comics.

_____. *Civil War* #7 (Jan. 2007). New York: Marvel Comics.

Millar, Mark and Tom Breevort. *Civil War Podcast.* Marvel.com. Accessed 12 Nov. 2014 at http://marvel.com/rss/podcasts/Civil_War_Podcast.mp3.

Reynolds, Richard. *Superheroes: A Modern Mythology.* Jackson: University of Mississippi Press, 1992.

Richards, Dave. "Our Marvels at War: Millar Talks *Civil War.*" *Comic Book Resources.* Accessed 14 Nov. 2014 at http://www.comicbookresources.com/?page=article&old=1&id=7088.

Spanakos, Tony. "Tony Stark: Philosopher King of the Future?" In *Iron Man and Philosophy: Facing the Stark Reality*, edited by Mark D. White. Hoboken: John Wiley & Sons, Inc., 2010.

White, Mark D. "Did Iron Man Kill Captain America?" In *Iron Man and Philosophy: Facing the Stark Reality*, edited by Mark D. White. Hoboken: John Wiley & Sons, Inc., 2010.

_____. "Superhuman Ethics Class with the Avengers Prime." In *Avengers and Philosophy: Earth's Mightiest Thinkers*, edited by Mark D. White. Hoboken: John Wiley & Sons, Inc., 2012.

"Whose Side Were You On? Marvel Civil War Forum" *Comic Book Resources.* Accessed 12 Nov. 2014 at http://community.comicbookresources.com/showthread.php?12760-Whose-Side-Were-You-On-Marvel-Civil-War.

Wright, Bradford W. *Comic Book Nation: The Transformation of Youth Culture in America.* Baltimore: Johns Hopkins University Press, 2001.

Feminizing the Iron
Tony Stark's Rescue

Jason Michálek

From its most elemental level to the abstractly symbolic, iron is an important aspect of human existence on Earth. Iron is not only a common element in the nature of Earth's crust, it is also involved in the processes of the body's hemoglobin and has been utilized in its metallic forms in the construction of early civilizations. More symbolically, the planet of Mars—the surface of which gets its reddish color from oxidized iron—lends its planetary symbol to the Greek representation of man, and thus the cultural significance of iron is rooted in history. But much like the composition of Mars, the depth of *man* is colored differently beneath the exterior.

Tony Stark, who also cast himself into Martian symbolism with the Greek god of war, constructed his iron exterior when he found himself in the middle of his own belligerence. Facing this situation—of Tony's creations threatening his own life—is one of the major themes that connect the modern trade, *The Invincible Iron Man*, debuting a new style of suit in the Mark 1616 that offers to change the face and history of Stark Industries and its employees. Along with the decline of Tony's empire, the erasure of his mind and the constant shifts in and out of this world, the series fills the iron with an often marginalized operator that offers to change the face of the company and the man behind it all: woman.

This essay will investigate the role of the feminine in the current era of *Iron Man* by identifying the roles of women throughout *The Invincible Iron Man*, exemplifying the features of Tony Stark's character that could be considered traditionally feminine, and exploring the interaction of Tony with women, both static and dynamic. This analysis of Iron Man comics will serve as a form for the relationship between the masculine and the feminine in the modern age of America and the structural framework that supports this progression. The intent is to evidence the multi-faceted culture that America has become and how it is reflected in one of its popular secular myths from Earth–616.

For the purpose of this analysis, the presence of the *content* in the comics should precede the conclusions drawn from scholastic application. The modern age of comics—and indeed, of academics—is very much a plural ethos. While I incorporate different schools of gender theory applicable to the narrative in the comics, the intent is to draw out essences of parallel between that narrative and American culture. Thus, authorial choice of theory should not dictate or limit the possibilities of analysis. However, the primary sources of (post-)structural theory are derived from translated readings of Jacques Derrida and Michel Foucault, and Feminist Critical Discourse Analyses are primarily from the intersectional work *Gender Trouble* by Judith Butler—scholarly work that has been popularized in the current era.

Beneath the Iron Wool

> I went from being a man trapped in an iron suit to a man freed by it.
> —Ellis, "Extremis (Part I)"

Tony Stark and the idea of Iron Man were born during the Cold War, in which America's weapons were quickly becoming a threat to their creators as well as the entire world. But the lineage of the empire of America, as well as the Stark empire, precedes the modern era. Just as America had to build a political defense against its own nuclear weapons, Tony encased himself in the shell of his own creation to hold in his strength, his masculinity, and perhaps his misogyny. Through the emergence and collapse of Extremis to the registration and identification of superheroes culminating during *Civil War*, ideas of identity performance are brought to the forefront of this comic narrative. From his very name, and his continual utterance of "I am Iron Man," readers can safely presume at least these things below the surface: (1) that Tony represents the traditions of American masculinity, (2) that his strength derives from what he is, as a *man* fortified with iron, and his creations are secondary and (3) that nobody else can fill his suit quite like he can.

From its beginning, the storyline titled *Extremis* rehashes the concept of Tony Stark *being* Iron Man while shifts are made in Stark Industries and in the Marvel universe that challenge the presumptions of what that means.

The series opens with the technology of Extremis injected into an unknown civilian while Tony—questioned by investigative documentarian John Pillinger—himself questions intentions and application of Stark technology. The contrast to his uncertainty doesn't arrive until two issues later—when Stark sees his reflection in a computer screen behind the Iron Man structure as a man enhanced by the essence of his technology—as he finally accepts himself: "Oh *now* you can look at me?" (Ellis, "Extremis [Part III]").

The screen identity of the suit is as essential to Tony's perception of himself as Iron Man as it is to his readers.[1] Throughout comic book and literary history, masks have served the dual function of hiding a hero's primary identity and creating a super-identity that empowers the individual to become. While Tony is conflicted when asked to account for *what* Iron Man is—in all his functions, no matter how shameful—he certainly is confident when acknowledging *who* Iron Man is, because Iron Man seems to be greater than Tony Stark. This reverence is due, in part, to the idea that it is simpler to account for what he has created that is tangible than to inspect the elements of *himself* that are also his creation—because it is easier to accept or reject the superficial than the authentic.

The preference for the mask over the man is displayed not only by Tony, but also by the culture surrounding him. While protesters reproach Stark for his résumé of evil, they also revere the presence of Iron Man—who is the screened version of Tony Stark—as he basks in the glory of their admiration (Ellis, "Extremis (Part II)"). This presentation of superiority is not only negligent of inner truth: it also fails to account for the maintenance and reproduction of the super itself; the plurality of personas; a genuine or authentic identity; and the cause, effects, and centers of their (re-)creation. As Stark flies away from the island he claims used to be "the most fabulous place in the world," he abandons not only the history of his home but also the present responsibility of confronting the retributions of his presence (Fraction, "The Five Nightmares, Part 1").

At the molten heart of the iron, Tony Stark is a man: another recreational mask that presents its own functions beneath the wool of the hero. The suits protect his physical form from the limitations of his biological nature, but they also stop him from being *exposed* to the world, and vice versa. Though his suits may adapt and react to their environments in programmable ways, it is essential to see them as an extension of the operator behind the mechanics, and that readers are also subject to this integration.[2] Thus origin stories of the archetypical[3] suit are as much a search for the genealogical connections of the present (iron) *man* to his creations and operations as they are for our own interactions with such a masquerade.[4]

The Man Behind the Mask

He's a biological combat machine ... and I'm just a man in an iron suit.—Ellis, "Extremis (Part IV)"

While Tony's analyses of himself are more pleasing to him than his unadulterated likeness when he reflects upon his identity in the image of the mask, the suits of armor that Stark creates can speak no less of the identities he personifies than his performative utterance, "I am Iron Man." Thus when his contributions to the world are attacked by John Pillinger with the notion that Stark's company capitalizes on belligerence, it appears only natural for him to retreat to the suit to consider the utilities of his creation from within. But the story reveals Iron Man to be merely another layer of Tony as he explores who he has been as a man from the safety and guise of the suit.

Later, his naturalization of the essential core and control of Iron Man—through the integration of Extremis with his body—evidences the problem of such an anchored identity. By assimilating the core element of Iron Man into a part of his physical and mental self that is less fluid—no matter how liquid the semiotic depictions of the art may suggest—Tony binds the identity of the suit with his *being*. Though the suit is quick to congeal upon Tony's body when needed—controlled through his brain "like it was another limb" (Ellis, "Extremis [Part V]")—its presentation is still a superficial covering of who he really is. Tony, as the man behind the mask, is a metamorphic being that envelops and develops the world around him; the suit becomes just another aspect of his malleable biology.

While "man" is an important linguistic label to the performative identity of Tony Stark, Iron Man becomes both a linguistic and physical element that Stark semiotically fuses with himself in both physical presence and superimposition. Tony asserts his position as the heart and mind of Stark Industries—and at the literal helm of the suit—but Extremis lets readers envision how essential Iron Man has become to Stark. Just as manliness is summoned as a product of hegemonic masculinity, Iron Man becomes summoned through Tony's egocentric control to project a façade of strength, superiority, and protection from the core of his own *human* being. As the inner layer of his suit becomes incorporated into the flesh of his body, it becomes easier for him to paradoxically ignore his internalized connection with the suit as well as to summon the proof that he is Iron Man. The choice between these distinctions falls upon his willingness to acknowledge or admit either.

When he finally fights Mallen, Tony is forced to face the mask-less equivalent of his *extreme* equal. As Tony verbally rejects the parallels of destructive belligerence drawn between them, he attempts to erase this reality by physically killing his opponent and what he represents: "You're my nightmare: the version of me that couldn't see the future" (Ellis, "Extremis (Part VI)"). As Mallen is destroyed by Stark, it provides Tony with immediate and overt renunciation of his old, destructive ways. But with the close of the issue and final restitution, Stark must reprimand Maya Hansen for creating belligerence by her sale of Extremis to terrorists. In accounting for the events that caused havoc with Extremis, he must face her accusation of his self-asserted impunity when she claims, "You're no better than me." As he turns to the readers for absolution, though, it is unclear upon which aspect of her identity this distinction falls when he asserts, "But I'm trying to be." The irony—that what he verbally rejects and what he enacts do not match up—is left to the readers to sort out (Ellis, "Extremis [Part VI]").

The Metaphysical Bond

> I am in absolutely no pain. I can hear better than ever, I feel *stronger* than I ever have in my life, and I'm totally mobile again. / I'm a walking, talking, billion-dollar miracle, Tony.
> —Fraction, "The Five Nightmares (Part 4)"

Returning to the idea of Iron Man as a suit of self-protection and preservation, *The Five Nightmares* opens with Tony revealing five insecurities to the reader. Among concerns about alcoholism and his technology becoming too cheap and reproducible, these nightmares include Tony's fear that someone else will pilot the suit, Iron Man will become disposable, and the disposability won't be his own doing (Fraction, "The Five Nightmares [Part 1]"). On a larger scale, these apprehensions would exemplify insecurities of postcolonial imperialism—which was certainly reflected in his resistance to appoint a CEO for Stark Industries other than himself (Ellis, "Extremis [Part II]"). But as an egocentric individual, these fears represent the loss of personal power; of being dominated; and of being less of an iron *man*.

Although Stark's nightmares are reasonable feelings that echo the current wave of the male identity crisis in America said to have spawned in the 1980s,[5] readers soon learn that the ubiquity he fears also comes standard with technology in the age of information. Through a new terrorist threat that becomes a reality with a narrative of suicide bombings, Tony must face the enemy of an all-too-familiar patrilineage in the blood of Ezekiel Stane. This familial opposition serves a dual function of retribution for Stark's patricide and as a historical reminder of the stain of his sins from the past—a pun that borders on camp.

Tony comes close to recognizing this horror in the gripping handshake of his opponent while caught in the bombing of the Starkdynamics Tower in

Taiwan. Moments after Stane reveals himself to Tony, he is caught in the devastation as his technology is used against him in a sort of self-destruction. In addition to the demolition of the physical structure of his company building, the blast also threatens the life of Tony's valued assistant, Pepper Potts, as rubble from the tower falls around her. When he pulls her from the wreckage, badly hurt and barely alive, Stane's smiling face is the image of successful domestic terrorism. In the melodramatic fashion that echoes post–9/11 warfare,[6] Tony is tasked with saving the woman dearest to him while watching his fears materialize.

But when Tony considers the recovery of Pepper Potts, it leads him to relinquish a part of his past and share his likeness with her—not through destruction but, rather radically, construction. In the operating room, Tony finds Pepper in the same predicament that he was in with shrapnel threatening her heart. While the implementation of a repulsor would materialize the distributed connection of an intimate center with Potts, he doesn't hesitate to integrate the repulsor technology with the woman he cares for the most, cautioning only: "We'll have to make *you* like *me*, Pep… / Like I *used* to be, back in the day" (Fraction, "The Five Nightmares [Part 3]"). The hesitation in this caveat is not the fear of sharing himself with her, as Tony has had little reason to hold himself back from women. Instead, Stark fears turning Pepper into what he was for concern that she may become what he *is*, thus placing her under equal danger.

Pepper's hesitation doesn't subtly reflect Tony's fears of the dangers inherent in his technology: she acknowledges them overtly as his subordination of her. Her regard of his phallic appropriation is even less subtle when she talks to Tony about the Repulsor tech: "Tony, I don't want this weapon of yours inside of me" and "Take it out." But his justification of its use to Maria Hill is equally personal as he defends Pepper's entitlement and his intentions as his own. When he reveals to Pepper that her repulsor is not weaponized, she becomes elated and keeps her enhancement—a decision that will expand the function and identity of Stark Industries (Fraction, "The Five Nightmares [Part 4]").

The series ends with Tony ruminating on the events that have passed, showing his human reflection in the window as that of the Iron Man suit, and readers see the multi*faceted* image of Tony's reality. As he reveals a sixth nightmare, Stark recognizes the construction of gender as he recounts the significance of the issues: "[Stane has] shown me what kind of man I have to become— / —what kind of things I have to do— / —to keep my nightmares from coming true" (Fraction, "World's Most Wanted [Part 1]"). Tony's admission of this new fear—one that is necessary to face—acknowledges at least two things: (1) that "man" is not simply a solid attribute of identity, but a process and/or performance, and (2) that a certain spectral plurality exists in the roles of what things must be done in order to become.

This idea—of *becoming* a man—is slightly expanded in an epilogue with Peter Parker. The reader is shown that the "kind of things" Tony has to do are enforcing the dominant order by seizing the paraphernalia of a black market dealer, and trying to convince Spider-Man to register his identity for the safety and order of all. But in his final pose, Tony himself is remarkably torn, as Spider-Man observes, "He was *confident*. Always. And now... // Now he doesn't even look like he knows what day it is. / I've never, ever seen him so... / so *unsure*" (Fraction, "World's Most Wanted [Part 1]"). As Tony sits amidst de(con)struction, readers can anticipate a paradigm shift in whatever he "[has] to do" and what this will make him *become* (Fraction, "World's Most Wanted [Part 1]").

A Room of One's Own[7] (The Rescue Suit)

I'll be nobody's weapon.—Ellis, "Extremis (Part IV)"

When Tony clears space in his company for people to become more, he creates room for others to gain power. While Maria Hill was regarded as a burden towards the end of *The Five Nightmares*, she opens *World's Most Wanted* with a narrative of loss and resilience as the now *former* Deputy Director of S.H.I.E.L.D: "This is the way the end of the world begins: / With Maria Hill standing over her desk" (Fraction, "World's Most Wanted [Part I]"). As her history is recounted as a death of the mother and rebuke of the father, Hill asserts her independence to distinguish between "guys like Walsh" that are unpleasant and "guys like Tony Stark" that are pleasant. Even while her asserted control is repeatedly given and taken away, Hill's strength is in her recovery of herself (Fraction, "World's Most Wanted [Part III]").

Similarly, Pepper Potts—once only a secretary, now "you don't get to call her a *secretary* again,"—becomes a new representative archetype of a woman with power (Fraction, "The Five Nightmares [Part 4]"). As Tony upgrades her suit and engages in banter with her about being a "dream girl," it is unclear whether he is sincere in his regard for her. But when he makes Pepper the C.E.O. of Stark Industries after having shrugged off the suggestion that he needed to let someone help him "to make the world a better place" (Ellis, "Extremis [Part II]"), it reflects not only his regard for her as an object of desire, but also a person of agency equally capable or sufficient for the role of a Chief Executive Officer as he was. Thus Stark's first act of empowering Pepper is not only an endowment of ability but also a release and transfer of control from the patriarch to the feminine. His second act is to give her a suit of her own desires and room of her own with which to use it while he instructs Maria Hill to destroy the other Iron Man suits he had created (Fraction, "World's Most Wanted [Part III]"). The juxtaposition of these gestures can be read as a re-appropriation of the masculine to the feminine or the blurring of both at the intentional restructuring and command of Tony Stark.

The gesture of releasing power to the feminine is not only embodied with Tony's appointments of Pepper, but also interiorized by his erasure of his structuralized mind with reliance on others—primarily Pepper Potts and Maria Hill in place of a traditional male doctor or engineer. Tony's choice not to disestablish and re-establish his patriarchal grasp on his company reflects a rejection of the traditional, hegemonic masculinity. Instead, Tony utilizes what is considered traditionally feminine—collaboration and nurturing—to become more than the prescript of "man." In essence, his erasure of self and tradition is a space-clearing mechanism that allows him to explore the desires of his own mind without relying on pre-established genealogy. This choice rejects a world that would seek to imperialize him—namely through Norman Osborn's desire for Tony's relinquished power—while creating a world beyond the modern.

While Stark's actions and intentions may be progressive, it is crucial to acknowledge the flaws and dangers in a deconstructed world. Juxtaposed with American disillusionment, distrust, and disunity, events through *World's Most Wanted* do evidence dangers of a progressive world, too, namely: the technologic control of an open-sourced systems and drone warfare; the disordered mental state of Tony's disillusioned mind; preference for the superficial over the genuine and the obscuring of history in the mask of Madame Masque; and lack of concrete systems of order upon which to rely.

However, these elements all exist, regardless of a progressive world from which they are seen, and they are merely amplified by the hostile state of deconstruction. It is equally valuable to admit that the freedom and transparency of information of what is already present allows the revision and reconstruction of flawed systems as well. Therefore, [R/r]escue is a natural response to the recognition of signification, and symbolically represents the element necessary to be salvaged from a post-modern, disillusioned world.

Stark's Rescue

Lady ... uh...Iron Man is.—Fraction, "Stark Resilient, Part 8"

To understand the significance of Tony's *creation* of other masks of armor, one must observe the manner in which masks create identity. In Joan

Riviere's analysis of "womanliness" and gender identities, the idea arises of gender performance as a mask that hides one identity within another in an attempt to create something else—something more desirable. While Riviere is referring primarily to sexuality, socialization, and order, perhaps one of her most important sentiments reflects upon the plurality of the masquerade: "My suggestion is not, however, that there is any such difference [between identity and the masquerade]; whether radical or superficial, they are the same thing" (Riviere 131). The implication of conjoining identity with its mask (or masque) does more than blend or blur the lines of difference in the roles of individuals: it also creates a consolidation of multifaceted identity into the performance of an individual.

The effect of identity performance throughout *The Invincible Iron Man* represents a depth of character(s) that has become commonplace in the academics of American society and reaches into popular culture. In Tony's persona, this has always been evident: his anxiety over the loss of the Iron Man identity (Fraction, "The Five Nightmares [Part 1]"); Obadiah Stane's denial of Stark's lineage and Tony's self-destruction (Fraction, "The Five Nightmares [Part 3]"); his self-labeling of "normal" (Fraction, "Counting Up..."); and the performative labeling of being "divide and conquer" instead of "falling apart" (Fraction, "Digging..."). But the progressive difference of this trade of comics—one that combats the critiques of misogyny launched against representation of the feminine across the spectrum of art and comics—is the amount of dynamic evidence of resilient female characters: Maria Hill's recovery from her past, torture, and rape, and her collaboration with other females; the operation of advanced technology by Pepper Potts and the increase of functioning her suit provides; and the female solidarity of Potts and Hill when they realize that Tony seduced them both (Fraction, "Ghost..."). In addition to the presence of female protagonists, the struggles of female antagonists—such as the H.A.M.M.E.R. girls and Madame Masque—also provide deeper female characters without merely demonizing them or making them objects of sexual desire and promiscuity.

While immoral and sexual actions are present in female characters—both pro- and antagonistic—these traits are similarly performed by male protagonists. Additionally, the failure of male characters is repeatedly highlighted by either female characters, male counterparts, the perpetrators themselves, or the narrative frame, and thus the human elements of traditional masculinity are brought to the attention of the reader. Most importantly, in Tony's most vulnerable state, he relies upon Pepper Potts and the core elements of Mark 1616 to rescue him by integrating with his body what was once inside Pepper *before* he needs his male friends (Fraction, "Digging"). If reliance on others, asking for help, and relinquishing his industrial, intellectual, and physical power weren't progressive enough, integrating pieces of a suit intended for a female operator with his body to save his life must provide symbolism of restructuring the patriarch with elements that the past would rebuke as inferior. Whatever is created as a result of this incorporation is secondary to its depiction and shouldn't be compared to any process Stark engages in to become.

In contrast with creating a new order, the importance of releasing elements of the past are vital to allow the new system to function. Though Tony's past is notably peppered with misogyny, belligerence, negligence, and other deplorable acts, neither continuity of those acts themselves nor the reverence of their past realities will compromise his virtuous regulation of the future. Instead of seeking an *origin* like these of gender, order, culture, and virtue, Jacques Derrida reformulated the concepts of Claude Lévi-Strauss to position new structures like this as original: "…the appearance of a new structure … always comes about … by a rupture with its past, its origin, and its cause. Therefore one can describe what is peculiar to the structural organization only by not taking into account … its past conditions…" (291). This regulation of new systems does not seek to forgive or even forget the conditions and problems of the past, but rather to construct a new lineage from which those elements of order that are desirable reproduce themselves by performance— one that neglects the search for a point of origin in order to create one.

Am I Iron… *Man?*

> Gender is a complexity whose totality is permanently deferred, never fully what it is at any given juncture in time. An open coalition, then, will affirm identities that are alternately instituted and relinquished according to the purposes at hand; it will be an open assemblage that permits of multiple convergences and divergences without obedience to a normative telos of definitional closure.
> —Butler, *Gender Trouble*, 16

Tony Stark, on the other side of his own (re-)construction, must account for the world around him and the elements of his identity that the world associates with him. As Tony works to recover the elements of his mind that are essential to operate in a post-world, he devises the new identity of Stark as Resilient. Through the shifts in the world, gains and losses, and assaults on his company, his friends, and himself, this identity represents the resilience of the company beyond the Tony that started it all. The strength of the iron did not rest in the immovable man that molded the initial armor to shield and protect himself from the world, but from the elemental ability of changing in changing times.

Throughout the series of *World's Most Wanted*, Tony's flight, rejection, and erasure of the elemental connection of "Iron" to "Man" to "Tony Stark" lead him to safety only by embracing an elastic identity that incorporates what we would traditionally consider as the feminine. However, a closer analysis would reveal this action, at the dynamic, to be a performance of those human aspects of existence that are productive to sustaining society and cohabitation. Though Tony may return to the image of a modern man—flawed in many of the ways the past has shown through both his character and in traditionalist American males—his noble actions of humanism cannot be removed from the narrative of gender reconstruction and resilience.

Some of Tony's final moments in the "Stark Resilient" series represent the confrontation of the old order of masculinity by a revised man. As H.A.M.M.E.R. calls off the attack on Iron Man and Tony has to face the pilot of Detroit Steel, their cooperation is clearly forced—evidenced by their side-commentary to each other and manner in which they try to dominate each other with labels. But as a contrast to the egocentrism that Tony could have enacted, his play in the image of solidarity ignores his (former) inclinations of aggression and he defers his rage into the cup of his soft drink that he crushes as he smiles for pictures (Fraction, "The Man..."). Embracing feminine aspects in his identity do not remove his inclinations to participate in the system of hegemonic masculinity, but he must continually confront its existence in such a dominating patriarchal society for "...the subversion of paternally sanctioned culture can not[sic] come from another version of culture, but only from within the repressed interior of culture itself, from the heterogeneity of drives that constitutes culture's sealed foundation" (Butler 86). Thus the new Iron Man is more eclectic and human as the traits of each camp converge within the frame of his performative identity.

The creation, incorporation, and eventual end of Mark 1616 was not a passing element of the Stark legacy, but a glimpse of possibilities behind the mask that represents it. Though the suit itself is eventually removed, its pilot has gained notoriety that cannot be forgotten—within the *Iron Man* storyline or the comic community at large. Likewise, while the specific elements of the story are constrained to the mythos of Earth–616, their representation and the characters developed therein reflect the current era of the culture from which it originates. As a representative creation of the change in roles of America, Mark 1616 and the continual advancement and empowerment of Pepper Potts reflects a changing role of feminine and female characters in the genre of comics and society.

From this era onward—in order to engage in change and truly benefit his culture—Tony Stark must be present and active in his performance of a new order. In the same way he changed his representative superidentity from within the Iron Man suit and himself from the deepest part of his mind, re-assembled Tony represents the man who was Rescued by his own creation and the woman he entrusted with it. He does not become less or more of an Iron Man by relying upon the people and mechanics around him, but they become an extension of him. His incorporation or rejection of the elements he has at his disposal reflect exactly who he is; moment to moment; to the world and to his friends; man or other. By his ingenuity he became Iron Man, but Tony Stark's strength rests in his resilient and constant commitment to his duties: constantly performing and becoming … whoever he is.

NOTES

1. The computer screen, like Freud's "screen memory," is a medium of analysis and perception. While this screen is more present and tangible than Freud's mental block, it is also more exploitable to perspective bias, and therefore no less subject to reality and veracity (Freud, "Screen Memories").

2. Scott McCloud's appropriation of Marshall McCluhan's theory shows that as Tony hides in his suit, we experience hiding in him in his suit. Therefore, we are doubly masked (McCloud, p. 38).

3. See Carl Jung's ideas of archetypes.

4. The genealogical process reflecting Michel Focoult's idea that geneology is not a linear search for origins or finite meaning, but rather connections; a "vast accumulation of source material" from which to make many meanings. The masquerade is the age of post-creation where archetypes are prescript. The return to origination throughout the *Iron Man* narratives subverts the neglect of these meanings (Foucault, p. 76–77, 94).

5. The literary prominence of the male identity crisis—with its development in the 80s, 90s, and now—is often credited to the success of American author Robert Bly's best seller from 1990. The book is titled *Iron John: A Book About Men* and it explores the tale of "Iron John" from the *Grimm's Fairy Tales* for the archetypes that frame male expectations for success and achievement.

6. See the works of Libby Anker on political melodrama.

7. The title borrowed from Virginia Woolf's notorious essay of the same title about the necessity of (equal) space for women to achieve in the way that men had been.

WORKS CITED

Butler, Judith. *Gender Trouble: Feminism and the Subversion of Identity*. New York: Routledge, 1990.

Derrida, Jacques. "Structure, Sign, and Play in the Discourse of the Human Sciences." In *Writing and Difference*. Chicago: The University of Chicago Press, 1980.

Ellis, Warren (w) and Adi Granov (a). "Extremis (Part I of VI)" *Iron Man Vol 4 #1* (Jan. 2005). New York: Marvel Comics.

_____. "Extremis (Part II of VI)." *Iron Man Vol 4 #2* (Feb. 2005). New York: Marvel Comics.

_____. "Extremis (Part III of VI)." *Iron Man Vol 4 #3* (Mar. 2005). New York: Marvel Comics.

_____. "Extremis (Part IV of VI)." *Iron Man Vol 4 #4* (Oct. 2005). New York: Marvel Comics.

_____. "Extremis (Part V of VI)." *Iron Man Vol 4 #5* (Mar. 2006). New York: Marvel Comics.

_____. "Extremis (Part VI of VI)." *Iron Man Vol 4 #6* (Apr. 2006). New York: Marvel Comics.

Foucault, Michel. "Nietzsche, Genealogy, History." In *The Foucault Reader*. New York: Pantheon, 1984.

Fraction, Matt (w) and Salvador Larroca (a). "Counting Up from Zero." *Invincible Iron Man #20* (Jan. 2010). New York: Marvel Publishing, Inc.

_____. "The Danger We're All In." *Invincible Iron Man #15* (Sep. 2009). New York: Marvel Publishing, Inc.

_____. "Digging in the Dirt." *Invincible Iron Man #21* (Feb. 2010). New York: Marvel Publishing, Inc.

_____. "The Five Nightmares (Part I): Armageddon Days." *Invincible Iron Man #1* (July 2008). New York: Marvel Publishing, Inc.

_____. "The Five Nightmares (Part 3): Pepper Potts at the End of the World." *Invincible Iron Man #3* (Sep. 2008). New York: Marvel Publishing, Inc.

_____. "The Five Nightmares (Part 4): Neutron Bomb Heart." *Invincible Iron Man #4* (Oct. 2008). New York: Marvel Publishing, Inc.

_____. "The Five Nightmares (Part 6): Irrational Actors." *Invincible Iron Man #6* (Dec. 2008). New York: Marvel Publishing, Inc.

_____. "The Five Nightmares (Epilogue): Clifton Pollard." *Invincible Iron Man #7* (Jan. 2009). New York: Marvel Publishing, Inc.

_____. " Ghost in the Machine." *Invincible Iron Man #23* (Apr. 2010). New York: Marvel Publishing, Inc.

_____. "The Man in the Box." *Invincible Iron Man #33* (Feb. 2011). New York: Marvel Publishing, Inc.

_____. "Stark Resilient, Part 8: Drones Scream Down." *Invincible Iron Man #32* (Jan. 2011) . New York: Marvel Publishing, Inc.

_____. "World's Most Wanted (Part I): Shipbreaking." *Invincible Iron Man #8* (Feb. 2009). New York: Marvel Publishing, Inc.

_____. "World's Most Wanted (Part III): No Future." *Invincible Iron Man #10* (Apr. 2009). New York: Marvel Publishing, Inc.

Freud, Sigmund. "Screen Memories." In *The Uncanny*. New York: Penguin Books, 2003.

McCloud, Scott. *Understanding Comics*. New York: Kitchen Sink Press, 1993.

Riviere, Joan. "Womanliness as Masquerade." In *Female Sexuality: Contemporary Engagements,* edited by Donna Bassin. Northvale, New Jersey: Jason Aronson, 1999.

Iron Icarus

Comics Futurism and the Man-Machine System

Rikk Mulligan

In 1956, the bolt of lightning that transformed Barry Allen into the Flash in DC Comics *Showcase* #4 also heralded the Silver Age of comics and a shift toward science fiction (SF) as the inspiration for superhero origins. Although Marvel Comics drew on myths and magic with Thor and Doctor Strange, SF in terms of radiation-induced abilities created the majority of its new heroes, including the Fantastic Four, Hulk, Spider-Man, Daredevil, and the X-Men. SF-derived androids and robots appear in both Gold and Silver Age stories, but where DC Comics introduced robots with human brains,[1] Marvel instead created the Iron Man—a suit of powered armor worn and operated by Tony Stark. Unlike his contemporaries, Iron Man owes his origin to an injury rather than supernatural events, arcane knowledge, deific intervention, mutant abilities, radioactive manipulations, aliens, or a laboratory accident. Successive writers have revised the details, but the general plot remains constant: Stark is in the field reviewing the performance of weapons he designed when he is injured in an explosion, and subsequently captured by enemies who demand that he make weapons for them. Instead, he builds the suit.

The armor was initially created as a prosthetic means of life support and to escape. Its later abilities are engineering upgrades that reflect developments in science and military technology, and trends in SF. From its inception, the armor was the superpower; therefore, to dramatically contrast the hero identity with that of the civilian, stories emphasize the vulnerability of the human within—physical, emotional, and psychological. The early stories of the 1960s stress Stark's weak heart and inability to remove the chestplate.[2] But as later medical advances provided routine treatments for once-crippling conditions, the stories of the 1980s and 1990s turned to spinal injury and paraplegia, extensive nerve damage, and the need for an artificial heart, conditions requiring neurological remedies and artificial organs created by biotechnology blending mechanical and biological engineering. The armor lost its early, primary purpose as life support and became a transferable "superpower" that anyone can wear[3] just as any technician can be trained to operate the most sophisticated military and aerospace technology.

Early SF speculated on automation—robots and androids—replacing man, and more recent works consider the blending of man and machine, including physical prosthetics, neural augmentation, and integrated expert systems or artificial intelligence (AI). At the dawn of the new millennium, writer Warren Ellis chose to tinker with Stark, but rather than returning to injury or medical crisis, it is through biotechnological enhancement. Ellis' "Extremis" storyline combines Stark's genius in electronics and cybernetics with biotechnicist Maya Hansen's revolutionary reprogramming of DNA and human autonomic systems. The Iron Man armor had become limited by its human pilot, so the Extremis process was used to rewrite Stark's DNA and enhances him with new abilities. These enhancements effectively give him superpowers and also make him an integral part of the suit. Matt Fraction then explored these changes as the source of greater vulnerability rather than strength, and as a danger to the very people Stark seeks to protect when his enhancements make him a slave to the machine, underscoring the limits of automated weapons technology and emphasizing the continuing need for human oversight of the machine.

The ethos of *Iron Man* has changed over its fifty-year continuity as America's international geopolitical role has evolved. Initially grounded in the Cold War stand-off between the U.S. and U.S.S.R., Stark began as a munitions maker, weapon designer, and military contractor, who then turns to the consumer electronics market, alternative energy, medical devices, space, and scientific research. Stark's early technology relied on transistors and miniaturization, later evolving into electromagnetic fields and high-energy particle physics, with advanced data processing, expert systems, and AI in particular echoing real-world weapons systems developed for use by the U.S. military and sold to allies. *Iron Man* has remained one of Marvel's more political titles; yet even as the geopolitical context changed—America withdrew from Vietnam, the Cold War ended, the United States became the sole global superpower and then became embroiled in post–9/11 wars in the Middle East—its stories continue to consider new technological innovations and threats in both SF and geopolitical contexts. The title's writers frequently return to the related themes of the armor as prosthesis, Stark's role as a weapon innovator, and his complex relationship with the U.S. government and military. Over this span weapons systems have become more complex and include automated systems that no longer speed up human responses, but frequently surpass operator reaction time. As Iron Man, Stark embodies the role of human conscience and judgment in the operation of sophisticated and often deadly weapons systems, a core aspect of his various suits of armor. What remains central to the series is the need to challenge integrating man more closely with the machine in sophisticated weapon systems while also retaining human oversight and control because expert systems have parameters, not ethics nor morals.[4]

The Iron Man armor piloted by Tony Stark is an example of a human-machine or man-machine system as the combination of human operators with machines, including those with automated subroutines and increasingly sophisticated expert systems that are the precursors to AI. The modern era of such systems began during World War II with gunners, radar operators, and bombardiers, with the incorporation of data processing by high-speed computers extending the ability of humans to control ever more sophisticated systems. Automation became part of such systems in attempts to improve their performance by increasing the response time and precision of operators. According to David Noble, early pioneers of AI "were involved in military-sponsored projects on what became known as 'man-machine' systems, which aimed to achieve a better match between complex aircraft, anti-aircraft and naval guns, and radar systems and the human personnel that manned them" (Noble 153). Military applications then drove the initial quest for AI as an improved control system with "pilots, gunners, and radar operators" as its first human models (Noble 153). However, Noble points out that many advocates for AI believed that the integration of man and machine was only a limited, temporary step on the way to "fully autonomous intelligent systems" (160). The expectation is that such expert systems could decrease the inefficiency of poorly trained humans and hesitation caused by second-guessing. Today the needs of the man-machine system are in part defined by the competition between contending offensive and defensive systems, both of which can launch attacks or countermeasures with blinding speed because of faster computer processing speeds and elaborate subprocesses defined as expert systems. The problem is that contemporary weapons and countermeasures now respond faster than humans can react or override, risking more accidents and greater collateral damage, including the loss of innocent lives.

Modern weapon systems retain a human governor or command element, limiting the response to human reaction time, although for many outside the military these remain abstract concepts. Automated weapons and autonomous systems using AI have long been the province of SF, with Hal, of Arthur C. Clarke's novel, *2001: A Space Odyssey* (1968), and James Cameron's Skynet, from the *Terminator* (1984) franchise, as some of the best examples. SF literature and media generally explores new social applications of technology well in advance of comic books, but comic books and graphic novels present images that help the reader understand the abstract through concrete example. Iron Man's battles often showcase Stark's ability to overcome the challenges of more advanced and powerful technology, but since the late 1980s as computers have become more powerful, the stories have increasingly depicted the man as the limiting element in the system. To speed up its response time the Iron Man armor became more sophisticated, but Stark's initial attempts at integrating artificial intelligence were disastrous,[5] and the only option that remained was to improve the pilot—Tony Stark himself. The man within the armor is its vulnerability; a weak heart, degraded nervous system, addictive personality, or slow reaction time limit the performance of the technology, but integrating the human too closely with the technology erodes the hero's morality and humanity, also exposing him to the vulnerabilities of the machine such as hardware exploits, hacking, and computer viruses.

Tin Man: The Armor as Prosthetic

Superheroes maintain a secret identity to protect friends and loved ones, but where most can take off their costume and lead a (relatively) normal life in their civilian identity, Tony Stark could not remove his chestplate in the early years of *Iron Man*. In his history of the character, Andy Mangels explains that Stan Lee decided to give Stark a weak heart to make him a tragic figure and increase his popularity by countering the stigma of being a munitions maker and a part of the military-industrial complex (Mangels 6–8). Although it provides power for weapons and gadgets, the chestplate is a prosthetic device that must be regularly recharged to keep Stark's heart beating; if he removes it, his heart stops. Writers and editors slipped on occasion and referred to the armor as a "pacemaker," but eventually the chestplate was explained as a means of generating a magnetic field that held the shrapnel that endangered Stark's heart in place. Comic historians Gerard Jones and Will Jacobs point out that this physical weakness caused a psychological weakness; because Stark could not take the chestplate off, he was cut off from humanity and companionship, most typically the women who contributed to his wealthy, playboy image, but more importantly close family, friends, and confidants (Jones and Jacobs 70).

In 1969, in a crossover story appearing in *The Avengers #68* and *The Invincible Iron Man #19*, Stark is operated upon to repair the damaged tissue with synthetic heart tissue, an example of SF medical technology given that the first successful heart transplant only took place in 1968. At the time, Stark briefly considered retiring as Iron Man, even hiring boxer Eddie March as his proxy to wear the armor, but instead he chose to remain active as the armored avenger. For the next ten years a variety or writers and editors fell back on Stark's "weak heart" as a plot device, even though he was at last free of the chest plate, and in 1978 when David Michelinie, Bob Layton, and John Romita, Jr., began their critically-acclaimed three-year run on the series, they dropped the heart problems.

The tin man may finally have gotten a heart, but the new creative team introduced another weakness, alcoholism, that interfered with Stark's use and control of the armor, providing another example of human limits to the human-machine system. After a series of personal and business reversals, including being framed for murder as Iron Man and SHIELD attempting a corporate takeover of Stark International, Tony descends into alcoholism.[6] Frustrated by his business problems, Stark dons the armor while drunk and accidentally drops a train tank car full of chlorine gas, making an accident a disaster and forcing the evacuation of a five-mile radius of Long island (Michelinie, "Demon..."). This accident is a wake-up call and, with the help of his current romantic interest Bethany Cabe, Stark wages a successful campaign to stop drinking. Only a few years later, the new writer Denny O'Neil creates an extended storyline where Stark is the subject of an intense campaign by Obadiah Stane to wreck him professionally and financially. Stark begins drinking again; his descent into alcoholism takes place over two years of the comic's continuity, during which time, he loses Stark International and eventually ends up homeless in New York City's Bowery neighborhood. As he begins to drink more heavily, Stark, in the Iron Man armor, not only commits expensive acts of vandalism and public destruction, he also manages to leave Stark Industries facilities vulnerable to attack and espionage. His collapse is so complete that he exposes his identity to James Rhodes while drunk and forces Rhodes to use the armor in his stead (O'Neil). His spiral into alcoholism ends around issue #200 (November 1985), when he resumes the mantle of the Iron Man, confronts Stane, and then goes on to recover his fortune and business (Mangels 43–7). Yet Stark continues to recover from his alcoholism to this day because his engineering expertise cannot cure this condition, leaving it one the character's central and humanizing vulnerabilities.

Bad Wiring: Integrating Technology into the Man

The second era of *Iron Man* returned to using the armor as a prosthetic, enabling Stark to physically control his damaged body, before retreading the old weak heart plot device. As a combination of creative teams worked through these stories, a central theme developed where the integration of technology into the man makes him more vulnerable to outside interference and control. When Michelinie and Layton returned to *Iron Man* shortly after O'Neil's departure in 1986, Stark was suffering nerve damage from the energy fields created by his Silver Centurion armor. Although this problem was quickly resolved with no lasting effects, several issues later his girlfriend, Kathy Dare, shoots him, damaging his spine and leaving him paralyzed from the waist down (Michelinie, "Heartbeaten"). Stark quickly realizes that wearing the armor allows him to be fully mobile. He is on the edge of retreating from his human identity altogether by giving up his business responsibilities and social activities as Stark, when a team of friends and scientists discover a way to heal him. Before the operation, Stark comes to realize that "Iron Man is like money, power, influence—just a tool to be used" and that "without the human being inside, shell-head's just a piece of amazing machinery" (Michelinie, "Footsteps"). This cure—a biochip—is a programmable organic "computer chip" that would "instruct the body's own cells to reconstruct torn nerves" (Michelinie, "Footsteps"). Within a matter of issues Stark has again seemingly returned to normal, though now with technology permanently embedded within his body.

The implanted biochip repairs his paraplegia, but is exploited by an outside agency in ways that create an even greater vulnerability, leading to Tony Stark's apparent death. What began as a series of aches and twinges is revealed as a corporate plot by the Marrs twins to take control of Stark Enterprises by taking physical control of his body. The corporate subsidiary that had created the biochip in #248 had once been owned by the Marrs, who use their technicians to incorporate a Trojan Horse virus (programmatic backdoor access) that allows their people to use a massive mainframe to take control of "ninety-seven percent of Stark's motor functions" (Byrne, "Put...")—to pilot him. While they can override Stark's conscious control of his body, they cannot see what he is experiencing without external surveillance. Stark uses his encephala-link (a mental link to the armor created in #258) to remotely operate the armor, allowing it to then control the motion of his body within. However, this method increasingly damages Stark's central nervous system because the muscles and nerves try to move against the armor and he, at first, cannot feel the pain, and then has it used as neurofeedback against him. Eventually this leads to a complete physical collapse in #264, trapping Stark in the armor by #268 until he creates a skin-tight neurosheath as a full-body prosthetic, though it is fragile and its circuits burn out under too much exertion (Byrne, "The Hollow...." Still, the neurosheath is a delaying tactic at best; Stark's CNS continues to degrade, leading to his apparent death in *Iron Man* #284.

The changes to Stark's neurosystem created by the biochip and new nerve growth, now referred to as a techno-organic parasite, also laid the foundation for his rebirth. According to Mangels, the writer who inherited Byrne's "Stark is going to die" plotline, Len Kaminski had a strong personal interest in science and technology, and particularly wanted to consider "computerized nervous system interfaces, biological engineering, and mapping the human genome" in his stories (Mangels 57–8). Kaminski also drew from SF literature, specifically the first wave of Cyberpunk and its focus on computers, biotech interfaces, and inserting the humans mentally into the realm of machines—cyberspace. The blend of human and machine as cyborg is one of the better known Cyberpunk tropes—like the Robocop and Marvel's Deathlok—but Kaminski turned Stark into a cybernaut, who, according to Scott Bukatman, "gains the ability to move within the worlds of information" (Bukatman 19) and tends to be able to manipulate data streams and virtual reality. Stark is placed in near-cryogenic suspension until his science team figures out a way to recode the parasite's DNA so that it would become his new nervous system. When they access the biochip's operating system they expose it to Stark's "conscious" control, and he debugs the new Operating System (OS) as it is uploaded, maintaining human control of this technology (Kaminski, "Soul...").

Stark's genius in electronic and computers—hardware and software—make him the perfect vehicle to further explore cyberpunk themes, especially through his artificial nervous system. In essence, his intellect becomes a superpower in and of itself. By the mid- to late–1990s, the cyborg could be seen as "a coupling between a human being and an electronic or mechanical apparatus, or as the identity of organisms embedded in a cybernetic information system" (Kaminski, "Soul...") like cybernauts. But Iron Man does not explore these themes until the early 2000s. Disappointingly, the series retreats back into its older plotlines regarding Stark's physical frailty in order to focus more on post–9/11 geopolitical plots. Within the space of a few years, Tony

Stark dies and is reborn several times; with each rebirth the editors and writers damage his heart in new ways as a means of highlighting different uses of the armor as a life-support prosthetic, rather than using his biotechnology upgrades.[7] After the conclusion of the *Heroes Reborn* "experiment" of 1996–1997, Stark's body appears to be that of a normal human; however, the third volume of *Iron Man* has Stark assaulted in and out of his armor, finally leading to a massive, near-fatal heart attack brought on by his now-sentient armor. The Sentient Armor is another example of a killer AI like Hal and Skynet, however it remains beyond the scope of this discussion. Instead of killing Stark, at the last minute it sacrifices itself by tearing out its own artificial heart, implanting it into Stark to save his life (Quesada). The artificial heart makes him stronger, but other than being used for minor plot points, as with the now forgotten artificial nervous system, its potential remains largely ignored and questions regarding the artificial enhancement of humans by implants disregarded.

Cyborg Forecast: More and Less Than Human

The first four decades of *Iron Man* incorporated elements of Hard SF, post-modern and often-dystopic cyberpunk, and the space operatic conflicts of galaxy-spanning empires with the Krees and Skrulls. Yet the title avoided the more subtle social and political ramifications of futurist projections, even those only predicting fifteen minutes into the future. Richard Reynolds, who considers superheroes as a whole a modern mythology, argues that "scientific concepts and terms are introduced freely into plots and used to create atmosphere … but the science itself is at most superficially plausible, often less so, and the prevailing mood is mystical rather than rational" (16). Reynolds' assertion is appropriate for many of the early stories, given Stan Lee's lack of scientific knowledge that he freely admits in interviews (Mangels 13), but later writers made a point to better incorporate contemporary technology. Mangels stresses that several creators, including Bob Layton and Len Kaminski, were very interested in contemporary trends in science and brought them into their storylines. More recently Warren Ellis and Matt Fraction not only track science and technology, but also focus on its social impact, going beyond the typical "scenario forecasting" of military strategists and government contractors. *Iron Man* editor Tom Brevoort, explains that Ellis "reads every contemporary science journal coming out and likes to be on the cutting edge" and uses technology such as "nanomachines and pharmaceuticals and gene tampering and DBA splicing to evolve and upgrade the human body" (Mangels 108). Much of Ellis' writing deals with the unexpected consequences of radical technologies, often in countercultural or political contexts, such as rightwing militiamen gaining access to a supersoldier biotechnology in the *Extremis* arc. Both Ellis and Fraction draw on contemporary discourses surrounding stem cell therapy, cloning, and invasive biotechnologies, while also tying them into the increasingly pervasive surveillance culture of post–9/11 America, complete with the last vestiges of the quickly fading 1990s dream of the U.S. leading a New World Order.

Volume four of *The Invincible Iron Man* begins with the six-part *Extremis* storyline, in which Stark epitomizes the ultimate combination of contemporary technology and man as a cyborg. Mallen, a superpowered terrorist, defeats the Iron Man in combat, leaving Stark critically injured and dying—he has to have his DNA recoded by Extremis to heal him and make him an integral part of the armor. Extremis is a form of biotechnology—a supersoldier solution—that "hacks" or rewrites the body's "repair center, the part of the brain that keeps a complete blueprint of the human body" (Ellis, "Extremis Part III") to alter DNA, redesign muscles, tissues, and create new organs. Stark uses Extremis to "be the suit … grow new connections" and "wire the armor directly into my brain" (Ellis, "Extremis Part IV") rather than to grow new organs or increase his body's strength or speed. Mallen is too fast for Stark to engage effectively in their first battle so Stark needs to become the armor to reduce the lag between his reaction and the machine's response. To achieve this end, he uses Extremis to upgrade his body in numerous ways. Once the transformation is complete the analogy he uses to explain the changes is that the Iron Man suit is the application, Extremis is the OS, and his body is now the hardware. Stark immediately shows that the undersheath control layer for the armor is now physically part of him, stored in the hollow of his bones, and wired directly into his brain. He can operate the armor without a lag in response, at the speed of thought. He demonstrates that his modifications extend beyond the armor, sending a wireless signal by thought alone to make a cellphone call, and "see through satellites" (Ellis, "Extremis Part V"). One of the most powerful applications of these new abilities allows him to operate a large number of Iron Man suits remotely, as a veritable army of drones, in multiple locations. Now, Stark is only limited by his ability to multitask (and the ambitions of his writers and artists).

The Extremis DNA rewrite not only makes Stark part of the armor, but it also directly connects him to all Stark digital technology and most modern communications and computer equipment, making him the post-information age cyborg. In *Being Digital* (1995), Nicholas Negroponte, the founder of MIT's Media Lab, offers a view of the future being created by advances in and the proliferation of digital technologies and media. Stark's Extremis upgrade is an example of the coming post-information age that Negroponte sees as an era in which, using virtual environments, "digital living will include less and less dependence upon being in a specific place at a specific time, and the transmission of place itself will start to become possible" (Negroponte 165). Soon after his upgrade, Stark uses such environments when he multitasks: simultaneously fighting the Crimson Dynamo (while wearing the armor), using telepresence (video phone) to spearhead the hostile takeover of another corporation, helping engineer a cooling system for a rail-gun, while also communicating via Bluetooth with an agent bidding on ancient armor in an auction (Knauf, "Execute Program: Part 1"). The post-information age is not wholly beneficial; Negroponte cautions it will instigate "cases of intellectual-property abuse and invasion of our privacy ... digital vandalism, software piracy, and data thievery ... [and] the loss of many jobs to wholly automated systems" (227). By becoming not just part of a machine, but part of an extended, global system of information, Stark stretches his the limits of his consciousness beyond those of a single person. His multitasking ability creates closed decision loops that raise suspicion in others—he investigates a problem or analyzes a threat using his immediate access to databases and networks, and then acts on them unilaterally. Stark can act in multiple locations, remotely, with the speed of thought, and so he explains fewer of his decisions and actions to others because bringing them into the decision loops is inefficient. The result is a complete change in personality in his dealings with others. The Avengers see him as increasingly arrogant and highhanded, and the commanders of SHIELD find him becoming reclusive, evasive, and secretive (Knauf, "Execute Program: Part 1"). In becoming more than human as part of the global network, he also alienates his human contacts and isolates himself.

Stark is now superhuman, a cyborg whose biotech upgrades have altered his physiology in ways that make him part machine and give him actual superpowers. But in doing so, he is now susceptible to a number of exploits and attacks that would be ineffective against a normal human. The suit no longer requires a pilot who is specially trained, but a physically integrated entity that is part of its technological infrastructure. Only Stark can operate the Extremis armor because only he has the biological modifications to do so. However, the "Execute Program" storyline (vol. 4, #7–12) uses some retroactive conversion to explain that Professor Yinsen, when he initially saves Stark's life, also implants a "biomechanic receiving unit" that allows an outside operator to take over "impulse control and voluntary motor functions"; in effect, turning Stark into a puppet, much as the Marr's technology had years earlier (Knauf, "Execute Program, Part 4"). The implant remains dormant until the Extremis upgrade creates a persistent connection to global wireless transmissions, therefore someone who uses a network connection to plug the controller into the Internet can activate Stark's receiving unit. Because Stark is now the Iron Man, the override grants full access and use of the armor, allowing the rogue operator to assassinate six people, down an airliner, and kill a large number of bystanders. The last command given before the rogue's death commandeers Stark's newly built set of specialized "satellite" armors and wreaks havoc with them until they are destroyed, an effort that requires the help of the Fantastic Four and the Avengers. The sending device is destroyed when the operator is killed, and the implant, after being activated, is then identified by Stark's Extremis-enhanced immune/repair system as invasive, and it too is destroyed. In his arrogance, Stark has not upgraded his own "security," and so falls victim to a biotech "backdoor exploit" similar to the intrusions network administrators have dealt with since the days of pre-Internet computer networks.

Even when the Yinsen override device is destroyed, Extremis still offers other ways that the armor might be shut down and Stark's abilities neutralized by outside agencies. The questions that arise regarding Stark's mental stability during "Execute Program" become more prominent during the "Haunted" story arc (vol. 4, #21–28 and Annual #1) that follows. Between his obsessive-compulsive multitasking and his guilt for the deaths caused by the armor, Stark seldom allows himself downtime; the pressure of the constant work drives him to the edge of burnout. He also begins to see "ghosts," although Dr. Leonard Sampson diagnoses these as his Extremis-enhanced subconscious communicating with his conscious mind—an effect of the massive amount of data his brain is absorbing but unable to immediately process (Knauf, "Haunted"). SHIELD and a government commission not only question his stability, but force Stark to wear a psionic damper after he refuses to undergo a full mental evaluation by Dr. Sampson. The Damper interferes with his ability to use Extremis as an operating system, disabling his capacity to interface with all digital systems, including the armor and wireless communication. The committee justifies their order citing erratic behavior, but the Deputy of Defense drives the decision in an attempt to hide his misappropriation of Extremis and its use in an illegal, secret weapon development project. Stark uses older versions of his armor to uncover the involvement of the Mandarin and to defeat him, allowing him to have the damper removed.

Arguably the greatest vulnerability created by the Extremis upgrade is still Stark's connectivity. A Skrull computer virus uses Tony Stark's link to the Stark Industries dataspire to infect all StarkTech operating systems during the Skrull Invasion Marvel crossover storyline.[8] The Skrull virus infects the Extremis operating system, Stark's armor, the Raft superprison, the Camp Hammond Initiative training center, the core of SHIELD's weapons and technology, and a great deal of U.S. and NATO military equipment, leaving Earth more susceptible to the alien invasion. The corruption of StarkTech, and Stark's inability to quickly marshal a defense, cost him the position of Director and leads to SHIELD being disbanded. After the Skrulls are defeated, Stark's Extremis operating system remains infected, forcing him to downgrade to older versions of his armor because he can no longer operate the Extremis armor. Matt Fraction's summary of the invasion is: "Shapeshifting aliens infiltrated all aspects of human life, and planted a destructive virus in Stark technology, causing it to fail around the world—from cell phones to toasters to the Extremis armor that made Tony Stark into Iron Man. In the ashes of the invasion, Stark technology is synonymous with failure" (Fraction, "World's Most Wanted"). Because Stark is directly connected to so many databases and networks, when he becomes infected it spreads globally through his Extremis-enhancements to all other technology using similar protocols, much as viruses created to exploit the Windows operating system can spread to a variety of computers and devices as long as they run the same OS. Rather than becoming stronger by being integrated into the machine, Stark has become a liability not only to himself and his company, but to the world at large.

Warren Ellis transformed Tony Stark into a superhuman, and Charles and Daniel Knauf explored the new vulnerabilities created by Extremis, but it took several stories created by Matt Fraction and Salvador Larroca to chart the fall of the iron Icarus as they disassembled the post-information age cyborg. The failure of Stark's technology left him disgraced, an easy political target for Norman Osborn at the end of the Skrull invasion. Osborn hates Stark for his greater genius and success as a businessman, and uses his position as the head of SHIELD's successor, HAMMER, to label Stark the world's most wanted man. This is not completely unwarranted; Stark does upload a virus to disable all remaining Stark technology now under HAMMER's control, as well as wiping all records and databases relating to the Superhuman Registration Act in order to keep Osborn from learning the identities of any masked heroes. Unfortunately, one of the Extremis biotech or exotech enhancements transforms Stark's brain into an organic flashdrive; unlike a normal brain, he worries that even if damaged, data might be recovered. To prevent Osborn or anyone else from accessing his knowledge, especially the Registration database and Repulsor technology, Stark begins to wipe his drive by "zeroing out" his brain cells—a process that will ultimately remove his memory, personality, and even his neural pathways, reflexes, and autonomic systems (Fraction, "World's Most Wanted, Part 2"). As Stark erases his brain, he experiences cognitive decay—his control of the armor's systems diminishes, his mind becomes less sophisticated, and he must fall back on older, "more commercial" models. Only repulsor power can activate this process, so Stark is forced to run from hidden armor depot to hidden lab, each time using an even more obsolete version of his armor, a swift fall down memory lane. After the final procedure, he is forced to wear his old Mark 0 armor, the clunky, scavenged gray shell, to confront Osborn in the Iron Patriot armor, a repurposed pre–Extremis Iron Man suit. Stark is nearly killed, goes into a seizure, and is left in a persistent vegetative state with machines breathing for him. He transforms from a human/machine hybrid—a fully integrated cyborg with near-unlimited capacity—to a physical shell that still relies on a machine to survive.

Fraction and Larroca's "Stark: Disassembled" story arc takes advantage of the Extremis exobiology to restore Tony Stark by reinstalling his memory from backup and implanting a new power source, as though he is a damaged computer in need of repair. Immediately after his Extremis upgrade, Stark backups up his memory; however, he never bothered to update this backup, and there are gaps in his long term memory including the Civil War, his role as Director of SHIELD, the Skrull Invasion, and the rise of Osborn and HAMMER. The backup is only of his memory, leaving him without a clean version of the Extremis OS and still unable to use his Extremis armor. Part of Stark's restoration requires that Pepper Potts' Stark-Rand electromagnetic repulsor generator (similar to the arc unit of the *Iron Man* film [2008]) be implanted into his chest, not to stabilize shrapnel, but to accelerate his healing system and provide autonomic or involuntary nervous control—the RP unit includes these processes as subroutines. The RP unit increases Stark's strength and stamina, enhances his healing system and intellect, and allows him to access some of his expanded digital connections if not control an army of Iron Men any longer.

Even without the Extremis OS, Stark's exobiology remains that of a cyborg; he is not only dependent on the RP unit to blink and breathe, but also subject to external manipulation and, worse, tampering. The RP unit is now part of his biological systems and he cannot survive without it, echoing the earlier reliance on the chest plate in previous incarnations. While rebuilt, the Extremis exobiology that allowed Stark to restore his memory leaves him susceptible to typical hardware exploits—his backup files have been tampered with and agents of the Mandarin have added a Trojan Horse that allows Stark's motor control to be overridden as others have done in the past. The Mandarin's control also allows him to conduct surveillance on Stark, giving him the ability to inform others of Stark's actions as an example of a pervasive surveillance. The Mandarin shares this intelligence with Stark's business competitor, Justine Hammer, and his enemy, General Bruce Babbage, who obtain a court order placing a governor on his RP unit that enables them to shut down his armor when they wish, often in the middle of a battle, much to Stark's endangerment and public embarrassment. The level of surveillance and infiltration given through Stark's corrupted files opens him to not just attack, but the theft of his designs and his corruption by the Mandarin's technicians, a reflection of contemporary issues such as Chinese hackers attacking U.S. federal government and Department of Defense systems, denial of service attacks aimed at key Internet service providers, and recent acts of corporate and military espionage involving stolen files for military systems. The man has been saved, but his control over the technology, over the man-machine weapons systems, has been compromised by his complete integration into the technology.

After the end of the Cold War, perhaps because of its Vietnam origins and frequently political storylines, the *Iron Man* stories had lost much of their focus and gotten lost in cycles of death and rebirth and new versions of armor that briefly explored and then dropped different "neat ideas." After 9/11, authors returned to stories of geopolitical and ideological conflict, many involving the Stark confronting a variety of problems human and alien technology used as weapons. Within Marvel Comics, the varieties of Iron Man (including War Machine) are regarded as the most powerful American weapons systems yet devised, but these systems are not perfect and different teams of artists and writers focus on weaknesses that reflect contemporary issues with the military and technology. Stark may have debugged and patched his data, insulated his "brain" and exobiological systems; he may have secured his communications protocols and channels from intrusions, but the exobiology remains. Stark is no longer just human. When he allows himself to become too dependent on his technology, it is used against him in ways that suggest that a human who relies too much on the crutch of automation loses some of their humanity when they abrogate their responsibility to decide how the technology should act. What is important is that the man remains in control, the new era that began under the writing of Matt Fraction—the turn away from military contracts and weapons with a repulsor-based green energy revolution may have been forgotten by Marvel, but it has redefined Stark's role in many ways and serves as a warning or criticism of the legacy of the Cold War and the military-industrial complex that Eisenhower once warned the American public against. Human needs take precedence, and a human must control the machine.

NOTES

1. The Golden Age Robotman, Robert Crane, first appeared in *Star Spangled Comics* #7 (April 1942); the Silver Age Robotman, Cliff Steel, a member of the Doom Patrol, first appeared in *My Greatest Adventure* #80 (June 1963).

2. During the 1960s, in *Tales of Suspense* and later in *The Invincible Iron Man* (volume one), most of the writers suggested or explained that the chestplate operated like a pacemaker, that it kept his weakened heart beating properly. Later writers explained that the chestplate generated a magnetic field that kept the shrapnel in place, in particular John Byrne, Len Kaminski, and Warren Ellis.

3. The Iron Man armor in different versions, has been worn by: Tony Stark, Happy Hogan, Eddie March, James Rhodes, Carl Walker, Michael O'Brien, Bethany Cabe, "Vor/tex" in Stark's body, and finally, the "Sentient Armor" as a consequence of downloading the artificial intelligence of Jocasta. Tales of Suspense #39, *Tales of Suspense* #84, *Iron Man* vol. 1, #21, #42, #170, #244, #299, #300, #308–309; *Iron Man* vol. 3, #27–31.

4. "Computers are not moral; they cannot resolve complex issues like the rights to life and to death."

5. Joe Quesada created the sentient armor in *The Invincible Iron Man* volume 3, #26–30.

6. The extended storyline begins in Iron Man #121 and runs through #128, co-plotted by David Michelinie (w) and Bob Layton (inker), with John Romita, Jr., handling the pencils. For an extended discussion, see Andy Mangels, 38–40.

7. The time-switched, young Tony Stark has his heart damaged by the "original" Stark in *Iron Man* #325 (vol. 1), and is saved, but fitted with a chestplate as prosthetic in *Avengers* #395 (vol. 1). In the *Onslaught Universe*, as part of the *Heroes Reborn* storyline, an again-adult Stark has his chest riddled with shrapnel, which requires him to wear the Prometheum armor to stay alive.

8. Because of the shear number of series and overlaps that include Iron Man, much of the detail regarding the Skrull Invasion is outside the scope of this paper as my focus is on the Iron Man comic books themselves. By the same token, I have not included Ultron's infestation of Stark through Extremis as it occurred in the pages of *The Mighty Avengers*, "The Ultron Initiative" (#1–6, May-October 2007).

WORKS CITED

Abnett, Dan (w/p), Terry Kavanaugh (p) and Jimmy Cheung, Jim Calafiore, and Hector Collazo (p). "Face to Face." *The Invincible Iron Man #325* (vol. 1) (February 1996). New York: Marvel Comics.

Balsamo, Anne. *Technologies of the Gendered Body: Reading Cyborg Women*. Durham and London: Duke University Press, 1996.

Bukatman, Scott. *Terminal Identity: The Virtual Subject in Post-Modern Science Fiction*. Durham and London: Duke University Press, 1993.

Byrne, John (w) and John Romita, Jr. (p). "Put Them All Together They Spell Laser!" *The Invincible Iron Man #260* (vol. 1) (September 1990). New York: Marvel Comics.

_____. "Where is Iron Man?" *The Invincible Iron Man #264* (vol. 1) (January 1991). New York: Marvel Comics.

Byrne, John (w) and Paul Ryan (a). "First Blood" *The Invincible Iron Man #268* (vol. 1) (May 1991). New York: Marvel Comics.

_____. "The Hollow Man" *The Invincible Iron Man #269* (vol. 1) (June 1991). New York: Marvel Comics.

Drake, Arnold (w) and Bob Haney (p). *My Greatest Adventure #80* (June 1963). New York: DC Comics.

Ellis, Warren (w) and Adi Granov (a). "Extremis: Part One of Six." *The Invincible Iron Man* #1 (vol. 4) (January 2005). New York: Marvel Comics.

_____. "Extremis: Part Three of Six." *The Invincible Iron Man* #3 (vol. 4) (March 2005). New York: Marvel Comics.

_____. "Extremis: Part Four of Six." *The Invincible Iron Man* #4 (vol. 1) (October 2006). New York: Marvel Comics.

_____. "Extremis: Part Five of Six." *The Invincible Iron Man* #5 (vol. 4) (March 2006). New York: Marvel Comics.

Fraction, Matt (w) and Salvador Larroca (a). "World's Most Wanted: Part 1: Shipbreaking." *The Invincible Iron Man* #8 (vol. 5) (February 2009). New York: Marvel Comics.

_____. "World's Most Wanted Part 2: Godspeed." *The Invincible Iron Man* #9 (vol. 5) (March 2009). New York: Marvel Comics.

Goodwin, Archie (w) and George Tuska (a). "What Price Life?!" *The Invincible Iron Man* #19 (vol. 1) (November 1969). New York: Marvel Comics.

Jones, Gerard and Will Jacobs. *The Comic Book Heroes: The First History of Modern Comic Books from the Silver Age to the Present*. Rocklin, Ca.: Prima, 1997.

Kaminski, Len (w) and Kevin Hopgood (p). "Legacy of Iron." *The Invincible Iron Man* #284 (vol. 1) (September 1992). New York: Marvel Comics.

Kaminski, Len (w) and Barry Kitson (p). "Soul on Ice." *The Invincible Iron Man* #288 (vol. 1) (January 1993). New York: Marvel Comics.

Knauf, Daniel and Charles Knauf (w) and Patrick Zircher (p). "Execute Program: Part 1." *The Invincible Iron Man* #7 (vol. 4) (June 2006). New York: Marvel Comics.

_____. "Execute Program: Part 4." *The Invincible Iron Man* #10 (vol. 4) (September 2006). New York: Marvel Comics.

Knauf, Daniel and Charles Knauf (w) and Roberto de la Torre (p). "Haunted." *The Invincible Iron Man* #25 (vol. 4) (February 2008). New York: Marvel Comics.

Lobdell, Scott and Jim Lee (w) and While Portacio (p). "Heart of the Matter." *The Invincible Iron Man* #1 (vol. 2) (November 1996). New York: Marvel Comics.

Mangels, Andy. *Iron Man: Beneath the Armor*. New York: Del Rey, 2008.

Michelinie, David (w/plot), John Romita, Jr. (p), and Bob Layton (inks/plot). "Demon in a Bottle." *The Invincible Iron Man* #128 (vol. 1) (November 1979). New York: Marvel Comics.

Michelinie, David (w/plot), Bob Layton (p/plot). "Heartbeaten." *The Invincible Iron Man* #243 (vol. 1) (June 1989). New York: Marvel Comics.

_____. "Footsteps" *The Invincible Iron Man* #248 (vol. 1) (November 1989) New York: Marvel Comics.

Morrison, Grant. *Supergods: What Masked Vigilantes, Miraculous Mutants, and a Sun God from Smallville Can Teach Us About Being Human*. New York: Spiegel & Grau, 2012.

Negroponte, Nicholas. *Being Digital*. New York: Vintage, 1996.

Noble, David F. *The Religion of Technology: The Divinity of Man and the Spirit of Invention*. New York: Penguin, 1999.

O'Neil, Denny (w) and Luke McDonnell (p). "Blackout!" *The Invincible Iron Man* #169 (vol. 1) (April 1983). New York: Marvel Comics.

Postman, Neil. *Technopoly: The Surrender of Culture to Technology*. New York: Vintage, 1993.

Quesada, Joe (w) and Sean Chen (p). "The Mask in Iron Man Part Five: Blood Brothers." *The Invincible Iron Man* #30 (vol. 3) (July 2000). New York: Marvel Comics.

Reynolds, Richard. *Super Heroes: A Modern Mythology*. Jackson: University Press of Mississippi, 1992.

Siegel, Jerry (w) and Leo Nowak (p). *Star Spangled Comics* #7 (April 1942). New York: DC Comics.

Wright, Bradford W. *Comic Book Nation: The Transformation of Youth Culture in America*. Baltimore: Johns Hopkins University Press, 2001.

About the Contributors

José **Alaniz** is an associate professor in the Department of Slavic Languages and Literatures and an adjunct in the Department of Comparative Literature at the University of Washington–Seattle. He is the author of *Komiks: Comic Art in Russia* (2010) and *Death, Disability and the Superhero* (2014). He chairs the executive committee of the International Comic Arts Forum and is working on a study of disability in Euro-American graphic narrative and a history of Czech comics.

Julian C. **Chambliss**, Ph.D., is an associate professor of U.S. history at Rollins College in Winter Park, Florida. His interests are in urban development and popular culture in the United States. His writing on comics has appeared in *Critical Survey of Graphic Novels* (2012) and the journal *Studies in American Culture*. He co-edited *Ages of Heroes, Eras of Men* (2013) and his commentary on comic culture has appeared in the *Los Angeles Times, USA Today,* and on National Public Radio.

Will **Cooley** is a historian of the twentieth century United States and an associate professor at Walsh University. He earned a Ph.D. from the University of Illinois and has published in the *Journal of Urban History* and the *Journal of Sport and Social Issues*. He has contributed to *American Sports: A History of Icons, Idols, and Ideas* (2013) and *Multicultural America: A Multimedia Encyclopedia* (2013).

John **Darowski** is a Ph.D. student at the University of Louisville, where he continues to indulge a life-long love of comic books by researching and writing about their role in society. Other areas of interest include anime and manga and the Gothic. He has essays in a number of superhero collections, including *The Ages of Superman* (2012), *The Ages of Wonder Woman* (2014), and *The Ages of the X-Men* (2014).

Joseph J. **Darowski** received a Ph.D. in American studies from Michigan State University. He taught in the English Department at Brigham Young University–Idaho and is a member of the editorial review board of *The Journal of Popular Culture*. He is the author of *X-Men and the Mutant Metaphor: Race and Gender in the Comic Books* (2014), and editor of *The Ages of Superman* (2012), *The Ages of Wonder Woman* (2014), and *The Ages of the Avengers* (2014).

Charles **Henebry** received a doctorate in English literature from New York University. Originally a student of emblems (black-and-white picture books from Shakespeare's day) he has recently focused his scholarship on the four-color world of comic books, delivering conference papers and contributing a number of entries to *Comics Through Time* (2014), a four-volume history of the form.

Richard A. **Iadonisi** teaches writing at Grand Valley State University in Allendale, Michigan. He is the editor of *Graphic History: Essays on Graphic Novels and/as History* (2012) and has written essays on Frank Miller's *Batman: The Dark Knight Returns*, Art Spiegelman's *Maus*, and the representation of Chinese and Korean soldiers in Korean War comics.

Jason **Michálek** is the creative content consultant in the marketing and communications division of Public Sector Consultants in Lansing, Michigan. His work has been published in both creative and academic journals. He has a B.A. in English language and literature from Grand Valley State University and he plans to continue his graduate work in the field of American studies.

Rikk **Mulligan** is the program officer for scholarly publishing at the Association of Research Libraries. He holds a Ph.D. in American studies from Michigan State University. He serves on the editorial board of the *Journal of Popular Culture* and *Dialogue: The Journal of Pedagogy and Popular Culture*. He has published on *Battlestar Galactica* and the zombie apocalypse in popular culture and has contributed to critical studies of graphic novels and comic books.

Brian **Patton** teaches English and film studies at King's University College at Western University in London, Canada. His research interests include post–1945 British literature, spy fiction and film, as well as comics and graphic narratives. He has essays in other multicontributor collections including *James Bond and Popular Culture* (2015*)* and *For His Eyes Only: The Women of James Bond* (2015).

Mark C. **Rogers** is a professor of communication and chair of the Division of Humanities at Walsh University. He has been teaching and writing about comics since the early 1990s. He is primarily interested in political economy and the influence of the economy on the content of mass media. His writing on comics and political economy has been published in the *International Journal of Comic Art* and *Critical Approaches to Comics* (2011).

Jason **Sacks** co-wrote and -edited *The American Comic Book Chronicles: The 1970s* (2014). He's also a contributing writer to *The American Comic Book Chronicles: The 1980s; Ages of the Avengers* (2014) and *The Flash Companion* (2008), and is a former editor at *Amazing Heroes* magazine. He is a software project manager for a small ebook company and moonlights as the publisher and frequent writer for the website Comics Bulletin.

Natalie R. **Sheppard** has a master's degree in English literature from the University of New Orleans. Her areas of interest are modern and contemporary American literature and popular culture. She has presented on the subject of comic books and popular culture at the University of Florida, the Rocky Mountain Comics Conference, the Comics and Popular Arts Conference, and the Popular Culture/American Culture Association in the South.

Craig **This** has a B.A. and M.A. in history and is a lecturer at Sinclair Community College in Dayton, Ohio. He teaches a course on comic books and American popular culture, has published essays in *Nazisploitation: The Nazi Image in Low-Brow Cinema and Culture* (2011) and *Icons of the American Comic Book* (2013), and is a member of CAPE (Comics Association of Professional Educators).

John M. **Vohlidka**, Ph.D., is an assistant professor of history at Gannon University. He specializes in early modern European history with emphasis on the Tudors and Stuarts and the Reformation. He teaches the courses Comics and Culture, History of the Future, and Post-Atomic Japan, and has contributed essays to several books on *Doctor Who*.

Jean-Philippe **Zanco** teaches economics and social sciences in high school and at the Institut d'Etudes Politiques of Toulouse. Among several books and articles, in 2012 he published *La Société des Super-Héros: Economie-Sociologie-Politique*. He also contributed an essay to the collection *The Ages of the X-Men* (2014).

Index